Visual Basic .NET
Codemaster's Library

Visual Basic® .NET Codemaster's Library

Matt Tagliaferri

SYBEX

San Francisco · London

Associate Publisher: Richard Mills

Acquisitions and Developmental Editor: Tom Cirtin

Editor: Sarah H. Lemaire

Production Editor: Mae Lum

Technical Editor: Greg Guntle

Electronic Publishing Specialist: Kate Kaminski, Happenstance Type-o-Rama

Proofreaders: David Nash, Laurie O'Connell, Nancy Riddiough

Indexer: Nancy Guenther

Cover Designer: Caryl Gorska, Gorska Design

Cover Photographer: Peter Samuels, Tony Stone

To Sophia, the stinker-doodle

Acknowledgments

This was a difficult book to write, and there were many people who made it possible. First, Tom Cirtin at Sybex receives thanks for shaping and focusing the idea of the book into its final form. The next round of kudos goes to Kylie Johnston, Mae Lum, Sally Engelfried, and Sarah Lemaire, who took my heap of manuscript and made a book out of it. I also need to thank Greg Guntle and John Godfrey for going over the thousands of lines of code with a fine-toothed comb and making sure it worked on more than the two PCs I have available for .NET testing at the moment.

Finally, I need to thank my ever-tolerant wife Janet, who was forced to stare at my back as I sat swearing in front of my PC these past few months.

Contents at a Glance

Contents

Introduction

About 18 months ago, I began reading about the forthcoming version of Visual Basic, and I was jazzed about it from the get-go. The early details were sketchy, but I did know that Microsoft was going to turn Visual Basic into a full object-oriented language. I had experience in some "full" object-oriented development and was quite impressed with the way that good OOP design seemed to naturally organize my thoughts (and my code). I was eager to begin using these design principles in Visual Basic.

Of course, such power was not to come without a price. The new Visual Basic, I would learn, was *not* to be backward compatible with VB6. Since all of my current day job development was in VB6, upgrading to the new language would not simply be a one-day slam-dunk, as it was when I moved from Visual Basic 4 to 5 or from VB5 to VB6.

VB .NET in Perspective

Visual Basic .NET is, simply put, quite a large hunk of new functionality to learn for the experienced Visual Basic developer. While Visual Studio .NET does ship with a VB6-to-VB .NET project converter, you'll quickly realize (maybe before even trying it out on one of your projects) that a strict conversion is probably the wrong solution for all but the most trivial of programs. The reason for this is that the VB .NET is much, much more than a list of syntactical differences. .NET development presents radically new language features and ways for programs to communicate with each other. For this reason, .NET applications will most likely be designed differently from the ground up.

The first major difference that you'll notice when perusing some VB .NET examples is the true object-oriented nature of the language. *Everything* is a class in Visual Basic .NET. Your application, the forms, all the buttons, labels, and Treeview objects are all instances of true objects. This gives the language a previously unknown uniformity. It also gives you the power to create descendant classes of common user interface classes should you need some enhanced functionality and/or some additional data-storing properties.

The VB .NET object-oriented nature is closely coupled with the .NET Framework. The .NET Framework is an object-oriented API of sorts. It represents hundreds of classes that encapsulate functionality found in the Windows operating system or in resources like Message Queue or SQL Server. These classes have been logically grouped into hierarchical organizational units called *namespaces*, which allow you to include only those namespaces in your program that you require. In truth, one cannot get very far learning about VB .NET without also learning about the .NET Framework upon which the language is built.

One of the primary features of the .NET Framework that will radically change your programming thought process is the concept of garbage collection. The .NET Framework manages the memory of all objects automatically, which makes it nearly impossible to write a program with old-style "memory leaks" caused by forgetting to free a resource. It also lets you concentrate on the logic of your procedures instead of matching up every object instantiation with a line of code that frees the object.

You'll also greatly benefit from structured exception handling, a vast improvement over the `On Error Goto` crud you've had to endure up to this point. An exception handler wraps a block of code with one or more lines of code that can handle different types of errors. The classes of exceptions range from very general to very specific, so you can handle a certain class of errors one way (like writing a message to the event log) and another class of errors in a different way (like warning the user about a problem through a message box). Exception handlers can also be nested, meaning you can·take care of problems within an inner block of code that doesn't affect outer blocks. Try accomplishing that in VB6 without convoluted coding!

One of the truly new innovations in the .NET Framework is the concept of XML web services. XML web services are objects that can be called over a standard HTTP protocol. The object is serialized and deserialized into an XML format for transport, and then arrives to your program as a standard .NET Framework object. This method of programming allows developers to make services available on the Internet for other programmers to use, either freely or against some type of payment model. The hope is that XML web services will be the next generation of ActiveX controls, giving third-party developers an excellent way to add value to developers by creating reusable objects that can be accessed over any Internet connection.

Of course, this overview only scratches the surface of what makes VB .NET something that gets you revved up. Microsoft took a step back and rethought the concept of the perfect development tool, and the .NET platform is the result of that. Even after over a year of playing with the language myself, I'm still learning about new classes in the .NET Framework and when to use certain new development techniques or technologies.

Who Am I?

I was one of only two sophomores in my high school way back in 1982 who was offered a computer class after the high school purchased six TRS-80s ("Trash-80s" we called them). I attended the PC classes in junior and senior year, as well. Those were fun times, because the teachers were pretty much learning to navigate the PC world at the same time we were, and we all kind of stumbled through those first years together.

Once I got my hands on software development in high school, I didn't let go. I got my B.S. in Information Systems at the Ohio State University (s'go Bucks!) and started work shortly thereafter for an insurance organization. My job there was pretty interesting: All their data was locked inside this legacy mainframe system (I couldn't even tell you what system), and one of their mainframe programmers wrote a custom query tool that extracted the data out of the mainframe and into PC text files. They hired me out of school to act as a "business analyst," which basically meant that I would do ad hoc projects for people in the company (spitting out mailing labels, summarizing data to back up research projects, and so on). My programming tool at the time was FoxPro 2 by Fox Software (before Microsoft swallowed them whole).

When I left the insurance company, I began a job-hopping journey (some my own doing, some the doing of layoffs and mergers) through several industries, including finance, retail, commercial software development (an antivirus package), and trucking. The main lesson that I learned during these sojourns was that, even though I was pretty much doing the same work (cranking out code) for all of these companies, I wasn't really happy in any job unless I personally found the industry interesting. Having had this epiphany, I set out to land a job in the coolest industry I could think of, which brought me to my current (and, I hope, final) position at the Cleveland Indians' front office, where I've been happily designing in-house systems for almost five years.

Not being satisfied with developing software a mere eight hours per day, I also write some code in my spare time. I became enamored with the PC game industry and found myself writing level-editing programs for games like Doom and Quake. I also wrote my first two books for Sybex on constructing levels for games. My Quake level editor, qED, enjoyed modest success as a shrink-wrapped, retail piece of software. I was doubly excited when I was offered the chance by Sybex to write a book highlighting some of the power of VB .NET for people just like myself—experienced Visual Basic programmers who want a crash course to help tackle the learning curve associated with learning the new language.

If something ever does manage to get me away from my PC, it's usually my wife and two little girls or a baseball game.

About the Book and CD-ROM

This book is aimed at the experienced Visual Basic programmer. Having stated this, I don't spend any time on a "Hello world" program of any type. I also wanted to stay away from the other extreme, however: writing a complete, fully functional application of some sort and then explaining every line of it. These "made for the book" applications are rarely of much use to the majority of readers. Instead, I chose to write small programs that embody one or two of the topics in the book.

I didn't waste time prettying up the interface on the programs or designing them to pretend that they were part of some productive application. Some of the programs are simply buttons that do their thing when clicked, along with a means to output the results (`Listbox`, `Label`, `Treeview`, `Console`, and so on). The focus here is on the nuts and bolts of the code that performs the task in question.

I hope you can take some of the example code and refer to it later as you start to develop your own applications. Need to read from a text file? One of the examples reads the contents of a text file and loads the results into a multiline `Textbox`. Need to read and write to `INI` files? The book contains a self-contained class for doing just that.

All of the projects that correspond to the example code are on the CD-ROM that accompanies this book. There is not always a one-to-one relationship between book section and project. For example, there is a project named `prjNetNotePad` that contains sample code for three of the topics (reading from a text file, writing to a text file, and owner-drawn menus). In many other cases, a single project does correspond to a single topic (the message-queuing section, for example). At the beginning of each topic, you'll find the name of the folder on the CD-ROM that contains the code corresponding to that section.

Onward to VB .NET

As you've probably already figured out, the .NET Framework is a brave, new world. It offers new capabilities to VB programmers but not without a cost: You have a few things to learn, and you'll change the way you approach programming. The mission of this book is to turn you from a VB .NET novice into an "experienced programmer." With any luck at all, it will give you the confidence to march into your boss's office and justify the need to rewrite all of your current VB code in the new version of the language using the .NET platform, thereby justifying your existence at your place of business for many years to come. And, if you're like me, you'll have a ton of fun doing it.

PART I

From VB6 to VB .NET

- Using the new operators

- Declaring variables in new ways

- Working with arrays

- Avoiding redundant function calls

- Speeding up string operations with `StringBuilder`

- Doing without the `Tag` property

- Linking several events to the same code

- Compound Boolean expressions

1   Using the New Operators

 The new operator code can be found in the folder prjOperators.

Visual Basic has always been a bit behind the curve in its use of operators. Fortunately, the .NET Framework has allowed Microsoft to easily make some old shortcuts and some new operators available to the VB programmer.

Operator Shortcuts

Borrowing from the C family of languages, you can now shorten the line of code

```
x = x + 1
```

with the following:

```
x += 1
```

Most of the other basic operators work the same way, as shown in the following table:

Operator Shortcut	Short For	Meaning
x += y	x = x + y	Add y to x and put result in x.
x -= y	x = x - y	Subtract y from x and put result in x.
x *= y	x = x * y	Multiply y by x and put result in x.
x /=y	x = x / y	Divide x by y and put result in x.
x \= y	x = x \ y	Divide x by y and put result in x (integer divide).
x ^= y	x = x ^ y	Raise x to the y power and put result in x.
x &= y	x = x & y	Concatenate y to x and put result in x (string).

All of the operators shown in this table are arithmetic operators, with the exception of the string concatenation operator &.

Bitwise Operators

Visual Basic has never had operators for performing bitwise functions—until now, that is. The following table shows the three bitwise operators available in VB .NET:

Operator	Short For	Meaning	Example	Result
And	Bitwise And	Both left and right side of operator are 1.	1 And 0	0
Or	Bitwise Inclusive Or	Either left or right side of operator is 1.	1 Or 0	1
Xor	Bitwise Exclusive Or	Either left or right side of operator is 1, but not both.	1 Xor 0	1

As a refresher, the following table shows the four possible combinations of left and right sides of bitwise operators and the result of each:

Left	Right	Bitand	Bitor	Bitxor
0	0	0	0	0
0	1	0	1	1
1	0	0	1	1
1	1	1	1	0

Still Missing

Here are some operators that you might be familiar with in other languages but that still haven't made their way into Visual Basic yet:

Mod Shortcut   Many languages use % as a shortcut for the modulus (remainder) operator and then use x %= y as a shortcut for taking the remainder of x divided by y and putting the result back in x. The Visual Basic modulus operator is still mod, and there is no corresponding operator shortcut.

Bitwise Shift   There are still no operators for shifting a set of bits left or right.

Postfix Increment/Decrement   The C language family allows you to write x++, which is short for x = x + 1, and x--, which is short for x = x - 1. These operator shortcuts are not available in Visual Basic. (One wonders why x += y was borrowed from C, but not x++.)

Using the Operators

The example program (illustrated here) shows all of the new Visual Basic arithmetic operators in action:

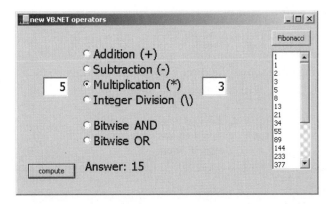

This program is divided into two sections. The left side of the program is a rudimentary calculator that takes the integer values entered into two text box controls and performs an operation on them, depending on the radio button selected. The code that determines what operation to take is as follows:

```
Private Sub cbCompute_Click(ByVal sender As System.Object, ByVal e As_
    System.EventArgs) Handles cbCompute.Click

        Dim iValueA As Integer
        Dim iValueB As Integer

      'exception handlers catch user putting
      'non-numbers in text boxes
        Try
            iValueA = CInt(tbA.Text)
        Catch
            tbA.Text = "0"
            iValueA = 0
        End Try

        Try
            iValueB = CInt(tbB.Text)
        Catch
            tbB.Text = "0"
            iValueB = 0
        End Try

        If rbPlus.Checked Then
            iValueA += iValueB   'this is short for iValueA =
                ➡iValueA + iValueB.
        ElseIf rbMinus.Checked Then
            iValueA -= iValueB
        ElseIf rbTimes.Checked Then
            iValueA *= iValueB
        ElseIf rbDiv.Checked Then
            Try
                iValueA \= iValueB
            Catch eErr As Exception
                Call MsgBox(eErr.ToString)
            End Try
        ElseIf rbAnd.Checked Then
            iValueA = iValueA And iValueB
        ElseIf rbOR.Checked Then
            iValueA = iValueA Or iValueB
        End If

        lbAnswer.Text = "Answer: " & iValueA
    End Sub
```

This procedure makes use of exception handling to make sure that numeric values are entered in the text boxes (zeros are used as the operands if nonnumeric values are supplied) and to trap any divide-by-zero errors that might occur. The rest of the routine merely checks which radio button is checked and performs the correct operation on the two numbers.

The second part of the program generates the beginning of the Fibonacci sequence of numbers and displays the results in a Listbox:

```
Private Sub cbFib_Click(ByVal sender As System.Object, ByVal e As_
    System.EventArgs) Handles cbFib.Click

        Dim i As Integer = 1
        Dim j As Integer = 1
        Dim t As Integer
        Dim iCtr As Integer = 0
        Dim arList As New ArrayList(20)

        arList.Add(i)
        arList.Add(j)

        For iCtr = 0 To 20
            t = i                   'save i
            i += j                  'add j to i
            j = t                   'put save i into j
            arList.Add(i)           'add result to arraylist
        Next

        lbFib.DataSource = arList    'bind arraylist to listbox
    End Sub
```

This procedure makes use of the ArrayList class to store the integers and then binds the ArrayList to the Listbox in the last line. The idea behind the Fibonacci sequence is to start two variables at value 1, add them together, and store the result back into one of the variables. You then repeat this process as long as desired. The preceding example generates the first 21 values in the Fibonacci sequence.

2   New Tricks in Variable Declaration

 The variable declaration code can be found in the folder prjVariables.

Usually, a book in this format might not cover something as rudimentary as variable declaration in a programming language. However, Visual Basic .NET has several significant differences in its base data types and variable declaration syntax. These differences bear discussion because not knowing about them can cause anything from temporary confusion to a hair-pulling bug or two.

Integer Type Changes

The first major change you need to be aware of is that an *Integer* is not an Integer anymore (huh?). Likewise, a *Long* is not a Long, either. In previous versions of Visual Basic, a variable declared as an Integer gave you a 16-bit variable with a range from –32768 to +32767. In VB .NET, an Integer is a 32-bit variable with a range from about negative to positive 2 million. In other words, it's what you used to call a Long. A variable declared in VB .NET as a Long is now a 64-bit integer. So, where did the 16-bit integer go? That's now called a Short. Here's a quick translation table:

What You Used to Call	Is Now Called
Integer	Short
Long	Integer
Really big 64-bit number that I can't define	Long

Why in the name of Sweet Fancy Moses did Microsoft change the integer type names in what seems to be the most confusing way imaginable? There's a good reason, actually. The answer lies in the fact that the .NET platform is Microsoft's attempt to bring all (or most, anyway) of their programming languages under a single runtime umbrella: the .NET Framework. One problem in attempting this was that Microsoft's C++ and Visual Basic languages did not use a common naming system for their data types. So, in order to unify the naming system, some changes had to be made in one or the other of the languages, and we VB programmers were chosen to take on the challenging task of learning a new naming convention (because of our superior intelligence, naturally).

If the new integer naming scheme is simply too much for you to keep track of, you have a nice, simple alternative, fortunately. The Short, Integer, and Long data types are the VB equivalents of the .NET Framework data types System.Int16, System.Int32, and System.Int64. You can always declare your integer variables using these types instead. This would certainly end all confusion as to what integer type is what size.

The *Dim* Statement Behaves Differently

Consider the following Visual Basic variable declaration:

```
Dim A, B, C as Integer
```

In VB .OLD, a line like this was the source of boundless confusion among programmers because the data type of variables A and B was not well defined. The intention of the programmer was probably to declare three Integer variables, but VB6 and below did not treat this line in this way. Instead, only variable C was declared as an Integer, and A and B were most likely each declared as a Variant.

VB .NET corrects this long-time confusion. The previous line behaves as God, Bill Gates, and most likely the programmer who wrote it intended it to behave: it declares three `Integer` variables.

You can still add each type explicitly, or you can mix types, as shown here:

```
Dim A as Short, B as Integer, C as String
```

No More Variants

The `Variant` data type has gone the way of the mastodon. Instead, the base, catch-all data type in Visual Basic .NET is the `Object`. The new `Object` type duplicates all the functionality of the old `Variant` data type.

Personally, I was never much for using the `Variant` data type because it seemed like all I was ever doing was explicitly converting the contents of my `Variant` variables into integers or strings or whatever in order to perform accurate operations on them. However, I find that I already use the `Object` data type much more frequently, because it's not just for holding base data types like integers and strings, but also for holding actual class instance types like a `Button`, a `Form`, or my own invented classes.

Initializers

Using initializers is a cute new feature that lets you declare and initialize a variable in the same line, as in these examples:

```
Dim X as Integer = 0
Dim S as String = "SomeStringValue"
Dim B as New Button()
Dim A(4) As Integer = {0, 10, -2, 8}
```

The first two lines declare and initialize simple data types to default values. The third line is a holdover from prior versions of VB—it declares an object of type `Button` and instantiates it in the same line. The last line creates an array of four integers and sets the initial values of all four elements in the array.

NOTE   Arrays in Visual Basic .NET are always zero-based arrays. The `Option Base` statement is no longer supported.

Local Scope

A variable can now be declared inside a statement block such as an `If` or `Do While` statement, and the variable will have scope only within the block in which it is declared, as in the following example:

```
Dim bDone As Boolean = False
Dim r As New Random()
```

```
Do While Not bDone
    Dim Y As Integer

    Y = r.Next(1, 100)
    bDone = (Y < 10)
Loop

Call Console.Writeline("Final value=" & Y)
```

This block of code will not compile properly because the declaration of Y is inside the Do While block, but Console.Writeline attempts to access it. Since Console.Writeline is outside the scope of the loop, the variable is also out of scope.

Most programmers might combat the potential for these local scope errors by putting every Dim statement at the top of the procedure or function. This can lead to an inefficient use of resources, however. Consider the following code fragment:

```
If not UserHasAlreadyRegistered() then
    Dim f as New RegistrationForm()
    f.ShowDialg
end if
```

In this code, some magic function goes off and checks if the program has already been registered. If not, then an instance of the registration form is declared and shown. If the user has already registered the software, why bother creating an instance of a form that will never be displayed? All this does is clog up the garbage collector later. As you can see, clever use of a local scope variable can save your program memory, making it run more efficiently.

3   An Array of Usefulness

 The arrays example code can be found in the folder prjArrays.

Variable arrays have been a useful tool in past versions of Visual Basic, and they remain so in Visual Basic .NET. An array is a group of variables, all of the same type or class, that are referred to by a single name and an index.

Declaring Arrays

Arrays are declared like any other variable, with the addition of parentheses after the variable name. The following line declares an array of string variables:

```
Dim a() As String
```

This declaration leaves the number of elements in the array as an unknown. You can also declare an array with a known upper bound as follows:

```
Dim a(3) As String
```

This declares an array of three strings. The indices on this array would be 0, 1, and 2.

NOTE All Visual Basic .NET arrays have a lower bound of 0.

Like non-array types, you can also initialize arrays in their declaration line, as seen here:

```
Dim aVals As Integer() = {-1, 8, 5, 2}
Dim aVals As Integer() = New Integer(){-1, 8, 5, 2}
```

These two lines are functionally equivalent—they each create an integer array of four elements.

Working with Arrays

It may seem odd to think of it this way, but an array is actually an instance of a class called `Array`. Because it is a class, it has properties and methods attached to it for performing work on the data within the array. The following table lists some useful properties and methods of the `Array` class:

P/M	Name	Function
Property	Length	Returns number of elements in the array.
Property	Rank	Returns number of dimensions in the array. (There's more information on dimensions later in this section.)
Property	GetUpperBound	The highest index in the array.
Method	Clear	Sets all array values to Nothing.
Method	Sort	Arrange the elements in order.
Method	BinarySearch	Looks for an element in a sorted array and returns the index of its location or the element nearest to the search element if not found.

The following code snippet shows some of these array methods in action. This code loads an array of strings (using the handy `Split` method of the string class), then prints the elements of the array by enumerating through them. It then sorts the array and reprints to show them in sorted order. Finally, it searches for two strings, one known to be in the array and one known not to be in the array.

```
Private Sub cbSingle_Click(ByVal sender As System.Object,_
    ByVal e As System.EventArgs) Handles cbSingle.Click

        Dim a() As String
        Dim s As String
        Dim iPos As Integer

        s = "Now is the time for all good men "
```

```
s &= "to come to the aid of their country"

a = s.Split()

Console.WriteLine("--straight enumeration--")
For Each s In a
    Console.Write(s & " ")
Next
Console.WriteLine(" ")

'note sort is a shared function (class method)
Array.Sort(a)
Console.WriteLine("--sorted enumeration--")
For Each s In a
    Console.Write(s & " ")
Next
Console.WriteLine(" ")

'note BinarySearch is a shared function (class method)
Console.WriteLine("--Binary Search--")
iPos = Array.BinarySearch(a, "good")
Console.WriteLine("found elt 'good' at position " & iPos)

Console.WriteLine("--(failed) Binary Search--")
iPos = Array.BinarySearch(a, "bad")
Console.WriteLine("elt 'bad' at closest to position " & (Not iPos))

    End Sub
```

A few additional notes about the preceding code example:

1. Note that the Sort method is a public class method. This means that the method is not called from an object instance, like this:

   ```
   a.Sort()
   ```

   Instead, the method is attached to the class name itself, and the array to sort is sent as a parameter, as follows:

   ```
   Array.Sort(a)
   ```

2. If the BinarySearch method does not find the desired string, it returns a negative number. If you use the bitwise Not operator on this value, it will return the element closest to the one you searched for.

Multi-Dimensional Arrays

Arrays can have multiple versions, but anything over two dimensions usually hurts my head to think about too hard. 2D arrays, however, have a myriad of uses, especially in computer

graphics (a topic I love but have almost no natural talent for). The following little class shows
the start of a matrix class that uses an array to hold its data:

```
Public Class Matrix3D
    Private a(2, 2) As Integer

    Sub New()

        Dim i, j As Integer
        For i = 0 To a.GetUpperBound(0)
            For j = 0 To a.GetUpperBound(1)
                a(i, j) = 0
            Next
        Next

    End Sub

    Public Sub Add(ByVal m As Matrix3D)

        Dim i, j As Integer
        For i = 0 To a.GetUpperBound(0)
            For j = 0 To a.GetUpperBound(1)
                a(i, j) += m.Element(i, j)
            Next
        Next

    End Sub

    Public Property Element(ByVal i As Integer, ByVal j As Integer) As Integer
        Get
            Return a(i, j)
        End Get
        Set(ByVal Value As Integer)
            a(i, j) = Value
        End Set
    End Property

    Public Sub Randomize(ByVal iUpper As Integer)

        Dim i, j As Integer
        Dim oRand As New Random()

        For i = 0 To a.GetUpperBound(0)
            For j = 0 To a.GetUpperBound(1)
                Me.Element(i, j) = oRand.Next(iUpper)
            Next
        Next
```

```
    End Sub

    Public Sub Display()

        Dim i, j As Integer
        Dim s As String

        For i = 0 To a.GetUpperBound(0)
            For j = 0 To a.GetUpperBound(1)
                s = Me.Element(i, j)
                s = s.PadLeft(4)
                Console.Write(s & " ")
            Next
            Console.WriteLine("")
        Next


    End Sub

End Class
```

The Matrix3D class contains methods for displaying the contents of the matrix in the console and for adding two matrices together. Running the example code will demonstrate the basic functionality.

As you can see, the Matrix3D class uses a simple 2D array of 3×3 elements to contain its data. A more full-featured matrix class would not be "hard-coded" to a 3×3 matrix, but would allow the user of the class to set the upper boundary.

4   Boxing, Unboxing, and a Bit of *ILDASM*

 The boxing/unboxing example can be found in the folder prjBoxing.

Most of the standard "off the top of your head" variable types you can think of fall under a category known as *value types*. These variable types include integers, singles, and all other numeric types, and Boolean, character, date, and enumeration types.

These variables are called value types because their data is held completely within their own memory allocation. Consider the following four lines of code:

```
Dim I, J as integer
I = 25
J = I
J = 101
```

In this example, variable J is set to the value of I, and then changed to a different value. The values of I and J after this code executes would be 25 and 101, respectively, even though one variable is set temporarily to the value of the other. This demonstrates that the memory space of each variable is distinct.

The other class of variables is called *reference types*. Reference types include all classes, strings, and arrays (even if the array elements themselves are value types).

The major difference between reference and value types is how the memory is allocated. Value types are stored on your program's stack, meaning that they can be accessed only while they're in scope. Reference types are stored in a place in memory called the *runtime heap*, and instance variables of reference types act more like pointer variables, which can be seen in the following sample code:

```
Dim I, J as SomeObject
I = new SomeObject()
I.SomeIntProperty = 25
J = I
J.SomeIntProperty = 101
```

This code, although extremely similar to the value type example, yields much different results. The assignment of variable J to I in this example means that both J and I point to the same object instance. This means that when the property SomeIntProperty on variable J is set to value 101, the same property on variable I will also be 101, since both variables point to the same object.

In many cases, you want a value type like an integer to be treated like a reference type like Object. Much of the standard .NET functionality requires this. For example, if you look in the Visual Studio .NET Help at the way to add an item to a Listbox, you'll see that the List-Box.Items.Add method takes a parameter of type Object. Does this mean that you cannot add integer values to a Listbox? In truth, you can add integers to a Listbox, but a special conversion happens automatically along the way. This conversion places the value type variable into an instance of type Object, or, in other words, into a reference type. This implicit conversion is called *boxing*. Here is a simple block of code that demonstrates boxing:

```
Dim a As New ArrayList()
Dim i As Integer

For i = 0 To 9
    a.Add(i)
Next
```

This simple loop is adding the values from 0 to 9 into a class known as an ArrayList, which is like an array with some special functionality. The Add method on the ArrayList requires a parameter of type Object, yet you're sending it an integer value. Since this program doesn't bark at you when you run it, it must be legal.

ILDASM

Microsoft provides a nifty little tool, called ILDASM.EXE, for learning about the .NET Framework at a lower level.

NOTE   The .NET tools can be easily located and executed by running the Visual Studio .NET command prompt, which is located in the Start menu after you install Visual Studio. This program looks like a DOS box, but has environment variables set to point to all of the .NET installation paths. You can run ILDASM from this command prompt simply by typing **ILDASM** and pressing Enter.

This program can be used to view the IL, or intermediate language, dump of a .NET executable. Viewing this IL dump can really teach you some of the under-the-hood workings of a .NET program. The following illustration shows the ILDASM program after opening the compiled prjBoxing.EXE that corresponds to this chapter.

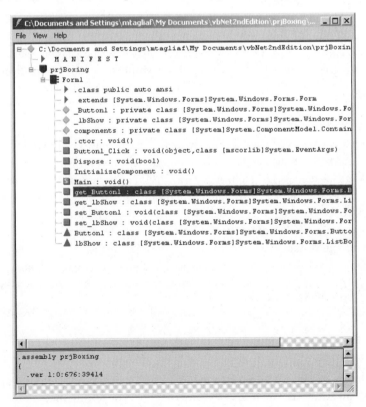

As you can see, the project consists of a class named Form1, and all the members of Form1 are listed in a Treeview form. Each member can be double-clicked to show the IL code that makes it up. Clicking the Button_Click member displays the following code:

```
.method private instance void  Button1_Click(object sender,
    ➡class [mscorlib]System.EventArgs e) cil managed
{
  // Code size       104 (0x68)
  .maxstack  2
  .locals init ([0] class [mscorlib]System.Collections.ArrayList a,
           [1] int32 i,
           [2] class [mscorlib]System.Collections.IEnumerator _Vb_t_ref_0)
  IL_0000:  nop
  IL_0001:  newobj      instance void [mscorlib]System.Collections.ArrayList::
      ➡.ctor()
  IL_0006:  stloc.0
  IL_0007:  ldc.i4.0
  IL_0008:  stloc.1
  IL_0009:  ldloc.0
  IL_000a:  ldloc.1
  IL_000b:  box         [mscorlib]System.Int32
  IL_0010:  callvirt    instance int32 [mscorlib]System.Collections.ArrayList::
      ➡Add(object)
  IL_0015:  pop
  IL_0016:  nop
  IL_0017:  ldloc.1
  IL_0018:  ldc.i4.1
  IL_0019:  add.ovf
  IL_001a:  stloc.1
  IL_001b:  ldloc.1
  IL_001c:  ldc.i4.s    9
  IL_001e:  ble.s       IL_0009
  IL_0020:  ldarg.0
  IL_0021:  callvirt    instance class [System.Windows.Forms]System.Windows.
      ➡Forms.ListBox prjBoxing.Form1::get_lbShow()
  IL_0026:  callvirt    instance class [System.Windows.Forms]System.Windows.
      ➡Forms.ListBox/ObjectCollection [System.Windows.Forms]System.Windows.
      ➡Forms.ListBox::get_Items()
  IL_002b:  callvirt    instance void [System.Windows.Forms]System.Windows.
      ➡Forms.ListBox/ObjectCollection::Clear()
  IL_0030:  nop
  IL_0031:  ldloc.0
  IL_0032:  callvirt    instance class [mscorlib]System.Collections.IEnumerator
      ➡[mscorlib]System.Collections.ArrayList::GetEnumerator()
```

```
IL_0037:  stloc.2
IL_0038:  br.s        IL_005e
IL_003a:  ldloc.2
IL_003b:  callvirt    instance object [mscorlib]System.Collections.
    ➡IEnumerator::get_Current()
IL_0040:  call        int32 [Microsoft.VisualBasic]Microsoft.VisualBasic.
    ➡Helpers.IntegerType::FromObject(object)
IL_0045:  stloc.1
IL_0046:  ldarg.0
IL_0047:  callvirt    instance class [System.Windows.Forms]System.Windows.
    ➡Forms.ListBox prjBoxing.Form1::get_lbShow()
IL_004c:  callvirt    instance class [System.Windows.Forms]System.Windows.
    ➡Forms.ListBox/ObjectCollection [System.Windows.Forms]System.Windows.
    ➡Forms.ListBox::get_Items()
IL_0051:  ldloc.1
IL_0052:  box         [mscorlib]System.Int32
IL_0057:  callvirt    instance int32 [System.Windows.Forms]System.Windows.
    ➡Forms.ListBox/ObjectCollection::Add(object)
IL_005c:  pop
IL_005d:  nop
IL_005e:  ldloc.2
IL_005f:  callvirt    instance bool [mscorlib]System.Collections.IEnumerator::
    ➡MoveNext()
IL_0064:  brtrue.s    IL_003a
IL_0066:  nop
IL_0067:  ret
} // end of method Form1::Button1_Click
```

Granted, this code is pretty daunting at first glance (especially if you consider that it represents only about 10 lines of VB .NET code), but you should be able to make out a few recognizable actions being performed after a bit of study. In particular, you should see two explicit box statements, at lines IL_000b and IL_0052. The first box statement happens right before an integer variable is going to be placed into the ArrayList, and the second box statement is right before an integer is going to be added as an item in a Listbox. Both actions require the integer to be boxed into a reference type before they can occur.

The unboxing (the act of turning the reference type back into a value type) is a bit harder to spot, but it can be found at line IL_0040. Here, you can see the line that reads:

```
Microsoft.VisualBasic.Helpers.IntegerType::FromObject(object)
```

This line tells you that an integer is being loaded from an object, which is exactly what unboxing is all about. In this code, unboxing must occur to get the integer back out of the ArrayList in the following VB .NET code:

```
lbShow.Items.Clear()
For Each i In a
```

```
        lbShow.Items.Add(i)
    Next
```

The enumeration of all the integers in `ArrayList a` is what requires the unboxing.

5   Avoiding Redundant Function Calls

 The redundant function calls code can be found in the folder `prjRedundantFunctionCalls`.

This little coding shortcut seems so obvious that I almost didn't consider it worth inclusion in the book, but I see this rule broken so frequently that I felt it worth repeating. The rule, in its most basic form, is as follows:

Why execute code more than once when running it once gives the same result?

To illustrate this rule with an absurd example, consider the following block of code:

```
For X = 1 to 1000
    Y = 2
Next
```

This loop assigns the value 2 to the variable `Y` 1,000 times in a row. Nobody would ever do this, would they? What's the point? Since no other code executes in the loop except for the assignment statement, you know that nothing could possibly be affecting the value of `Y`, except the assignment statement itself.

When the previous loop is complete, `Y` has the value of 2. It doesn't matter if this loop runs 1,000 times, 100 times, or simply once—the end result is the same.

While I've never seen code quite as worthless as this, the following block of code is very close to one that I read in a Visual Basic programming article a while back:

```
Do While instr(cText, "a") > 0
    cText = Left(cText, instr(cText, "a") - 1) &
            "A" & mid(cText, instr(cText, "a") + 1)
Loop
```

This code scans through the contents of a string variable and replaces all of the lowercase letter *a*'s with uppercase *A*'s. While the function performs exactly what it's intended to perform, it does so in a very inefficient manner. Can you detect the inefficiency?

A Simple Speedup

To determine what rankled my feathers so much about this block of code, you need to think about how long it takes your lines of code to run. All Visual Basic lines of code are not created equal in terms of the length of time they take to execute. Take the `instr` function, for example. The `instr` function scans through a string looking for the occurrence of a second string. Imagine that you had to write a Visual Basic replacement for the instr function. You would start at the beginning of the string, compare it to the comparison string, and keep looping through each character until you either found the comparison string, or got to the end of the original string.

The instr function built into Visual Basic probably does the same thing, albeit in some optimized fashion. However, you don't get anything for free. If you call instr, Visual Basic internally loops through the test string looking for the comparison string. This loop is going to take some finite amount of time (a very small amount of time, to be sure, but a finite amount, nonetheless). Following my rule, why would you want to run this loop more than once when running it once gives the same result?

The previous tiny little block of code calls the exact same instr function three times every time the loop is iterated. If you assume that the instr call itself runs as I surmise (some linear search through the input string), the instr call will take longer to run on larger input strings because the code has to loop through every character in the string. What if the input string to the loop was the entire contents of all the books in the Library of Congress? Let's say, for the sake of argument, that the instr call takes one minute to run on a string as large as the entire contents of the Library of Congress. Since the loop executes the instr call three times, the loop will require (at least) three minutes for each iteration of the loop. Multiply that by the number of *A*'s found in the Library of Congress, and you'll have the total operating time of the loop.

If I make a simple change to the loop, I can reduce the number of instr function calls from three to one:

```
iPos = instr(cText, "a")
Do While iPos > 0
    cText = Left(cText, iPos - 1) & "A" & mid(cText, iPos + 1)
    iPos = instr(cText, "a")

Loop
```

The new loop stores the result of the instr function call into a variable and uses that variable in the first line of the loop, where the lowercase *a* is replaced by an uppercase *A*. The loop result is the same, but the instr function is called only once per loop iteration.

Does a change like this really make a difference in speed? The example program proves the difference. The program creates a large string of random letters (with spaces thrown in to make them look a bit more like words) and then runs through one of the previous loops to replace all of the lowercase *a*'s with uppercase *A*'s. The "fast" loop (one instr call per loop iteration), runs at about 75 percent of the speed of the "slow" loop (three instr calls per loop iteration). A 25 percent speed saving is considered quite good. If a loop of this type were called repeatedly in your application, a 25 percent speed increase might make your application feel faster to the end users. I've learned that the feel of an application is of primary importance to the end user—if the program feels slow, the user might not use the application.

This example program contains a brief example of random number generation in Visual Basic. A class called Random is included in the .NET Framework that handles all types of random number generation. The Random class contains methods for generating floating-point random numbers between 0.0 and 1.0 or between a numeric range. See the example program function named RandomBigString for some sample uses of the Random class.

6   Even Speedier—The *StringBuilder*

 The StringBuilder code can be found in the folder prjStringBuilder.

The preceding section teaches a good general-purpose rule of thumb when writing code: Don't run code multiple times when running it once produces the same result. The example program in that section demonstrates how a sizable speedup can be achieved by following this rule of thumb. Unfortunately, that example program is still relatively dog-slow compared to yet another method, built right into the .NET Framework, for string searching and replacing.

You see, the code was one of the earliest sections I wrote for the book, and it has a decidedly VB6 feel to it. The Instr function and the use of standard strings is exactly the way a VB6 programmer would write a program to replace all lowercase letter *a*'s with uppercase *A*'s in a program. What I didn't understand at the time, however, was the unique way that strings are handled in Visual Basic .NET compared to VB6. In Visual Basic .NET, strings are *immutable*, which is a fancy word meaning that once a string is assigned, its value cannot change. So, consider the following code:

```
Dim s as string = "I'm immutable…."
s = "Yet I've just changed!"
```

What happens here is that the original string instance is destroyed and a new instance is created to hold the second string. The string variable s points to this new instance.

Armed with this new knowledge, I looked back on my original, "fast" method of string replacement in the original example, and was horrified by what I saw:

```
Do While instr(cText, "a") > 0
        cText = Left(cText, instr(cText, "a") - 1) &_
            "A" & mid(cText, instr(cText, "a") + 1)
    Loop
```

This code is destroying and creating the value of variable cText (a string of 16,384 characters) in a loop, one time for every lowercase *a* in the string. If you assume an even distribution of letters (and spaces), this averages out to about 607 destroy/recreate cycles of the giant string. No wonder the loop (even the "fast" one) takes 100+ milliseconds!

Fortunately, the .NET developer brain trust knew that string manipulation couldn't be a slow thing, so they provided some tools in the .NET Framework that speed up string operations. Specifically, they provided the `StringBuilder` class. This class allows for the modification of strings without the recreation of a string instance during each modification. This means that you can probably speed up your character replacement loop measurably using a `StringBuilder` instead of a standard string class. It gets even better than that, though. The `StringBuilder` class has some methods built into it to perform many common string manipulations without us having to write VB code to do it. As an example, here's a new function to replace all the lowercase *a*'s in a string with uppercase *A*'s:

```
Protected Function StringBuilderTextConvert(ByVal cText As String)_
    As String

    Dim sb As New StringBuilder(cText)

    Return sb.Replace("a", "A").ToString

End Function
```

All that is required is to initialize a `StringBuilder` class with the contents of the passed-in string variable `cText`, and then to call the canned `Replace` method. I modified the program from the previous section to add this new method of string replacement so that I could compare the execution times. I had one problem, though—around 9 times out of 10, running the `StringBuilder` replacement method yielded a time of 0 milliseconds! (Occasionally I got a time of 10 ms.) In any event, it's pretty obvious that the `StringBuilder` method is significantly faster than either of the VB methods I had developed in the prior section.

The sample project `prjStringBuilder` shows some other timing comparisons between the `StringBuilder` and an "old school" way of performing string manipulation. On the Insert tab, 1,000 character *x*'s are inserted into the middle of a large string. The `Remove` demonstration is the same for a `StringBuilder` as a `Replace`, with the replacement character being an empty string.

7   Delving into Docking and Anchoring

 The docking and anchoring code can be found in the folder `prjAnchors`.

Finally, finally, finally! I am so tired of writing code to resize controls on a form. How many third-party auto-resizer VBXs and OCXs and ActiveX controls have been put on the commercial and freeware market? Being the type of person who would only use a third-party control when its functionality couldn't be duplicated with good old VB code, I never used one of these controls. Instead, I used to spend an hour writing silly little snippets of code in the Resize event of my VB forms to do things like:

- Making sure the Treeview got longer as the form did
- Making sure the grid got wider as the form did
- Keeping the OK and Cancel buttons near the bottom of the form

Visual Basic GUI components finally have two properties that save me from having to write this kind of time-wasting code ever again. These are called the Dock and Anchor properties. (Any reason why they chose two maritime references?)

The Dock property can be set to one of the following values: None (the default), Top, Left, Right, Bottom, or Fill. Setting the property to None causes the control to stay right where you put it on the form. A setting of Top, Left, Bottom, or Right causes the control to remain attached to that side of the parent of the control. Setting these properties in the Visual Studio Property Editor is done with a little graphical representation, as shown here:

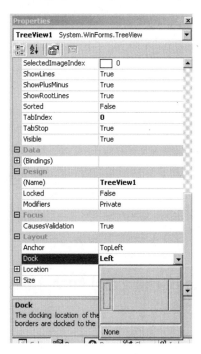

In the sample project, the Treeview is set with a Dock of Left, so it remains attached to the left side of its parent, which is the main form. The control lbDirections is set with a Dock of

Top, which causes it to remain docked with the top of its parent, which is the upper-panel control. The following illustration shows a picture of the project while it's running:

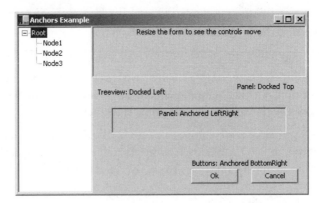

Docked controls grow appropriately if the edges of the parents to which they are docked grow in the following manner:

- A control with a Dock set to Left or Right grows in height as its parent grows in height.

- A control with a Dock set to Top or Bottom grows in width as its parent grows in width.

The Anchor property is somewhat similar to the Dock property, but the control doesn't attach itself directly to the edge of the form. Instead, its edges maintain a constant distance to the edges defined by the property.

Setting the Anchor property is also done graphically, as shown in this illustration:

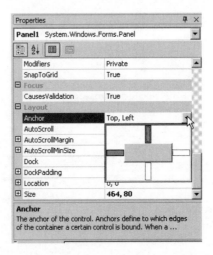

The available settings are some combination of Top, Left, Bottom, and Right. The default Anchor value is Top, Left meaning that the control's top and left side will remain a constant distance from the top and left edges of its parent. If you set a control to Left, Right, the left and right edges stay anchored to the left and right edges of the form—meaning that the control has to resize as the form was resized. The lowermost panel in the sample project has an Anchor property of Left, Right so you can see it resize as the form is resized and it maintains its left and right anchors.

The next illustration shows the same project with the form made both taller and wider. Note how all of the controls on the form have fallen into line without a single line of code!

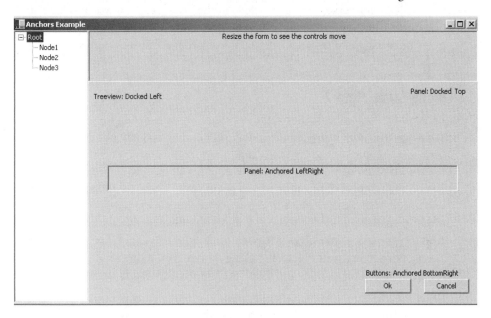

Looking at the illustration should give you a pretty good idea of the Dock and Anchor properties in action, but things should really click into place when you run the provided project. Watch all of the controls conform to their Dock and Anchor properties as you resize the form.

8   Beyond the *Tag* Property

The Tag property code can be found in folder prjCustomTreeNode.

"What? No Tag property? Why would they remove that? I use that property in at least 100 different ways. What the heck am I supposed to do now?"

The hue and cry came from all directions when developers learned that Microsoft had removed the Tag property from all of their controls in the .NET Framework. That Tag property serves as a catch-all property to store user-defined data. It originally started as an Integer property but changed over to a String property to meet user demand.

People found myriad uses for the Tag property. For example, suppose you were populating a Treeview with the names of employees from a corporate database for the purposes of creating an org chart. While loading each employee into a TreeNode object on the Treeview, you could store the primary key for each employee (be it the social security number, a GUID, or some other unique identifying element) into the Tag property on the TreeNode. Then, when the application user selected a TreeNode in the Treeview, you would have instant access to the primary key of the table from which you loaded these employees. This would allow you to query the database to return additional information about the employee (date of birth, service time, current title, and so on).

Along Came Beta 2

I guess Microsoft actually heard the developer screams when they attempted to remove the Tag property. As of Visual Studio .NET beta 2, they actually put the user-defined property back, as a member of the Control class. Apart from almost rendering this part of the book useless, all Microsoft did was anger the *other* developers, the ones who liked the reasoning behind the removal of this property to begin with. These developers argue that you really don't need Microsoft to give you a property for supplying user-defined data, because the object-oriented features of VB .NET make it really easy (almost trivial, really) to add user-defined properties yourselves. I happen to fall into this camp. I submit that by removing the Tag property, Microsoft is actually taking away a crutch that might prevent you from using object-oriented techniques and therefore not use the new language in the way in which it was intended.

Furthermore, having a Tag property on every single component can add up to a great deal of overhead. Do you really need a Tag property on every label and button on every form in your application? Perhaps, but probably not. Why have properties on controls that you'll never use? In the long run, it's better to run with stripped-down versions of all the controls and use other tools to bolt new things on the side, as you need them. This is a core component of object-oriented programming.

To demonstrate the power of using object-oriented programming, I'll take an existing component and bolt a few new properties onto it. In this example, the goal is to load up a Treeview with a list of files on the machine's hard drive. When the user clicks one of the nodes in the Treeview, I would like the program to display the date and size of that file.

There are two basic ways to solve this problem. The first way is to wait until the user clicks a file in the Treeview, then go back to the file system to load the file date and time and display it. This method might be a bit difficult to implement, mainly because the Treeview node isn't going to have the filename with its complete path on each node. I'd probably have to iterate through the parents of the node to reconstruct the full path of the file.

Instead, it's much easier to store the date and time of each file somewhere as I'm iterating through the file system and loading the filenames into the Treeview. The only question is where to store these date and time variables. Since I need a date and time variable for each file I was going to load into the Treeview, it makes sense to bolt these variables onto the TreeNode class, as shown here:

```
Class FilePropertitesTreeNode
    Inherits TreeNode

    Private FFileDate As DateTime
    Private FFileSize As Long

    Property FileDate() As DateTime
        Get
            Return FFileDate
        End Get
        Set
            FFileDate = Value
        End Set
    End Property

    Property FileSize() As Long
        Get
            Return FFileSize
        End Get
        Set
            FFileSize = Value
        End Set
    End Property

End Class
```

The class is called FilePropertiesTreeNode. It inherits off of the base TreeNode class, found in the System.Windows.Forms namespace. The purpose of the class is to add two additional properties to the standard TreeNode. These properties store a date and a number representing the size of a file.

The intention is to use a new TreeNode instead of the standard TreeNode when filling a Treeview with file/directory information. While loading the Treeview, I can put the date and time of each file in these new properties, thus giving me easy access to them as a node is selected in the Treeview. I can easily create more properties that further describe each file, such as hidden/read-only attribute information, the file extension, the bitmap associated with this file type, and so on.

Using an Inherited Class

To use your custom inherited TreeNode instead of the base TreeNode, you merely create an instance of your new class and add it to the Treeview using the same Add method you'd normally use. The Add method takes a TreeNode as its parameter—this includes TreeNode objects or direct descendants of TreeNode objects, like my FilePropertiesTreeNode. Here is some example code to add a new TreeNode to a Treeview named tvStuff:

```
oNode = New FilePropertitesTreeNode()
oNode.Text = "C:\WINDOWS\SOMEDUMMYFILE.TXT"
oNode.FileDate = "Jan 1, 2001"
oNode.FileSize = 65536
tvStuff.Nodes.Add(oNode)
```

Of course, this file information is all made up. What would be more useful would be to load actual filenames off a disk and store their properties in the new TreeNode class instances. This would be the first step in writing a Windows Explorer–like program. The sample project prjCustomTreeNode does just that. It fills a Treeview with instances of my new FilePropertiesTreeNode class, reading files on the C drive as the source of the file information. The main recursive function that loads the Treeview is as follows:

```
Protected Sub FillTreeView(ByVal cFolder_
    As String, ByVal oParentFolder As_
    FilePropertitesTreeNode, ByVal iLevel As Integer)

        Dim d As DirectoryInfo
        Dim f As FileInfo
        Dim o As Object
        Dim oFolder As FilePropertitesTreeNode
        Dim oNode As FilePropertitesTreeNode
        Dim cName As String

        'for this demo, we're only going
        '3 levels deep into the file structure
        'for speed reasons
        If iLevel > 3 Then Exit Sub

        d = New DirectoryInfo(cFolder)
        cName = d.Name
```

```
'fix the entry 'C:\', so we don't
'have double \\ in filenames

If cName.EndsWith("\") Then
    cName = cName.Substring(0, cName.Length - 1)
End If


'create node for this folder
oFolder = New FilePropertitesTreeNode()

'fill the custom properties
oFolder.Text = cName
oFolder.FileDate = d.LastWriteTime

'add this node. May have to add to Treeview
'if no parent passed in
If oParentFolder Is Nothing Then
    tvFileListing.Nodes.Add(oFolder)
Else
    oParentFolder.Nodes.Add(oFolder)
End If

Try
    For Each f In d.GetFiles()

        oNode = New FilePropertitesTreeNode()
        'set up folder
        oNode.Text = f.Name

        'fill in our custom properties
        oNode.FileDate = f.LastWriteTime
        oNode.FileSize = f.Length
        'add this node
        oFolder.Nodes.Add(oNode)
    Next

    For Each d In d.GetDirectories
        Try
            Call FillTreeView(d.FullName, oFolder, iLevel + 1)

        'catch errors, like access denied
        'errors to system folders
        Catch oEX As Exception
            Console.WriteLine(oEX.Message)
        End Try
```

```
        Next
Catch e As Exception
        Console.WriteLine(e.Message)
End Try

    End Sub
```

The FillTreeView procedure expects a folder name as its first parameter. It creates an instance of a DirectoryInfo object based on this folder name. The DirectoryInfo object returns useful information like the name of the directory and the last time it was written to. It also contains methods for looping through all of the structures inside it.

The first step is to create a FilePropertiesTreeNode and add it as a child to the passed-in parent node, also a FilePropertiesTreeNode. This routine has a depth tester that makes sure that the routine stops loading after four levels of depth in the file system. This is done only as an optimization, so the load routine takes a shorter amount of time.

There are two For…Each loops in the routine; the first loops through all the subdirectories in the current directory, and the second loops through all the files in the directory. For each subdirectory, the same procedure is recursively called against the new subdirectory name. For each file, one of the FilePropertiesTreeNode instances is created, loaded with the file date and time information, and added to the parent (folder) node.

Once the Treeview is filled, the OnAfterSelect event is set up so that the following code runs when the user clicks on a node in the Treeview:

```
Private Sub tvFileListing_AfterSelect(ByVal sender_
As System.Object, ByVal e As_
System.Windows.Forms.TreeViewEventArgs)_
Handles tvFileListing.AfterSelect

        Dim oNode As FilePropertitesTreeNode

        oNode = CType(e.Node, FilePropertitesTreeNode)
        If Not oNode Is Nothing Then
            lbFileName.Text = oNode.FullPath
            lbDate.Text = "File Date: " & oNode.FileDate()
            lbSize.Text = "File Size: " & oNode.FileSize() &_
            " bytes"
        End If

    End Sub
```

This code first returns the node that was clicked and typecasts it to the special node class. (The typecast is necessary because the Node property on the System.Windows.Forms.Tree-ViewEventArgs object is of the normal TreeNode class.) If the typecast is successful, some labels are filled with the contents of the custom `FileDate` and `FileSize` properties, as illustrated here:

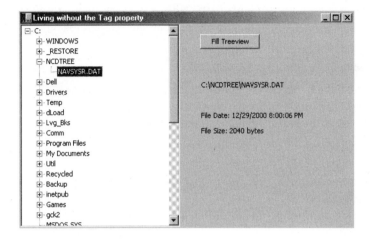

9   Handling Control Arrays Another Way

 The control array code can be found in the folder `prjNoControlArrays`.

From my very first days of Visual Basic, I was enamored with using control arrays. My first "real" Visual Basic program was a card game, and it seemed a perfect solution to create an array of picture box controls with the appropriate bitmaps for playing cards. I completed my card game, uploaded it to a local BBS (this was a few years before the Internet), and received a few comments about it.

My use of control arrays didn't stop with that first card game. I must have written a half dozen card games, as well as some crossword-type games, the mandatory number-scramble game, and a few other simple games that gave me fun projects to work on while I learned

Visual Basic. I'll bet almost all of those early programs used control arrays to handle the game elements.

Before I got my first copy of VB .NET, I was reading an online summary of some of the language changes, and one of the differences mentioned that control arrays were no longer a feature of the language.

The main benefit of having an array of controls is, of course, being able to write the same event-handling code for multiple controls and the ability to easily tell which control fired the event, as seen here:

```
Sub pnPanel_Click(Index as Integer)
    Msgbox("Panel index" & index & "was clicked")
End Sub
```

This piece of VB6 code handles the Click event for an array of controls named pnPanel and displays a message about which one was picked.

So what's a closet game programmer like me to do? If I have several similar user interface elements that I want handled all the same way and I can't group them with a control array, is there some other means to have all of these controls share the same event code? The answer is, of course, yes. Visual Basic introduces a Handles clause on procedures that allows you to link many event procedures to the same code. Here is an example of the Handles clause in action:

```
Public Sub PanelClick(ByVal sender_
    As Object, ByVal e As System.EventArgs)_
    Handles Panel1.Click, Panel2.Click, Panel3.Click,_
    Panel4.Click, Panel5.Click, Panel6.Click,_
    Panel7.Click,Panel8.Click, Panel9.Click

        Dim p As Panel
        p = CType(sender, Panel)
        If p.BackColor.Equals(Red) Then
            p.BackColor = Blue
        Else
            p.BackColor = Red
        End If
        p.Invalidate()
    End Sub
```

This Click event is wired up to nine different Panel controls here. The parameter sender is the control that caused the event. There is nothing that forces you to link the same event to controls of all the same class, so the sender parameter gets passed in with generic type Object. The programmer has to help out in determining what class of object caused the event. In the example program the choice is easy, because I purposely wired this Click event up to only Panel controls. Because I know this, I am able to typecast the sender parameter to a Panel variable, and I now have access to the panel that was clicked.

The rest of the Click event checks the color of the clicked panel and switches the color between blue and red. The last line, p.Invalidate(), forces the panel to repaint itself. This brings me to my second event, which is helped out by a Handles clause:

```
Protected Sub PanelPaint(ByVal sender As Object, ByVal e As_
    System.Windows.Forms.PaintEventArgs) Handles Panel1.Paint,_
    Panel2.Paint, Panel3.Paint, Panel4.Paint, Panel5.Paint,_
    Panel6.Paint, Panel7.Paint, Panel8.Paint, Panel9.Paint

        Dim p As Panel
        p = CType(sender, Panel)

        e.Graphics.FillRectangle(New SolidBrush(p.BackColor), p.ClientRectangle)

        If p.BackColor.Equals(Red) Then
            e.Graphics.DrawEllipse(New Pen(System.Drawing.Color.Green, 3),
               ➥p.ClientRectangle)
        Else
            e.Graphics.DrawEllipse(New Pen(System.Drawing.Color.Yellow, 3),
               ➥p.ClientRectangle)
        End If

    End Sub
```

Again, the paint event for all nine panels is handled by this single event, in which I again typecast the sender variable to a local Panel variable so I can do stuff to it. I then write some custom painting code. First, I fill the panel with its defined BackColor, and then (just for fun), I draw a circle within the boundary of the panel.

The final effect is that clicking any of the nine panels switches their color from red to blue. You can easily see how this might be the beginning of a tic-tac-toe game or something similar:

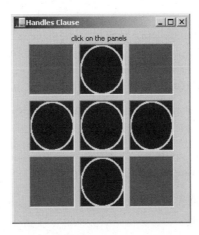

10   Letting Go of the Windows API

The Windows API code can be found in the folder prjApi.

When doing some of the earliest research into what VB .NET was all about, I read that while it would still be possible to access the standard Windows API calls I knew and loved, it wasn't recommended. Of course, I completely ignored this lack of a recommendation at first.

Old habits die hard, so they say. When trying something new in a program, my first instinct was to solve the problem using the same tools I've used to solve similar problems in the past. The example program in this section is a good example of how trying to use the old methods was unbelievably more trouble than it was worth.

The problem I was trying to solve was drawing a hole. The hole is an irregular polygon drawn into a window, with which I could do some cool things (like screensaver effects, for example). In older languages, I was able to draw my hole by creating an array of points that make up the polygon, then defining what's called a *region* in Windows-API speak, and then outlining and/or filling the region with further GDI calls. Of course, there's all the messy handle management to worry about when using API calls, but I've had enough experience in making these types of calls before, so that didn't bother me.

I started my Hole class. It consisted of some properties to specify the number of points that make up the hole, and the default radius (the hole is actually a regular polygon with each point shifted slightly in or out along its radius), a background color, and an outline color. Then, using the trusty API Viewer program found in Visual Studio 6, I began collecting the API declarations I would need for my hole drawing. Here is one such declaration:

```
Public Declare Function SelectObject Lib_
"gdi32" Alias "SelectObject"_
(ByVal hdc As Long, ByVal hObject As Long) As Long
```

This is the VB6 version of the API declaration, and this was only one of seven I would eventually need for my hole drawing. What struck me immediately about this declaration were the parameters and return type of variable type Long. I remembered that a Long in VB6 is a different animal than a Long in VB .NET. Since the DLLs holding these API calls on my PC aren't changing, I would probably have to change my function declaration to get these functions working. I changed all the Long references to Integer in the seven functions.

Then I wrote the Draw method of my Hole class. It looked something like this:

```
Public Sub Draw(ByVal theHDC As Integer)

        Const PS_SOLID = 0
        Const WINDING = 2

        Dim hRgn As Integer
```

```
        Dim hBrush As Integer
        Dim hPen As Integer
        Dim hOldPen As Integer
        Dim r As Integer
        Dim aPoint(pNumPoints) As POINTAPI

        Call GeneratePoints(aPoint)

        hRgn = CreatePolygonRgn(aPoint(0), pNumPoints, WINDING)
        If hRgn = 0 Then Exit Sub

        With pBackgroundColor
            hBrush = CreateSolidBrush(RGB(.R, .G, .B))
        End With

        With pOutlineColor
            hPen = CreatePen(PS_SOLID, 1, RGB(.R, .G, .B))
        End With

        hOldPen = SelectObject(theHDC, hPen)

        Call FillRgn(theHDC, hRgn, hBrush)
        Call Polyline(theHDC, aPoint(0), pNumPoints + 1)

        r = SelectObject(theHDC, hOldPen)
        r = DeleteObject(hPen)
        Call DeleteObject(hBrush)
        Call DeleteObject(hRgn)
    End Sub
```

Again, this is very VB6-like code. I was pretty confident that if I could pass a device context into this method, it would draw my hole for me. Next, I had to find out how to get the device context of a form. This turned out to be a bit harder than I thought (I figured there might just be a property on each form named .hDC or something), but after about 30 minutes of digging, I found a way to do it. The code to get and use the device context of a form looks similar to the following:

```
Dim gr As Graphics = Graphics.FromHwnd(Me.Handle)
Dim iPtr As IntPtr

iPtr = gr.GetHdc
Try
   (do stuff with iPtr here)
 Finally
    gr.ReleaseHdc(iPtr)
End Try
```

The trick here is that you have to release the device context handle when you're done with it. The other trick is that the device context is returned in a variable type named `IntPtr`, which I quickly found didn't work properly when I passed it to my seven various API calls. Once again, after some playing around, I found I had to change my API declarations further to declare some of the parameters as `IntPtr`s (others remained `Integer`s).

The final result of all this research can be found in the class `GraphicHoleAPI`. The problem was solved, but had I really solved it "the right way?" One of the things that told me I hadn't was that interesting `Graphics` class I stumbled across when looking for the device context handle. Was it possible that the `Graphics` class might have some drawing abilities itself?

I'll spare you the morbid details of discovering some of the basic .NET drawing classes, and instead I'll simply present you with the same hole drawing method done using .NET Framework objects:

```
Public Sub Draw(ByVal g As Graphics)

    Dim gp As New GraphicsPath()
    Dim aPoint(pNumPoints - 1) As Point

    Call GeneratePoints(aPoint)

    Call gp.AddPolygon(aPoint)
    g.FillPath(New SolidBrush(pBackgroundColor), gp)
    g.DrawPath(New Pen(pOutlineColor), gp)

End Sub
```

Huh, that's it? After the same basic `GeneratePoints` method, the drawing of the hole happens in two lines of code! In those lines, I'm creating instances of the .NET Framework classes `SolidBrush` and `Pen`, and using those to draw something called a `GraphicsPath` onto one of those fancy `Graphics` class instances. Yes, it seems a bit complicated using all those classes at first, but note there's no messy cleanup of all the objects. (I sound like an infomercial, don't I?) The objects are all garbage collected by the .NET Framework automatically, so you don't have to worry about destroying handles and selecting things in and out of device contexts.

The point here is that the research required to learn my way around the .NET Framework to solve this problem was probably equal to the time needed to retrofit my "old school" API solution into the .NET world anyway. And, by using the .NET Framework, I get the benefit of smaller code that prevents memory problems due to the garbage collector. So, while I know it's hard for some of you to let go of the old world, it's time. As final proof, you can see from the following illustration that each of the hole drawing methods are equivalent:

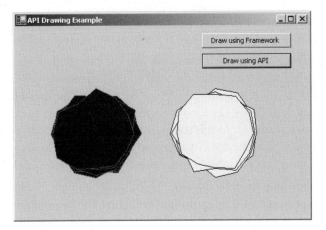

11   Short Circuiting

 The new operator code can be found in the folder prjShortCircuit.

Visual Basic has always been a bit different in its treatment of compound Boolean expressions. A Boolean expression, of course, is any expression that evaluates to a final value of true or false. Here are some simple Boolean expressions:

- X < 45 (True if integer variable X is less than 45.)
- lbOut.Items.Count = 0 (True if there are no items in the Listbox lbOut.)
- cbOk.Enabled (True if the button cbOk's Enabled property is set to true.)

A *compound* Boolean expression is two or more simple expressions grouped together by one of the Boolean operators, like And, Or, or XOR. Some examples of compound Boolean expressions are as follows:

- X < 45 And lbOut.Items.Count = 0 (True if both the left and right side are true.)
- lbOut.Items.Count = 0 Or cbOk.Enabled (True if either the left or right side are true.)

The Potential Inefficiencies of VB

As mentioned, Visual Basic treats these compound Boolean expressions differently than other languages do. In particular, Visual Basic always evaluates both sides of the expression, regardless of the outcome of the left side of the expression. Consider the following pseudocode:

```
If Day(Now) < 8 And TotalWarehouseInventory() < 200000 then
    <Do some stuff>
End If
```

The Boolean expression checks to see that the current date is in the first week of the month, then calls a function to calculate the total number of units in the fictitious warehouse, and then compares those units to a constant. Now, because of how the And operator works, you know that if the current day of the month is greater than 7, then the result of the warehouse counting function is irrelevant in this code—the If statement will always evaluate to false. Now, let's further suppose that the TotalWarehouseInventory function is a very "expensive" function because it opens up a database connection and runs a long query. Why should you run this expensive function if the result is irrelevant?

Many experienced VB programmers recognize this potential inefficiency, and they rework their code slightly to avoid calling the expensive function, as shown here:

```
If Day(Now) < 8 then
If TotalWarehouseInventory() < 200000 then
        <Do some stuff>
    End If
End If
```

This prevents the expensive function from running during most of the month, therefore being much more efficient. VB .NET, however, gives us two new Boolean operators that can also assist in code speedup.

The Short Circuit

Language compilers like C++ perform a simple optimization on compound Boolean expressions. In the case of two expressions linked by the And operator, the compiler skips evaluating the right side of the expression if the left side evaluates to false. Likewise, if two expressions are being combined by an Or operator, the right side evaluation is skipped if the left side evaluates to true. The optimization is known as *short circuiting* the expression.

Early beta versions of VB .NET actually changed the function of the And and Or operators to support short-circuiting functionality. They decided to remove that change, however, when they realized that developers used to the old function of the operators might come up with some unintended results if they didn't realize this changed functionality. For example, let's go back to the original pseudocode:

```
If Day(Now) < 8 And TotalWarehouseInventory() < 200000 then
    <Do some stuff>
End If
```

As mentioned before, VB6 code would always execute the `TotalWarehouseInventory` function. Although the primary purpose of this function appears to return a unit value that represents the inventory in the warehouse, the function might do some other things as well, such as create some roll-up tables or perform some logging. If this little code snippet were to be converted over to a language that short circuits the `And` statement, then those functions wouldn't be executed.

Microsoft realized the potential use for short-circuiting Boolean expressions, so they decided to introduce two new operators that provide this functionality. These operators are the `AndAlso` and the `OrElse` operators. They are used in place of the standard `And` and `Or` operators. So with these new operators, the example pseudocode would look like the following:

```
If Day(Now) < 8 AndAlso TotalWarehouseInventory() < 200000 then
    <Do some stuff>
End If
```

This statement makes sure that the potentially expensive `TotalWarehouseInventory` function runs only when needed. Now you just have to make sure that this is how you intend the flow of the program to be!

The example program in the following illustration demonstrates the difference between short-circuiting and standard Boolean operators:

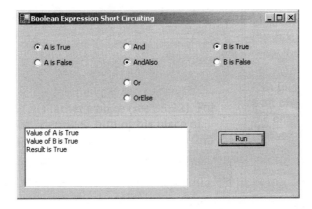

This program lets you set the value of the left and right sides of a compound Boolean expression (called A and B, respectively), and then run one of four Boolean operators on it—`And`, `AndAlso`, `Or`, and `OrElse`. To demonstrate short circuiting, the value of the variables are determined using a simple function:

```
Private Function ValueOfA() As Boolean
```

```
Dim cMsg As String = "Value of A is "

cMsg &= IIf(rbAYes.Checked, "True", "False")

Call lbOut.Items.Add(cMsg)
Return rbAYes.Checked

  End Function
```

The ValueofA function returns True or False based on the value of the radio button rbAYes, but it also adds a line of output to a Listbox. The screen shot in the preceding illustration shows the program when running A=True, B=True, with the AndAlso operator. Note that there are three lines in the output Listbox, meaning that both the ValueOfA and the ValueOfB functions were executed, as well as the end result entry. The following illustration, however, shows the program when running A=False, B=True with the AndAlso operator:

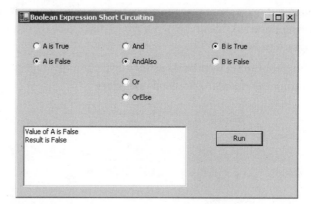

The important thing to notice here is that the ValueOfB function never ran. You can see only two lines in the output Listbox. This is expected because the left side of the AndAlso expression evaluated to false, meaning that there was no need to evaluate the right side.

As you can see, short-circuiting can help optimize your code. Why evaluate expressions whose result is irrelevant? Depending on what you put in the right side of your compound Boolean statements, you can greatly speed up your applications.

PART II

The .NET Framework

- Coding for multiple language sets

- Reading and writing to text files and the Registry

- Event logging

- Evaluating regular expressions

- Improving file copies, moves, and deletes

- Threaded programming

- Writing a Windows service

- Using and creating collections

- Going beyond comments: Writing code for your code

- Using event timers

- GDI+ development

- Reflection

- Automating programming with CodeDOM

- Monitoring your application's performance

12   Getting Resourceful

The resource code can be found in the folder prjResources.

The Web has turned all facets of computer use into a set of global communities. Whether your computer-related interests include programming, game playing, shopping, the arts, or one of dozens of other topics, using the Web to engage these interests means dealing with people from all over the world—they don't call it the World Wide Web for nothing. It's not the least bit unusual for me to converse with a fellow developer from Australia via a Usenet post minutes after Instant Messaging an old school friend living in London.

Developing software in the Internet age should be a global endeavor now, as well. Why cut off a huge portion of your potential user base just because your software can be understood only by those who can read English?

Resource Strings

Coding for multiple language sets can be made easier with the use of *resource files*. A resource file is a list of string constants that are to be used in your application. Such strings might be used to display messages or as the captions to other user interface elements. By giving your program the ability to display these messages in multiple languages, you increase the potential audience for your software. More users is always better, right?

A string resource file is a text file with a familiar INI file format to it. Here is the resource file for a small subset of words in Italian:

```
Language=Italiano
Hello=Ciao
Goodbye=Ciao
Door=Porta
Window=Finestra
House=Casa
Dog=Cane
Cat=Gatto
```

The idea is to create a separate resource file for each language that you plan on supporting. Each resource file would contain identical strings (the left side of the equal sign in the preceding lines of code), with only the strings themselves changing from file to file (the right side of the equal sign).

Once the resource files are created, they must be converted to an XML-style format using the command-line resource generator program named resgen.exe. The resgen program is a command-line utility that can be accessed from the Visual Studio .NET Command Prompt, which can be found in your computer's Start menu under Programs ➤ Microsoft Visual Studio

.NET ➤ Visual Studio .NET Tools. Running `resgen` to convert the preceding text file into a format usable by your program is as follows:

```
resgen.exe resITA.txt resITA.resx
```

Running the `resgen.exe` program with these parameters takes the `resITA.TXT` file, which has the INI-like format shown previously, and converts it to a `resITA.resx` format. The RESX format is used by Visual Studio programs to refer to on-disk resources to be embedded into the application. Adding these resources to your application involves the simple matter of adding the new RESX file to your project, as shown in this illustration:

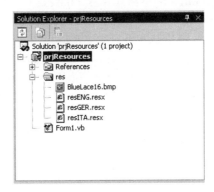

Once added to the project in this way, you can open the resource file and access any of the strings therein by using the following code:

```
Dim ResMan As System.Resources.ResourceManager
Dim cResource as string

ResMan = New System.Resources.ResourceManager("prjResources .resITA", _
System.Reflection.Assembly.GetExecutingAssembly) _

cResource = ResMan.GetString("Language")
```

The `ResourceManager` class is used for getting embedded resources out of your application. To instantiate a `ResourceManager` object, you pass the name of the RESX file (removing the extension, but adding the project name) and the name of the assembly in which the resources reside, which can usually be retrieved using the `System.Reflection.Assembly.GetExecuting-Assembly` method. Retrieving a string within the file is done using the `GetString` method on the `ResourceManager` object.

The sample project in this section uses the basic techniques just described to create three different resource files in English, Italian, and German, only one of which I know with any fluency—guess which one! As the user clicks each of the radio buttons, the corresponding resource file is loaded from the application and the strings are displayed in a Listbox. You can easily see how to extend this functionality to load resource strings for different languages to be used as all of the internal messages and labels in your application, instead of simply hard-coding those values into the source code. (Now if someone could just teach us to speak all of the languages we need to support, we'd all be rich!)

Bitmaps, Too

Resources are not limited only to strings. One can turn just about any disk-based file into a resource and embed it into the application. This can be a much better alternative than installing a bunch of "loose" files with the application and hoping nobody deletes them.

Bitmaps are a good example of a type of resource that you might want to embed into your application. To add a bitmap resource to your application, select Add Existing Item from the context menu in Solution Explorer, select the BMP file that you wish to add, then make sure that the file properties include Embedded Resource, as shown here:

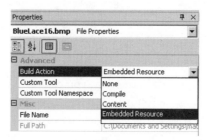

Once you've compiled a bitmap into your application in this fashion, you can retrieve it using the following code:

```
Dim a As Reflection.Assembly = _
System.Reflection.Assembly.GetExecutingAssembly()

Dim b As New _
Bitmap(a.GetManifestResourceStream("prjResources." & _
"BlueLace16.bmp"))
```

This code retrieves a resource by name into a Stream object, and that stream is passed to the Bitmap class constructor. You can now use the bitmap object normally in your code.

13   Reading from a Text File: An Introduction to Streams

The streams code can be found in the folder prjNetNotePad.

The VB6 syntax for reading from a text file seemed archaic at best: You had to keep track of file handles, use strange commands like Line Input #1, and you didn't have much support for handling errors like opening files that didn't exist or trying to overwrite a file for which you didn't have rights. You might figure that the .NET Framework handles text files in a more elegant fashion, and you're correct. In fact, an entire set of classes exists that handles the I/O of not only text files, but also data of all types. This set of classes is known collectively as *streams*. According to the .NET Framework help file, a stream provides a way to read or write data from a *backing store*. A backing store can be a file on disk, an area of RAM, or even a variable like a large string.

There are different types of Stream classes to handle the reading and writing of different types of data from different types of backing stores. A short summary of all the stream classes used for reading is as follows:

Class	Inherits From	Notes
Stream	System.Object	Abstract class, cannot use. Must use a class inherited from Stream.
BufferedStream	Stream	Provides a memory buffer to cache reads and writes in a loop.
FileStream	Stream	Provides random access to a disk file.
MemoryStream	Stream	Provides I/O to a block of memory.
TextReader	System.Object	Provides an abstract class to read text.
StreamReader	TextReader	Reads text from a Stream object.
StringReader	TextReader	Reads text from a string variable.
BinaryReader	System.Object	Provides an abstract class to read binary data.

All of these classes can be found in the System.IO namespace. They handle reading different types of information from many different types of sources.

Reading data from a text file is best done using the StreamReader class. The following code comes from the prjNetNotePad project. It populates the Textbox control tbMain with the contents of the passed-in file:

```
Protected Sub LoadTextFile(ByVal cFilename As String)

    Dim sIn As StreamReader
    Dim cLine As String
    Dim bDone As Boolean = False

    tbMain.Text = ""
    sIn = New StreamReader(cFilename)
```

```
Try
    While Not bDone
        cLine = sIn.ReadLine()
        If cLine Is Nothing Then
            bDone = True
        Else
            'note: carriagereturn = environment.newline
            tbMain.Text = tbMain.Text & cLine & Environment.NewLine
        End If
    End While
Finally
    sIn.Close()
End Try

End Sub
```

After clearing the Textbox, a StreamReader class is instantiated, passing the filename as the parameter on the constructor. (The StreamReader class has no fewer than nine different overloaded constructors, so some study might be warranted to learn all of the options available.)

The main reading loop might look different from file-reading loops you've set up in prior versions of Visual Basic. The main difference is that the StreamReader class does not have an .EOF (End of File) method. Instead, a ReadLine method is called, and the contents of this read are compared to Nothing. If the string is equal to Nothing, then you are at the end of the file. If you're not at the end of the file, then the string is appended to the Textbox.

The last three lines of the procedure close the StreamReader, inside a Finally block. Note that the entire read loop is inside this Try...Finally block. This guarantees that the Stream-Reader will be closed when the procedure returns.

14   Writing to a Text File: More on Streams

The code for writing to a text file can be found in the folder prjNetNotePad.

A bunch of classes for reading data isn't much good if there aren't equivalent writing capabilities to go along with it. As you might expect, all of the Stream reading classes have writing classes right alongside of them. A summary of output-specific classes is listed in the following table:

Class	Inherits From	Notes
Stream	System.Object	Abstract class, cannot use. Must use a class inherited from Stream.
BufferedStream	Stream	Provides a memory buffer to cache reads and writes in a loop.

Class	Inherits From	Notes
FileStream	Stream	Provides random access to a disk file.
MemoryStream	Stream	Provides I/O to a block of memory.
TextWriter	System.Object	Provides an abstract class to write text.
StreamWriter	TextWriter	Writes text to a Stream object.
StringWriter	TextWriter	Writes text to a string variable.
BinaryWriter	System.Object	Provides an abstract class to write binary data.

Like their reader equivalents, all of these classes can be found in the System.IO namespace. Writing data to a text file is best done using the StreamWriter class. The following code comes from the prjNetNotePad project. It takes the contents of the tbMain Textbox control and writes the result to the passed-in filename parameter:

```
Protected Sub SaveTextFile(ByVal cFilename As String)

    Dim sOut As StreamWriter
    Dim i As Integer

    sOut = New StreamWriter(cFilename)
    Try
        For i = 0 To tbMain.Lines.Length - 1
            Call sOut.WriteLine(tbMain.Lines(i))
        Next
    Finally
        sOut.Close()              'make sure the stream closes
    End Try

End Sub
```

This procedure is quite simple. A StreamWriter object instance is created, and the contents of the Textbox tbMain is written to it line by line. The loop is enclosed in a Try…Finally block to make sure the StreamWriter gets closed before the procedure exits.

> **NOTE**   You can access the contents of a Textbox either line by line using the Lines property or all at once using the Text property.

15   Reading and Writing to the Registry

 The Registry code can be found in the folder prjRegistry.

The largest obstacle to learning Visual Basic .NET, in my opinion, isn't going to be the new language features or syntactical changes. Instead, becoming familiar with all the ins and outs of the common language runtime (CLR) should prove to be the biggest hurdle for most .NET programmers regardless of their language of choice. Learning a class framework has proven to be difficult in the past, as well. I recall hearing and reading numerous statements claiming that learning the Microsoft Foundation Classes (MFC) was the hardest part about learning Microsoft Visual C++.

One example of functionality built into the CLR is accessing the Windows Registry. I had written my own little Registry class in VB6 for setting and retrieving values. A quick search in the Visual Studio .NET help file, however, told me that classes were already in place to handle that same functionality.

NOTE   Chances are, if you used any Windows API call in the past, there's some type of class in the CLR to handle that same functionality. This rule of thumb is a good starting point in learning about the CLR.

There are two Registry-specific classes in the CLR. The first class is called simply Registry. The only purpose of this class is to store the Registry constants that make up the roots of each Registry branch: HKEY_LOCAL_MACHINE, HKEY_CURRENT_USER, and so on. These constants, and the properties on the Registry class that represent each constant, are as follows:

Constant	Registry Property Name
HKEY_LOCAL_MACHINE	LocalMachine
HKEY_CURRENT_CONFIG	CurrentConfig
HKEY_CURRENT_USER	CurrentUser
HKEY_DYN_DATA	DynData
HKEY_CLASSES_ROOT	ClassesRoot
HKEY_PERFORMANCE_DATA	PerformanceData
HKEY_USERS	Users

Besides storing these constants, the Registry class isn't used for anything. Most of the work that you'll be doing is with the RegistryKey class. Here's a small procedure taken from the sample program that writes a value to the Registry:

```
Private Sub cbWrite_Click(ByVal sender As System.Object, _
    ByVal e As System.EventArgs) Handles cbWrite.Click


        Dim aKey As RegistryKey
        Dim iSec As Integer = Now.Second

        'start at HKEY_LOCALMACHINE
        aKey = Registry.LocalMachine
```

```
'create a subkey. trap any error (security, etc)
Try
    aKey = aKey.CreateSubKey(TESTSUBKEY)
    aKey.SetValue(TESTSTRING, iSec)
Finally
    Call aKey.Close()
End Try

lbStat.Text = "read registry value " & cFullKeyName _
& " set to " & iSec

    End Sub
```

The constants TESTSUBKEY and TESTSTRING are defined as form-level variables, so they are not shown in this procedure. As you can see, the RegistryKey variable aKey is initialized to the constant Registry.LocalMachine. From here, you can traverse down into this branch of the Registry using the CreateSubKey method. This method opens a key if it exists and creates it if it does not. Writing to the key is done using the SetValue method.

Note that I wrap the Registry functions in a Try…Finally block. Many users do not have permission to write to the system Registry. (In an NT/2000 environment, for example, people without local Administrator privileges cannot write to the Registry.) The Try…Finally block handles any errors that might occur while writing to the Registry and allows the program to continue. One could further enhance the exception handling with a message box to the user, logging to the event log, or some other notification that the Registry write failed.

The sample procedure to read a value from the Registry is almost identical:

```
Protected Sub cbRead_Click(ByVal sender As Object, _
  ByVal e As System.EventArgs) Handles cbRead.Click

    Dim aKey As RegistryKey
    Dim iSec As Integer

    'start at HKEY_LOCALMACHINE
    aKey = Registry.LocalMachine

    'create a subkey. trap any errors (security, etc)
    Try
        aKey = aKey.CreateSubKey(TESTSUBKEY)
        iSec = CInt(aKey.GetValue(TESTSTRING, -1))
    Finally
        Call aKey.Close()
    End Try
```

```
lbStat.Text = "read registry value " & cFullKeyName _
    & " as " & iSec
```

```
End Sub
```

The only difference between this procedure and the previous procedure is that the `GetValue` method is used instead of `SetValue`. The `GetValue` method has two parameters:

- The name of the variable to read under the current key

- The default value to return if the read fails (because the variable does not exist, for example)

In this procedure, the result of the read is converted to an integer. Once again, the Registry-handling code is wrapped around an appropriate `Try…Finally` block.

The Registry is the logical place to store user-specific settings for your application, like font and color choices, file history lists, or other properties that can be changed from user to user. It is also a veritable fun house of operating system and other application settings that you can mine for your own purposes. For example, I was recently writing a program that exported its data to an Excel spreadsheet. Knowing that many end users have trouble with the concept of drives and folder locations (especially in a networked environment), I decided that it would be useful for my program to store the spreadsheet in whatever folder the user had specified as his default Excel file location. That way, when the user opened Excel and clicked Open, the new file would be right there in front of him. I searched the Registry, found the desired key, and implemented this feature in less than 30 minutes. My end users were very impressed with this little functionality because it saved them the headache of finding the exported Excel spreadsheet themselves.

16   Keeping Regular with Regular Expressions

 The regular expressions code can be found in the folder `prjRegularExpressions`.

Any developer writing text-parsing software has probably found regular expressions to be an important tool in their toolbox. Regular expressions can be useful in programs such as log file parsers, HTML readers/extractors, and string search engines.

Regular expressions allow for the fast searching (and optional replacing) of text that matches a certain pattern. For the inexperienced, consider regular expressions to be like the VB `Instr` function to the hundredth power. While `Instr` allows you to look for a hard-coded occurrence of one string within another, one can use regular expressions to look for patterns of strings in extremely complex queries.

The different types of regular expressions that can be composed could easily themselves be the subject of a book, so trying to cover them in any detail here would be, as they say, "beyond the scope of this text." Indeed, the building of regular expressions requires its own separate language, which is outlined in good detail in the *.NET Framework Developer's Guide*. This text, along with the sample program in this section, which gives a half dozen or so examples, can serve as the start of your journey into regular expression expertise.

The sample program creates a class named `StringValidator` that contains several validation functions that use regular expressions to perform their validation. The following code shows one of those functions:

```
Shared Function IsAlpha(ByVal s As String) As Boolean

    Dim r As New Regex("[^a-zA-Z]")
    Return Not r.IsMatch(s)

End Function
```

This two-line function, `IsAlpha`, declares an instance of the `RegEx` class, and then returns whether the passed-in string `s` is a match to the regular expression [^a-zA-Z]. This regular expression is true if any letter in the function is not in a letter, either uppercase or lowercase. The caret (^) in front of the expression negates the expression, which means the `IsMatch` method returns true of any character is not an uppercase or lowercase letter. Note that the `IsAlpha` function itself returns `Not r.IsMatch(s)`, meaning if any character is not an alpha character, `IsAlpha` returns false; the function reads like a double-negative, so it might take a bit of time in your thinking chair to figure out the logic.

The rest of the `StringValidator` class contains more methods identical to this one, but looks for different types of strings. There are methods to test if a string looks like a phone number, a Social Security number, or ends in the letter *k*.

The program itself shows a `Listbox` containing several strings of different formats. Clicking each string shows the result of each `StringValidator` method as a check in a check box control, as seen here:

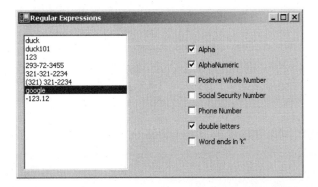

17   Improving File Copies, Moves, and Deletes

The copy, move, and delete code can be found in the folder `prjEnhancedFileOperations`.

One of my pet peeves is that when a new version of Windows introduces new functionality, Microsoft makes it maddeningly difficult for the Visual Basic programmer to take advantage of that functionality. In the old days, this was usually because of some limitation of the older versions of Visual Basic: no function callbacks, no function address pointers, unwieldy API parameters, and so on.

Two such examples of "new Windows functionality" have been around so long that I can hardly call them new anymore without smirking. Both are file-based features, introduced way back in Windows 95. The first is the "progress dialog box" that comes up when you're copying a large file, as seen here:

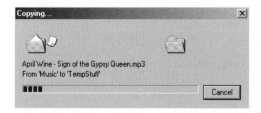

This little nicety is something I've often wanted to toss into my programs, and, until recently, didn't know exactly what mysterious incantation (or API call) I had to make.

The second example is the use of the Recycle Bin. When I want to delete a file in one of my programs, I often want it to go live in the Recycle Bin with the other "almost" deleted files, so the user can bring the file back from the dead if the need arises.

The VB6 `FileCopy` and `Kill` statements did not take advantage of these Windows features. `FileCopy` simply locks up your program until the copy is performed, which makes it pretty difficult to give the user feedback as to what your program is doing. Likewise, the `Kill` statement banishes a file to Nowhere Land with no chance for revival.

I was hoping VB .NET would have these two new features built right into the `File` class. As of this writing, this functionality is not present out of the box. However, due to the new object-oriented methodology, you can easily construct a little class that handles these functions for you. Thus, the `EnhancedFileOps` class was born!

Using the *EnhancedFileOps* Class

The most logical method of designing the `EnhancedFileOps` class would have been to inherit a new class from the existing `File` class. Unfortunately, this isn't possible because the `File` class is marked as NonInheritable, which means that you cannot create a new class under it. Instead, I decided to create a base class named EnhancedFileOps (which inherits right from System.Object) that does the work I need it to do.

The API call that handles both file copying (with a progress dialog box) and moving files to the Recycle Bin is called SHFileOperation. It takes as its lone parameter a structure called SHFileOpStruct. The declaration for the function and the structure are shown here:

```
Private Declare Function SHFileOperation _
Lib "Shell32.dll" Alias "SHFileOperationA" (ByRef _
lpFileOp As SHFILEOPSTRUCT) As Integer

Structure SHFILEOPSTRUCT
        Public hwnd As Integer
        Public wFunc As Integer
        Public pFrom As String
        Public pTo As String
        Public fFlags As Integer
        Public fAnyOperationsAborted As Integer
        Public hNameMappings As Integer
        Public lpszProgressTitle As Integer
End Structure
```

There are also a fair number of private constants declared in the class that represent constants placed into various fields of the SHFileOpStruct. Those constants are as follows:

```
Private Const FO_MOVE As Integer = &H1
Private Const FO_COPY As Integer = &H2
Private Const FO_DELETE As Integer = &H3
Private Const FO_RENAME As Integer = &H4

Private Const FOF_MULTIDESTFILES As Integer = &H1
Private Const FOF_CONFIRMMOUSE As Integer = &H2
Private Const FOF_SILENT As Integer = &H4
Private Const FOF_RENAMEONCOLLISION As Integer = &H8
Private Const FOF_NOCONFIRMATION As Integer = &H10
Private Const FOF_WANTMAPPINGHANDLE As Integer = &H20
Private Const FOF_CREATEPROGRESSDLG As Integer = &H0
Private Const FOF_ALLOWUNDO As Integer = &H40
Private Const FOF_FILESONLY As Integer = &H80
Private Const FOF_SIMPLEPROGRESS As Integer = &H100
Private Const FOF_NOCONFIRMMKDIR As Integer = &H200
```

Sending a File to the Recycle Bin

To send a file to the Recycle Bin, you make the API call with the wFunc parameter set to FO_DELETE, and the fFlags parameter set to FOF_ALLOWUNDO, as shown here.

```
Public Function SendToRecycleBin() As Boolean

    Dim sOP As New SHFILEOPSTRUCT()

    With sOP
        .hwnd = FhWnd.ToInt32
        .wFunc = FO_DELETE
        .pFrom = FFilename & Chr(0) & Chr(0)
        .fFlags = FOF_ALLOWUNDO
    End With

    Return (SHFileOperation(sOP) = 0)
End Function
```

Note that the pFrom parameter requires termination in two nulls, written as chr(0) in VB-speak. The reason for this is that the SHFileOperation API call can actually work on more than one file at a time. To process multiple files, you fill the pFrom parameter with each filename, separated by single nulls, and then you end the whole file list with two nulls. My example class does not take advantage of the multiple file functionality, but it would be easy enough to add in.

Take special note of the last line in the SendToRecycleBin function, because there are a few different little tricks going on there. The first is that VB .NET functions can return their value by using the special keyword Return. Older versions of Visual Basic required that you assign a value to a variable whose name was the function name. This was a big pain when you decided to change the function name but forgot to change the result assignment at the bottom.

The second little trick is a programmer's preference that I like to use to compress my code into fewer lines. The last line of code is exactly equivalent to the following statement block:

```
iResult = SHFileOperation(sOP)
If iResult = 0 then
    Return True
Else
    Return False
End If
```

This block is a bit easier to read, perhaps, but it takes six lines of code, whereas my replacement takes a single line. The trick here is to note that (SHFileOperation(sOP) = 0) is itself a Boolean expression—that is, it has a value of True or False. If the SHFileOperation API call returns 0, then the expression is true. If the API call returns non-zero, then the expression is false. Instead of writing all that out, I find it easier to compress it on one line. I call the function, compare the result to 0, and return the result of that comparison as the result of my SendToRecycleBin function.

Copying or Moving a File

Copying (or moving) a file using the API call is equally simple. In addition to the pFrom parameter that specifies the source file, you must also fill in the pTo parameter, which gives the destination. This is usually a folder name, as shown here:

```
Private Function InternalCopy(ByVal cDestination _
As String, ByVal bMove As Boolean) As Boolean

    Dim sOP As New SHFILEOPSTRUCT()

    With sOP
        .hwnd = FhWnd.ToInt32

        If bMove Then
            .wFunc = FO_MOVE
        Else
            .wFunc = FO_COPY
        End If

        .pFrom = FFilename & Chr(0) & Chr(0)
        .pTo = cDestination & Chr(0) & Chr(0)

        .fFlags = FOF_SIMPLEPROGRESS Or _
            FOF_FILESONLY Or FOF_NOCONFIRMMKDIR
    End With

    Return (SHFileOperation(sOP) = 0)

End Function
```

I made the InternalCopy function private because it handles both the moving and copying of large files, based on the function parameter bMove. I then created easy-to-read methods named CopyWithProgress and MoveWithProgress that in turn call this private function.

The function itself simply sets up the API structure and makes the call. Note the FOF_SIMPLEPROGRESS constant as part of the fFlags parameter; that's what displays the progress dialog box when large files are copied.

The example application allows you to pick a file, which it copies to hard-coded folder C:\tempvb when a button is clicked. Select a large file (100MB files are pretty commonplace these days on many hard drives) to make sure you see the progress dialog box in action. The second button on the form deletes this newly copied file by placing it in the Recycle Bin.

18   Detecting File Changes in a Folder

 The file changes code can be found in the folder prjFileSystemWatcher.

Necessity is the mother of invention, or something like that. Take, for example, the project that accompanies this section. While researching potential topics for my book, I came across the FileSystemWatcher class in the CLR. Thinking this might be a good candidate for a topic, I began writing a program to demonstrate the functionality of this class. After just over an hour, however, I couldn't get my example to work. I thought I was using the class correctly, but it just wasn't detecting file changes in the folder I specified.

As a wise help desk clerk once told me, "RTDM!" (Or "Read the Darn Manual," although the actual phrase most help desk clerks say substitutes a much less family-oriented word into the phrase.) A quick consultation into the Visual Studio .NET help gave me my answer: It seems the FileSystemWatcher class works only on Windows NT or 2000 platforms. My recently purchased PC was equipped with Windows Me.

Warning Unsuspecting Users

This turn of events got me thinking, "If the FileSystemWatcher class doesn't work on Windows 95/98/Me platforms, shouldn't there be some type of programmatic warning when trying to use it in that type of environment?" Therefore, before I show you how to use FileSystemWatcher, I'll show you how to create an error message for those who try to use it on unsupported platforms.

Thanks to the power of object-oriented programming, I can easily solve my own problem. With just a few short lines of code, I can write a descendant of the FileSystemWatcher class that displays an error message if someone attempts to use it in the wrong operating system environment. Here is the entire code for that class:

```
Class tagFileSystemWatcher
        Inherits FileSystemWatcher
        Overloads Property EnableRaisingEvents() _
        As Boolean
            Get
                Return MyBase.EnableRaisingEvents
            End Get
            Set(ByVal Value As Boolean)

                If Environment.OSVersion.Platform() = _
                System.PlatformID.Win32NT Then
                    MyBase.EnableRaisingEvents = Value
                Else
                    Console.WriteLine"& _
                    "("the FileSystemWatcher does not work in _
```

```
                    this operating system")
                    Console.WriteLine("Windows "& _
                    NT or Windows 2000 required.")
                    MyBase.EnableRaisingEvents = False
            End If
        End Set
    End Property
End Class
```

What I'm doing here is overriding the `EnableRaisingEvents` property in the `FileSystem-Watcher` class. A simple test is performed to see what operating system is being used. If it is a Windows NT system (including Windows 2000), then the ancestor `EnableRaisingEvents` property is set to the appropriate value. If the operating system test fails, then a warning message is written to the console, and the setting is left as false.

Not long after I completed this class, I upgraded my new PC to Windows 2000, which not only gave me about 3000 percent fewer crashes, but it also got me the benefit of using the CLR `FileSystemWatcher` class as shown in the example project.

Watching for Files

I decided to use a form-level property for this project to track the directory that I wanted the `FileSystemWatcher` to watch. Properties are useful because you can place code inside the `Set` procedure, which causes the code to execute whenever the property changes. Here is the code for that form-level property:

```
Property pFolderName() As String
        Get
            pFolderName = llFolderName.text
        End Get

        Set(ByVal Value As String)

            llFolderName.text = Value

            oWatcher = New tagFileSystemWatcher()
            oWatcher.Path = Value
            oWatcher.IncludeSubdirectories = False
            'oWatcher.Target = WatcherTarget.File

            oWatcher.NotifyFilter = NotifyFilters.Attributes Or NotifyFilters.
                ➥LastAccess Or NotifyFilters.LastWrite Or NotifyFilters.
                ➥Security Or NotifyFilters.Size

            AddHandler oWatcher.Changed, AddressOf FolderChanged
            AddHandler oWatcher.Created, AddressOf FolderCreated
```

```
        AddHandler oWatcher.Deleted, AddressOf FolderDeleted
        AddHandler oWatcher.Renamed, AddressOf FolderRenamed

        oWatcher.EnableRaisingEvents = True
    End Set
End Property
```

The Get procedure simply returns the value of the LinkLabel control as the value of the property. When the property is set, the LinkLabel value is also set (keeping the LinkLabel and the property values in sync). After this, the FileSystemWatcher is initialized. (Actually, my descendant tagFileSystemWatcher class is used, so I can get the benefit of my new operating system version check.) The oWatcher variable instantiates, and several properties are set to control the functionality. The ChangedFilter property controls what types of file changes to report on. The sample procedure reports on all available changes. (The values are combined using the VB .NET bitwise OR operator Or.) Then, events are tied to the object using the AddHandler procedure. This procedure connects an object's events to an event handler at run-time. The event handler's parameters have to match the parameters required by the event type.

Once a folder is selected in the sample application, you can see it in action by starting an instance of Windows Explorer and playing around in that folder. Try creating a new file, moving files in and out of the folder, deleting files, and renaming files. Each time, the tag-FileSystemWatcher instance should diligently report each of your actions.

19   Thinking in Threads

The thread code can be found in the folder prjThreads.

Threaded programming has been around for several versions of Windows now, but it was scarcely available to the Visual Basic programmer of yesterday. Thread support was not built into prior versions of Visual Basic, and some third-party control or DLL was usually needed to accomplish any type of threaded programming. Those days have left the building. Support for threads is built into the .NET Framework, so if you can find an application or routine that would be best served running in its own thread, you can now easily make this happen.

The most "famous" example of threaded programming (at least to me) is the spell checker in Microsoft Word. You can see the little book and pencil icon running in the lower toolbar as you type, and if you happen to mistype a word, you see the little red squiggle underneath the word as soon as you hit the spacebar to start a new word. This process is running in its own thread, so that the constant icon updating, spell-checking, and red-squiggle drawing code doesn't (apparently) take CPU cycles away from you while you type. Actually, the threaded spell checker in Word was somewhat of a revolution in spell-checking, because all prior spell checkers were a separate process that you performed after you were done typing.

Taking advantage of threads allowed the Microsoft programmers to implement the live, red-squiggle spell checker that you're all familiar with today.

The sample program in this section borrows a bit from the Microsoft Word spell-check idea. I decided to implement a letter-occurrence counter that runs in its own thread, as shown in the following illustration. The Listbox at the right of the text keeps a running count of the letters that you type and performs this counting in a separate thread so as to not disturb your typing.

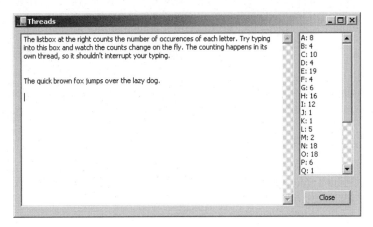

Starting a thread is done just like instantiating any other .NET Framework object. As a parameter on the New constructor, you pass a pointer to the code you want the thread to run when it begins. This is done using the AddressOf operator, as shown here:

```
aThread = New Thread(AddressOf ThreadBegin)
aThread.IsBackground = True
aThread.Start()
```

This code instantiates a thread and sets it to run the ThreadBegin procedure when it starts. It then sets the thread to run as a background thread, and gets things rolling by calling the Start method.

Let's jump ahead to the ThreadBegin routine to see how that does its job:

```
Private Sub ThreadBegin()

    Do While True
        CountTheLetters()

        'sleep for 1 second, then start the loop over
        Thread.CurrentThread.Sleep(1000)
    Loop

End Sub
```

By looking at this code, you can see how almost trivial it is to set up a background thread. The routine runs in an endless loop. A second routine is called that counts all the letters in the Textbox and reports them in the Listbox. (The details of that procedure are not important in the threading example.) Then, the current thread is told to sleep for one second (1000 milliseconds), and the infinite loop is resumed. Since the loop runs forever, you need to shut it down gracefully when the program is closing. This is done in the Closing event of the form:

```
Public Sub Form1_Closing(ByVal sender As Object, ByVal e As System.
   ➥ComponentModel.CancelEventArgs) Handles Form1.Closing
      Call aThread.Abort()
End Sub
```

That's about it. Try running the example program and see how smooth it feels to type in the Textbox while the letter counter on the right keeps updating at the same time.

Once you find out how easy it is to program using threads, you may find yourself rethinking how you might use them in some of your current projects. For example, I'm currently writing a VB6 project that builds a little summary bar graph in the upper-right corner of the screen as a set of data is loaded. This bar graph adds an extra second to the loading time of my data set, but it isn't really used by the application except for the user to view. My thought was that I could make my application feel faster by loading that bar graph in a separate thread, which might cut down the total loading time of the large data set into the application.

20   Timing Up Events with Timers

 The events and timer code can be found in the folder prjScreenSaver.

Timer controls have been around VB for a long time, but now you can create them on the fly without having to drop a placeholder component on the form. Declaring and initializing a timer dynamically can be done as follows:

```
oTimer = New Timer()
oTimer.Interval = 100           '10 ticks per second
AddHandler oTimer.Tick, AddressOf oTimerTick
oTimer.Enabled = True
```

This code creates a timer, sets it to fire its Tick event every 100 milliseconds, attaches the Tick event to the procedure named oTimerTick, and then turns the timer on.

NOTE   You can still use the old way to add most nonvisual controls into VB6-created projects. However, instead of being right on the form, there is a special location in the IDE below the form design area that shows the nonvisual controls.

The most interesting part of this code is the AddHandler statement. While the end result here is the same as if you had dropped a timer control into your project, double-clicked it, and then written code for the Tick event, being able to dynamically add and remove event handlers at runtime can be very powerful. You can, for example, write two different event handlers for the Tick event and then switch between them when desired—something like the pseudo-code here:

```
If (some value is even) then
    RemoveHandler oTimer.Tick, AddressOf OddEvent
    AddHandler oTimer.Tick, AddressOf EvenEvent
Else
    RemoveHandler oTimer.Tick, AddressOf EvenEvent
    AddHandler oTimer.Tick, AddressOf OddEvent
End if
```

You would then have distinct event handlers for the same Timer control.

This ability to dynamically assign events doesn't just apply to the Timer control. It opens the door to being able to create any type of control at runtime and hook up the controls' events to code you have written.

21   At Your (Windows) Service

 The Windows service code can be found in the folder prjWindowsService.

Now here's something that prior-generation VB programmers could never do—write a working Windows NT (or Windows 2000) service. In the past, if you wanted to write a Windows service you had to ask your C++ buddy to do it for you, who would usually just laugh at your "inferior" programming language. (Meanwhile, it took the C++ guys seven hours to get a dialog box with four buttons and a Listbox laid out, but nobody ever seemed to call them on *that* little problem in the language, did they?) In any event, you can now thumb your nose back at the world, for you have the power to write Windows services as well.

What kind of program is useful as a Windows service? Any program that needs to run all the time but (normally) not be seen can be a good candidate for a Windows service. Monitor programs, virus checkers, and security watchdog programs all fall into this category.

My example Windows service is a RAM monitor. It uses a performance counter object to poll the amount of available RAM and to write this number into the event log. My service is hard-coded to perform its polling every 10 seconds; a real-world application would probably wait a bit longer between polling times (or even be user configurable). However, I was impatient and wanted to see my results quickly, so 10 seconds was my choice.

Setting up a Windows service is one of the project types you can choose when you create a new project, as seen in this dialog box:

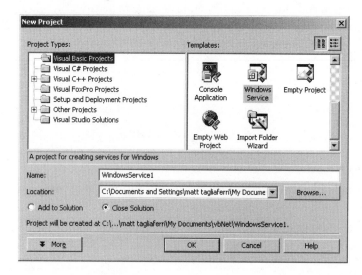

Once you create a project of this type, you will be given a base project with a predefined class that helps get the service installed on a computer. The first thing you need to do is change the `ServiceName` property on the main object to a memorable name for what your service does. This name is important to remember because you'll see it in the list of available services on your PC once you've installed it correctly.

Once you've named the service, you can go into the predefined code and start working on what your service will actually do. The default service class gives you empty `OnStart` and `OnStop` methods, which are called when the service is started (either manually or on system bootup) or stopped on the computer. The `OnStart` method is where you should claim any resources and initialize any data your service needs. Likewise, the `OnStop` method can clean up such resources.

If you only code within the `OnStart` and `OnStop` methods, it will be pretty hard to write a service that does anything useful. Some type of "hook" mechanism is needed to keep your service doing work while it's running. This hook can be a `Timer` object, a `FileSystemWatcher` object, a `Scheduler` object, or anything that gives you the means to run code at a specified time. I chose a `Timer` object for my sample class. The `OnStart` method enables the timer, as seen here:

```
Protected Overrides Sub OnStart(ByVal args() As String)
    oEventLog.WriteEntry(Me.ServiceName & " service started")
```

```
    oTimer.Enabled = True
End Sub
```

On every tick of the timer, the sample service updates a counter, and if the magic 10-second milestone is reached, a procedure named RecordAvailableRAM is called to write the available RAM to the event log. Both the timer tick and the RAM writing routines are shown here:

```
Private Sub oTimer_Elapsed(ByVal sender As System.Object, ByVal _
  e As System.Timers.ElapsedEventArgs) Handles oTimer.Elapsed

        Const RECORDEVERY As Integer = 10

        iCtr += 1
        If iCtr Mod RECORDEVERY = 0 Then
            Call RecordAvailableRAM()
            iCtr = 0
        End If

End Sub

Private Sub RecordAvailableRAM()

        Dim oCounter As PerformanceCounter
        Dim r As Long

        Try
            oCounter = New PerformanceCounter("Memory", _
            "Available Bytes")
            r = oCounter.RawValue()
            oEventLog.WriteEntry("RAM: Available Bytes = " & _
            r.ToString)

        Catch oEX As Exception
            oEventLog.WriteEntry("tagTestService failed: " & _
            oEX.Message)
        End Try

End Sub
```

Once the service is compiled, it is installed from a command line using the InstallUtil program:

```
Installutil prjWindowsService.EXE
```

You should get a message stating that your service was installed correctly. A quick look at your Windows services should confirm this. My test service (named `tagTestService`) is shown in the following illustration, properly installed, waiting to be started:

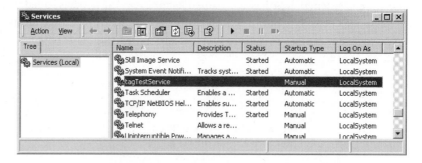

After testing my service by starting it and then stopping it a minute or two later, a quick check to the event log proved that my service was executing properly:

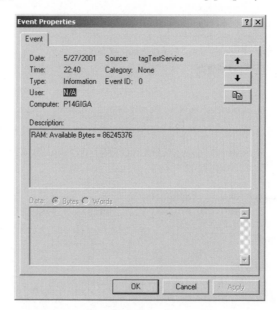

22   Actively Researching Active Directory

 The Active Directory example can be found in the folder `prjActiveDirectory`.

Many modern (as in Windows 2000) networks are using Microsoft Active Directory (AD) as their primary directory service. Active Directory services allow for the easy grouping and management of network resources like users, printers, folders/files, e-mail mailboxes, address lists, and other important objects. The Active Directory Services interface (ADSI) is a set of COM components that allow access to Active Directory objects on a network.

ADSI functionality is encapsulated in the .NET Framework under the System.Directory-Services namespace. There are two primary classes with which you need to become familiar: the DirectoryEntry class and the DirectorySearcher class.

The *DirectoryEntry* Class

The DirectoryEntry class encapsulates a single entry in the Active Directory. Directory entries are arranged in a tree structure (like a standard hard drive folder structure), so that a given DirectoryEntry may have any number of DirectoryEntry child objects under it. These objects can be accessed from the Children property.

A DirectoryEntry class is obtained by passing in a valid LDAP address, as well as a username and password that contain appropriate rights for reading the network's Active Directory. The following code snippet shows a DirectoryEntry instance being instantiated:

```
Const USERNAME = "CN=putusernamehere,CN=Users,DC=mydomain,DC=com"
Const PASSWORD = "putpasswordhere"

Dim cAddress = "LDAP://OU=putOUhere,DC=putdomainhere,DC=com"

Try
    Dim oDir As DirectoryEntry = New _
       DirectoryEntry(cAddress, USERNAME, PASSWORD)…
```

Once obtained, you can use the DirectoryEntry object to parse downward through the tree, using this object as the root.

The example program in this section loads up part of the Active Directory tree into a Tree-view for display. Borrowing from an earlier example, I created a simple descendant class of the TreeNode that could hold a DirectoryEntry object:

```
Protected Class DirEntryTreeNode
    Inherits TreeNode

    Sub New(ByVal oDir As DirectoryEntry)
       MyBase.New()

       'text of the node defaults to the name prop of the directoryentry
       Me.Text = oDir.Name
       FDir = oDir
    End Sub

    Private FDir As DirectoryEntry
    Property DirEntry() As DirectoryEntry
       Get
```

```
            Return FDir
        End Get
        Set(ByVal Value As DirectoryEntry)
            FDir = Value
        End Set
    End Property
End Class
```

This code allows me to fill a visual control (a `Treeview`) with a hierarchical data structure (the tree-like structure of the Active Directory), and keep the tree nodes linked to the `Directory-Entry` classes.

Iterating through any tree-like structure screams out for a recursive routine. Here is the code that loads the `Treeview`:

```
Private Sub cbLoad_Click(ByVal sender As System.Object, _
    ByVal e As System.EventArgs) Handles cbLoad.Click

    Const USERNAME = "CN=putusernamehere,CN=Users,DC=mydomain,DC=com"
    Const PASSWORD = "putpasswordhere"

    Dim cAddress = "LDAP://OU=putOUhere,DC=putdomainhere,DC=com"

    Try
        Console.WriteLine("trying " & cAddress)
        Dim oDir As DirectoryEntry = New DirectoryEntry(cAddress, USERNAME,
            ➥PASSWORD)

        Me.Cursor = Cursors.WaitCursor
        tvDir.BeginUpdate()
        tvDir.Nodes.Clear()
        Call AddToTreeview(oDir, Nothing)
    Finally
        tvDir.EndUpdate()
        Me.Cursor = Cursors.Default
        tvDir.Nodes(0).Expand()
    End Try

End Sub

Private Sub AddToTreeview(ByVal oDir As DirectoryEntry, ByVal oRoot As TreeNode)

    Dim oChild As DirectoryEntry
    Dim oNode As New DirEntryTreeNode(oDir)

    If oRoot Is Nothing Then
        Call tvDir.Nodes.Add(oNode)
```

```
Else
    Call oRoot.Nodes.Add(oNode)
End If

For Each oChild In oDir.Children
    Call AddToTreeview(oChild, oNode)
Next

End Sub
```

The cbLoad_Click routine instantiates the root DirectoryEntry that's loaded into the Tree-view, clears the Treeview, and then calls the recursive routine AddToTreeview. Recursive routines are unusually elegant in their simplicity, and this one is no exception. The passed-in DirectoryEntry object is used to create one of the descendant TreeNode classes, and this class is added to the Treeview, either as a parent of the node that is passed in, or as the root node itself. The code then iterates though all the children of this DirectoryEntry and calls the same routine. The following illustration shows the populated Treeview:

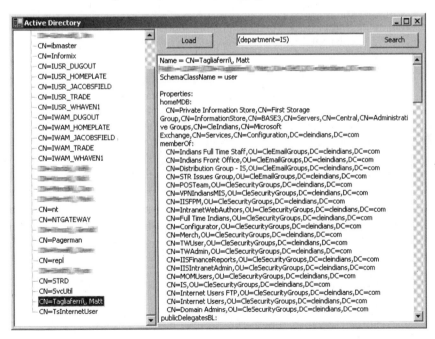

The *DirectorySearcher* Class

The contents of the Active Directory can be simply enormous on a big corporate network. The DirectorySearcher class can scan through Active Directory entries and return those that match a specified condition. For example, you can look for all entries whose Name property matches a certain string or who have a given Department property. The DirectorySearcher will return multiple results (with an optional maximum that you specify), and can be given a maximum amount of time before it returns the results (for those absolutely enormous Active Directory structures).

The sample program in this section shows an example of how the DirectorySearcher class works. It takes the contents of the Textbox named tbFilter and uses that as the Filter property for the DirectorySearcher.

See the VB .NET help for the syntax requirements for the Filter property on the DirectorySearcher.

```vbnet
Private Sub cbSearch_Click(ByVal sender As System.Object, _
ByVal e As System.EventArgs) Handles cbSearch.Click

    Dim cAddress = "LDAP://DC=putdomainhere,DC=com"
    Dim NL As String = Environment.NewLine

    Dim oDir As New DirectoryEntry(cAddress, USERNAME, PASSWORD)
    Dim oSearch As New DirectorySearcher(oDir)
    Dim cOutput As String

    oSearch.Filter = tbFilter.Text

    oSearch.PropertiesToLoad.Add("path")
    oSearch.PropertiesToLoad.Add("cn")
    oSearch.PropertiesToLoad.Add("title")
    oSearch.PropertiesToLoad.Add("department")

    Dim oResults As SearchResultCollection = oSearch.FindAll()

    Dim oRes As SearchResult
    For Each oRes In oResults
        With oRes
            cOutput &= "--------------------------"
              ➡& NL
            cOutput &= .Properties("cn").Item(0).ToString & NL
            cOutput &= "   Path: " & .Path & NL
            Try
                cOutput &= "   Title: " & .Properties("title").Item(0).ToString
                  ➡& NL
            Catch
                cOutput &= "   Title: <not specified>" & NL
            End Try
            Try
                cOutput &= "   Dept : " & .Properties("department").Item(0).
```

```
            ➥ToString & NL
        Catch
            cOutput &= "    Dept : <not specified>" & NL
        End Try
    End With
Next
tbInfo.Text = cOutput

End Sub
```

The `DirectorySearcher` class starts searching at the root node that you specify. (This example starts at the beginning of the domain.) You must also specify which properties you want to return on each object that it finds that matches the search criteria. Once set up, use the `FindAll` method to return the results, which are returned in a collection of objects of class `SearchResult`. The code then prints the name of each object returned, as well as the title and department property values. Note how the code that outputs these values is wrapped in exception handlers. This is because there is no guarantee that every Active Directory object will have a `Title` or `Department` property. If one of these properties is missing, the exception handler allows the loop to gracefully continue.

The following illustration shows the results of an AD search on the corporate network where I work. (Don't tell my network admin that I was snooping around her AD; she'll have my head!)

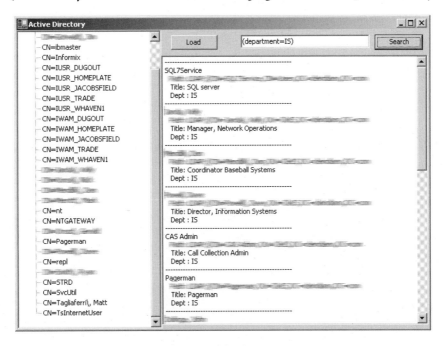

23   Diving into Collections

 The collections code can be found in the folder prjCollections.

A *collection* is a class that manages a related group of objects. Collections vary in how objects are added and removed, how they are stored, and how they are accessed. Numerous collections are built into the .NET Framework, or you can create your own collection classes. This section describes some common collection types and provides some usage examples.

The *NameValueCollection*

The NameValueCollection class is designed for storing string key-value pairs. For example, you might have a list of employee names and their Social Security numbers. The Social Security number of each employee (because each is unique) could be used as the key to look up the name of the corresponding employee. You can use a NameValueCollection object to store the employee/Social Security number pairs.

The following code demonstrates common usage of the NameValueCollection. First, five items are added to an instance of the NameValueCollection object. To return the value corresponding to a given key, use the Item property. You can also enumerate through all the keys or all the values using the AllKeys property, respectively, as shown here:

```
Private Sub cbNameValueCollection_Click(ByVal sender As _
System.Object, ByVal e As System.EventArgs) Handles _
cbNameValueCollection.Click

        Dim oNVC As New NameValueCollection()
        Dim s As String

        Console.WriteLine("---------NameValueCollection " & _
        "example-----------")
        oNVC.Add("000-00-0001", "Mother Goose")
        oNVC.Add("000-00-0002", "The Frugal Gourmet")
        oNVC.Add("000-00-0003", "Pokeman Master")
        oNVC.Add("000-00-0004", "Simpsons Compendium")
        oNVC.Add("000-00-0001", "Real Estate Tycoons")

        Console.WriteLine(oNVC.Item("000-00-0001"))

        Console.WriteLine("enumerate the keys" & _
        "(notice how duplicates are handled)")
        For Each s In oNVC.AllKeys
            Console.WriteLine("-- key " & s & " ----")
            Console.WriteLine(oNVC.Item(s))
        Next

    End Sub
```

Note that duplicates are allowed in a `NameValueCollection`. If a duplicate key is added, the two values corresponding to that key are displayed, separated with a comma. In the preceding code, the return value for property `oNVC.Item("000-00-0001")` is `Mother Goose, Real Estate Tycoons`.

The *HashTable*

While the `NameValueCollection` is made purely for string storage, the `HashTable` is a general-purpose collection that can hold any group of objects. Each object must be associated with a unique key. The most common use of a key is a string value. For example, one could store a collection of `Employee` objects using the employee Social Security number as the key. Instead of associating the key with a simple string like in the `NameValueCollection`, however, you can put any Visual Basic .NET object in the `HashTable`.

NOTE   The rest of the collection examples create collections of a simple business object named `BookEncapsulater`. This class contains the properties for a book ISBN (the unique identifier used by the book industry to identify a title), a title, and a date of publication. Obviously, a fully functional class would include many more properties to fully describe a book title. The code for the `BookEncapsulater` class can be found in the `mBook.vb` module in the sample project `prjCollections`.

The following code adds four instances of a `BookEncapsulater` object into a `HashTable`, and then demonstrates both retrieving one of the objects by its hash code and enumerating through all the objects in the collection:

```
Private Sub cbHashtable_Click(ByVal sender As _
System.Object, ByVal e As System.EventArgs) Handles _
cbHashtable.Click

    Dim oHash As New Hashtable()
    Dim oBook As BookEncapsulater
    Dim d As DictionaryEntry

    "Console.WriteLine("--------HashTable " & _
    "example----------")
    Try
        oBook = New BookEncapsulater("000-00-0001", _
        "Mother Goose", #6/24/1966#)
        oHash.Add(oBook.ISBN, oBook)

        oBook = New BookEncapsulater("000-00-0002", _
        "The Frugal Gourmet", #2/21/1951#)
        oHash.Add(oBook.ISBN, oBook)
```

```
        oBook = New BookEncapsulater("000-00-0003", _
        "Pokeman Master", #11/2/1964#)
        oHash.Add(oBook.ISBN, oBook)

        oBook = New BookEncapsulater("000-00-0004", _
        "Simpsons Compendium", #3/18/1945#)
        oHash.Add(oBook.ISBN, oBook)

        'uncommenting this will produce
        'an exception because you can't
        'have a duplicate key (ISBN)
        'in the hashtable
        'oBook = New BookEncapsulater("000-00-0001",
        '"Real Estate Tycoons", #7/11/1969#)
        'oHash.Add(oBook.ISBN, oBook)
    Catch oEX As Exception
        Console.WriteLine("exception alert: " & _
        oEX.Message)
    End Try

    'return one of the objects in the
    'hashtable using the 'Item' property
    Console.WriteLine(oHash.Item("000-00-0003"))

    'enumerating the elements in the
    'hashtable requires a typecast
    For Each d In oHash
        oBook = CType(d.Value, BookEncapsulater)
        Console.WriteLine(oBook.Name & ", " & oBook.ISBN)
    Next

End Sub
```

One of the minor problems with the HashTable (and most of the other collection classes) can be seen at the end of the preceding code, where you're enumerating through it to return the individual items. Once you get an item back, you have to do a typecast using a CType() function to get the object back into a usable state. This isn't too big a deal, but having to typecast as you take objects out of all your collections is something that's easy to forget and can lead to problems. It seems that it would be much easier to iterate through a HashTable this way, for example:

```
For each oBook in oHash
    Console.WriteLine(oBook.Name & ", " & oBook.ISBN)
Next
```

However, trying to pull the class directly out of the HashTable in this way causes a runtime InvalidCastException error, unfortunately.

The *Stack*

The Stack collection implements the adding of objects in a last-in, first-out order. Think of a stack of trays in the cafeteria. If someone puts one on the top of the stack right before you show up, that is the one you'll take. The tray at the bottom was the first one on the stack, and it'll be the last one off.

In the following code, the Stack implements a Push method to add an object and a Pop method to remove an item. In addition, you can use the Peek method to check out the item on the top of the Stack without actually removing it:

```
Private Sub cbStack_Click(ByVal sender As System.Object, ByVal _
e As System.EventArgs) Handles cbStack.Click

        Dim oStack As New Stack()
        Dim oBook As BookEncapsulater

        Console.WriteLine("---------Stack example----------")
        oBook = New BookEncapsulater("000-00-0001", _
        "Mother Goose", #6/24/1966#)
        Call oStack.Push(oBook)

        '-- other items pushed onto stack here,
        'removed for brevity

        Console.WriteLine("stack being emptied, note order")
        Do While oStack.Count > 0
            oBook = CType(oStack.Pop, BookEncapsulater)
            Console.WriteLine(oBook.ISBN)
        Loop

    End Sub
```

Note that you must once again perform a typecast during the Pop to cast the object coming off the Stack into a strongly typed object variable.

The *Queue*

The Queue collection implements the removal of objects in a first-in, first-out order, like the line for an amusement park ride. The first person in the line is the first person to come out the other end. Adding an object to a Queue is done using the EnQueue method; removing an object is done using the DeQueue method. You may also Peek at the top object without removing it.

Creating a Type-Safe Collection

You've already seen the minor hassle of having to typecast all of the objects coming out of the collection classes in order to use the objects in the code. In addition, you might run into problems putting objects into a collection. All of the methods used to add an object to a collection take any object as a parameter. What if, for example, you create a collection variable meant to hold BookEncapsulator objects, and you accidentally put a MagazineEncapsulator object in the collection? The compiler isn't going to bark at you—you can put any type of object you want into a collection. However, the problem will show up when you try to remove that rogue object at runtime, because the typecast you attempt will more than likely fail.

What would be really useful would be to create a type-safe collection—one that allows you to add and remove objects of one certain type only. In addition, you could perhaps handle all the messy typecasting inside your type-safe collection, making the usage of that collection all the easier.

This sounds like an object-oriented programming slam dunk, but in practice it's not all that easy. Here is what looks like a perfectly good inherited class for storing my BookEncapsulator object in a Stack:

```
Class SimpleBookStackEncapsulator
    Inherits Stack

    Public Overloads Sub Push(ByVal b As BookEncapsulater)
        Call MyBase.Push(b)
    End Sub

    Public Function Pop() As BookEncapsulater
        Return CType(MyBase.Pop(), BookEncapsulater)
    End Function

End Class
```

Easy as pie, no? Unfortunately, the Pop method on this class is illegal. It is not permissible to have an overridden function that differs only by return type. That is, my BookStackEncapsulator Pop function is identical to the Stack Pop function, except for the type of object it returns, and this is illegal.

This problem is easily fixed by adding a Shadows keyword to the Pop definition:

```
Public Shadows Function Pop() As BookEncapsulater
    Return CType(MyBase.Pop(), BookEncapsulater)
End Function
```

The Shadows keyword allows me to completely ignore the base class Pop method and replace it with my own.

A Second Type-Safe Solution

Just to play devil's advocate here, what if there was no such thing as a Shadows keyword? Could you still write a type-safe stack? The answer is yes, but you'd need to do a bit more work.

```
Class BookEncapsulaterStack

    Dim oStack As New Stack()

    Sub Push(ByVal oEmp As BookEncapsulater)
        oStack.Push(oEmp)
    End Sub

    Function Pop() As BookEncapsulater
        Return CType(oStack.Pop, BookEncapsulater)
    End Function

    ReadOnly Property Count() As Integer
        Get
            Return oStack.Count
        End Get
    End Property

    Sub Clear()
        oStack.clear()
    End Sub

    Function Peek() As BookEncapsulater
        Return CType(oStack.Peek, BookEncapsulater)
    End Function
End Class
```

This class does not inherit from a Stack. Instead, it inherits directly off an object and contains a Stack inside it. It has Push, Pop, Peek, and Clear methods, just like a Stack object would, but you don't run into override problems because these methods aren't overriding methods in a lower class.

Yet Another Type-Safe Solution

There is a third way you can implement type-safe collections. This method is built right into the .NET Framework. It involves creating your class by making it a descendant of the class CollectionBase, as shown here:

```
<Serializable()> Class AnotherBookEncapsulaterStack
Inherits System.Collections.CollectionBase

    Sub Push(ByVal oEmp As BookEncapsulater)
        MyBase.InnerList.Add(oEmp)
    End Sub

    Function Pop() As BookEncapsulater
```

```
        Dim iCtr As Integer = MyBase.InnerList.Count
        Dim oBook As BookEncapsulater

        If iCtr > 0 Then
            oBook = CType(MyBase.InnerList.Item(iCtr - 1), _
            BookEncapsulater)
            MyBase.InnerList.RemoveAt(iCtr - 1)
            Return oBook
        Else
            Dim e As New _
            Exception("error: cannot pop, stack is empty")
        End If

    End Function

    Function Peek() As BookEncapsulater
        Dim iCtr As Integer = MyBase.InnerList.Count

        If iCtr > 0 Then
            Return CType(MyBase.InnerList.Item(iCtr - 1), _
            BookEncapsulater)
        Else
            Dim e As New
            Exception("error: cannot peek, stack is empty")
        End If

    End Function
End Class
```

The CollectionBase class has an Innerlist property that should be used to store all of your typed objects. The Innerlist property is protected, meaning it is available only to descendants of the class, not to anyone outside the class. To implement my type-safe stack, I implemented the Push, Pop, and Peek methods by manipulating this inner list and by performing the necessary typecasts on the objects on the way out of the list.

Both of the later solutions work fine, but they aren't nearly as elegant as the first solution—simply creating a descendant of the Stack class. For starters, you have to duplicate every property, event, and method from the Stack class in your new class that you want to support. Suppose, for example, that a new version of VB .NET comes out in a few years, and some useful feature is added to the base Stack class. You would have to open up this new class and add that feature manually. By inheriting right off the Stack class, your new object automatically inherits those new features when you start using the new version of Visual Basic. This example shows one of the reasons why object-oriented programming is so powerful.

24   Pass the Collection Plate One More Time

 The additional collections code can be found in the folder prjSpecializedCollections.

Collection classes are an extremely useful and important tool in your VB .NET arsenal. You can find some really interesting types of collections if you dig deep enough in the .NET Framework documentation. I came across an interestingly named namespace, System .Collections.Specialized, and decided to see what types of cool goodies might be hiding in there.

StringCollection

The StringCollection is named appropriately—it represents a strongly typed collection of strings. Unlike many other collections, the StringCollection can contain duplicate elements (in this case, strings). For example, this class might be useful in parsing out text into word elements.

The following code loads a sentence of words into the StringCollection, binds the collection to a Listbox, and then sets the SelectedIndex property of the Listbox based on a search through the collection using the IndexOf method:

```
Private Sub cbStringCollection_Click(ByVal sender As _
        System.Object, ByVal e As _
        System.EventArgs) Handles cbStringCollection.Click

        'stringcollection is a strongly typed collection of strings.
        'duplicates are allowed
        'searches are linear (read: slow if many elts)
        Dim c As New StringCollection()

        c.Add("Now")
        c.Add("is")
        c.Add("the")
        c.Add("time")
        c.Add("for")
        c.Add("all")
        c.Add("good")
        c.Add("men")
        c.Add("to")
        c.Add("come")
        c.Add("to")
        c.Add("the")
        c.Add("aid")
        c.Add("of")
        c.Add("their")
        c.Add("country")
```

```
        lbElts.DataSource = c
        lbElts.SelectedIndex = c.IndexOf("good")
End Sub
```

The *ListDictionary*

The ListDictionary class implements a collection of objects as a linked list. The linked-list architecture is internal—you do not have to lie awake nights remembering how to keep all those pointers straight during linked-list adds, deletes, and balancing operations like back in school. Linked lists are pretty cool structures when dealing with small numbers of elements, but they don't fare well as the number of elements in the list starts to increase. In fact, the .NET Framework documentation recommends using the ListDictionary only when the elements in your list number 10 or less; otherwise a HashTable structure is more efficient. (The ListDictionary beats the HashTable when dealing in 10 elements or less.)

To prove this theory, I decided to write a little program that timed the searching through both a ListDictionary and a HashTable. I made the number of elements to add to each collection a constant that I could easily change. The code that adds the elements, searches for an element, and reports the time elapsed is as follows:

```
Private Sub cbListDictionary_Click(ByVal sender _
    As System.Object, ByVal e _
    As System.EventArgs) Handles cbListDictionary.Click

    Const NUMELTS = 16384

    Dim oListDictionary As New ListDictionary()
    Dim oHashTable As New Hashtable()
    Dim i As Integer
    Dim o As SomeSillyClass
    Dim t As New tagElapsedTime()
    Dim cVal As String
    Dim iValToFind As Integer = NUMELTS \ 2 - 1

    t.StartTimer()
    For i = 0 To NUMELTS - 1
        o = New SomeSillyClass()
        o.p = i
        oListDictionary.Add(i.ToString, o)
        If i Mod 100 = 0 Then
            lbStat.Text = "adding item " & i.ToString & " of " &
                ➡ NUMELTS.ToString
            lbStat.Refresh()
        End If
    Next
```

```
        o = oListDictionary.Item(iValToFind.ToString)
        Console.WriteLine("listdictionary: ")
        Console.WriteLine(o.p.ToString & " found in " & t.MilliSecondsElapsed
            ➥.ToString & " ms.")
        Console.WriteLine("")

        t.StartTimer()
        For i = 0 To NUMELTS - 1
            o = New SomeSillyClass()
            o.p = i
            oHashTable.Add(i.ToString, o)
            If i Mod 100 = 0 Then
                lbStat.Text = "adding item " & i.ToString & " of " & NUMELTS
                    ➥.ToString
                lbStat.Refresh()
            End If
        Next

        o = oHashTable.Item(iValToFind.ToString)
        Console.WriteLine("hashtable: ")
        Console.WriteLine(o.p.ToString & " found in " & t.MilliSecondsElapsed
            ➥.ToString & " ms.")
    End Sub
```

For the most part, the reported times matched the claims in the .NET Framework documentation. Searching through 16,384 elements was done almost 50 times faster by the HashTable than the ListDictionary class. The search took 180 milliseconds for the HashTable compared to 8,552 milliseconds for the ListDictionary. When searching through 10 elements, the ListDictionary was usually faster (0 milliseconds vs. 10 milliseconds), but these extremely small values are at the lower bound of my little timer class, and the resolution is not as perfect as I would want to do a truly accurate reading.

My own conclusion is that the times are so close in the small elements case, why bother with the ListDictionary at all? The HashTable is clearly superior as the number of objects added gets larger, and if the number of objects stays small, the searches will be quick anyway (only infinitesimally slower than searching the ListDictionary). If you're a real nut for optimization, you could look into a third class, called the HybridDictionary, that uses a ListDictionary in the beginning, and switches over to a HashTable when the number of objects gets large enough to warrant the speed increase. However, there is a performance penalty at the point where the objects are moved from the one class into the other.

Don't Be So Insensitive

Most of the string-based collections classes use a case-sensitive matching algorithm when doing searches. This means that you could add *MATT*, *Matt*, and *matt* to the collection. You may want to create a string collection that does not allow multiple entries that differ only in the case of the letters.

This type of class is created in a somewhat unusual way, using a kind of parent class called `CollectionsUtil`. This class contains a method named `CreateCaseInsensitiveHashtable`. This specialized `HashTable` will throw an exception if a duplicate string is added, as shown here:

```
Private Sub cbHashes_Click(ByVal sender As _
System.Object, ByVal e As _
System.EventArgs) Handles cbHashes.Click

    Dim cu As New CollectionsUtil()
    Dim h As Hashtable

    Try
        Console.WriteLine("case INsenstive hashtable ")
        h = cu.CreateCaseInsensitiveHashtable()
        Call h.Add("apple", "apple")
        Call h.Add("APPLE", "APPLE")
    Catch
        Console.WriteLine("error adding element")
    End Try
End Sub
```

This code will throw the exception because *Apple* is added twice.

25   System Trays in Their Full, Upright Positions

 The system tray code can be found in the folder `prjSlashdotReader`.

NOTE   The SlashDot reader program was originally conceived by John O'Donnell and was the source for an article at `http://www.c-sharpcorner.com`. This article was the first in a two-part series that explained how to retrieve and parse the XML data from SlashDot, but it had not yet placed the article titles into a system tray icon. Given proper permission, I "borrowed" this excellent idea, completed the program, and used it in this book. Check out the C# Corner website for more excellent .NET programming ideas and tutorials.

Everybody wants to put their program in the Windows system tray these days. My system tray at one point or another has been bursting at the seams with icons for AOL Instant Messenger, Napster (well, not anymore), WinAmp, Trend Anti-Virus, speaker volume control, and a few others that I clicked once to find out what they did and then promptly deleted from my system.

You too can clog up your users' system tray with your own program by using the `Notify-Icon` class in the .NET Framework. As mentioned earlier, I borrowed the idea for a system tray program from an online .NET programming colleague who displayed the headlines of the SlashDot news service (`http://www.slashdot.org`) as a series of menu items.

Tray icon programs are created using the `NotifyIcon` class. Creating a `NotifyIcon` to show up in the Taskbar is as easy as the following few lines of code:

```
aNotifyIcon = New NotifyIcon()
aNotifyIcon.Text = "Slashdot Today"
aNotifyIcon.Icon = Me.Icon
aNotifyIcon.Visible = True
```

With this code, the icon displayed in the system tray is whatever icon is defined for the main form of the application. The `Text` property defines the ToolTip that appears when the user holds the mouse over the icon. Finally, the icon is made visible.

NOTE   As of Windows XP, the system tray is no longer referred to as such—it's called the *notification area*.

What's on the Menu?

The pop-up menu that appears when the user right-clicks the icon in the system tray is the `ContextMenu` property of the `NotifyIcon` class. The `ContextMenu` class can be used to display a pop-up menu on any control. Setting up a `ContextMenu` in code is done exactly as normal menus are—by appending `MenuItem` objects to the `ContextMenu` object.

For my example, I knew that I was going to be displaying SlashDot article titles in the menu, and that each of these articles was going to be associated with a web address that the user could navigate to by accessing that menu item. To easily store the web address with each `MenuItem`, I decided to create a descendant of the `MenuItem` class with a string property to store the URL:

```
Class MenuItemWithURL
    Inherits MenuItem

    Sub New(ByVal cText As String, ByVal cURL As String)
        Call MyBase.New(cText)
        URL = cURL
    End Sub

    Private FURL As String
    Property URL() As String
        Get
            Return FURL
```

```
            End Get
            Set(ByVal Value As String)
                FURL = Value
            End Set
        End Property
    End Class
```

This short code creates a new type of `MenuItem` object with one additional string property for storing the URL associated with the article. It also creates a new constructor so that I can easily pass in the menu text and the URL as I create each instance.

Once armed with my new `MenuItem` descendant, building the `ContextMenu` was done as follows:

```
Dim cTitle As String
Dim cURL As String
Dim aMenu As ContextMenu
Dim aUMenuItem As MenuItemWithURL
Dim aMenuItem As MenuItem

Try
    aMenu = New ContextMenu()
    aMenu.MenuItems.Clear()
Catch oEX As Exception
    MsgBox(oEX.ToString)
    Exit Sub
End Try


' **** start: code simplified for this section --
For Each (something) In (somethingelse)
    cTitle = ObtainTitle()
    cURL = ObtainURL()
'**** end: code simplified for this section --

aUMenuItem = New MenuItemWithURL(cTitle, cURL)
AddHandler aUMenuItem.Click, AddressOf MenuClick
aMenu.MenuItems.Add(aUMenuItem)
End If
Next

aMenuItem = New MenuItem("-")
aMenu.MenuItems.Add(aMenuItem)
aMenuItem = New MenuItem("Exit")
AddHandler aMenuItem.Click, AddressOf AppExit
aMenu.MenuItems.Add(aMenuItem)
aNotifyIcon.ContextMenu = aMenu
```

I purposely left out the code that figures out how to loop through and load the headlines and URL strings so that I might better explain them in their own chapter. Thus, the code between the obvious comments in the preceding code is merely placeholder pseudocode to show you that a loop is in fact being executed and that an article title and URL are being somehow loaded into string variables.

Once these variables are loaded, one of my snazzy new `MenuItemWithURL` classes is instantiated. These two variables are passed in to the constructor, and the object is added to a `ContextMenu` instance named `aMenu`. The `Click` event for each of these menus is set to a procedure named `MenuClick`.

Next, two standard `MenuItem` objects are added to the `ContextMenu`. The first object is simply a divider line, and the second object is the option to exit the program. This last `MenuItem` has its `Click` event set to a procedure named `AppExit`.

Finally, the `ContextMenu` for my `NotifyIcon` object is set to point to the `aMenu` variable that I just built. This allows the pop-up menu to appear when the user right-clicks my tray icon.

When the user selects one of the `MenuItemWithURL` objects from the menu, the following two-line procedure is called:

```
Private Sub MenuClick(ByVal sender As Object, ByVal e As _
EventArgs)

    Dim aItem As MenuItemWithURL

    aItem = CType(sender, MenuItemWithURL)
    Process.Start(aItem.URL)
End Sub
```

This code typecasts the passed-in `Sender` variable back to my `MenuItemWithURL` class and then calls the `Process.Start` method on the URL that is stored in this menu item. This has the effect of starting the machine's default browser and navigating to that site. Thus, when the user selects one of the articles from the menu, their browser opens and they can read the text of the article, as seen in this illustration:

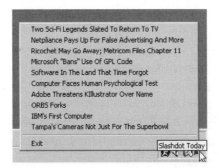

The program is rounded out by adding a timer that reloads the ContextMenu at a regular interval. I set this interval to two minutes while testing my program; a production version of the program would probably reload the menu at a more sane level, say once or twice per hour.

26   Seeing the Inner Workings of Your Code

The StackFrame code can be found in folder prjStackFrames.

Writing code that displays information about your code—now *that's* pretty cool. The .NET Framework allows you to access information about the procedure-calling stack using the StackTrace and StackFrame classes. The following procedure gives an example:

```
Private Sub DisplayStackFrameReport()

    Dim oST As New StackTrace(0)
    Dim oSF As StackFrame
    Dim oMeth As MethodBase
    Dim oParm As ParameterInfo
    Dim i As Integer

    Call lbOut.Items.Clear()
    For i = 0 To oST.FrameCount - 1
        oSF = oST.GetFrame(i)
        oMeth = oSF.GetMethod
        lbOut.Items.Add("----- stack frame " & i _
        & " -----")

        lbOut.Items.Add("MethodName=" & oMeth.Name)
        lbOut.Items.Add("Private=" & oMeth.IsPrivate)
        lbOut.Items.Add("Public =" & oMeth.IsPublic)
        For Each oParm In oMeth.GetParameters
            lbOut.Items.Add(" Parameter=" & oParm.Name)
            lbOut.Items.Add(" Type=" & _
            oParm.ParameterType.ToString)
        Next
    Next

End Sub
```

The StackTrace constructor in this procedure takes a single integer parameter that defines how many frames to skip in this trace. This functionality is provided so that you might skip reporting on procedures dealing only with the debugging code you are writing. In this example, however, I chose to not skip any frames by providing a 0 as the parameter.

The available frames are then iterated with a For loop. For each frame, the method (procedure) name is obtained by returning the MethodBase object tied to the current StackFrame object. The `MethodBase` class also provides detailed information on each parameter passed in as a collection of `ParameterInfo` objects. The last part of the procedure shows each parameter's name and type.

The following is the full output to this simple procedure. You can learn an enormous amount of information about the inner workings of your program, VB .NET, and Windows in general by studying the full stack trace of even a simple program like this one:

```
----- stack frame 0 -----
MethodName=Button2_Click
Private=False
Public =False
 Parameter=sender
 Type=System.Object
 Parameter=e
 Type=System.EventArgs
----- stack frame 1 -----
MethodName=OnClick
Private=False
Public =False
 Parameter=e
 Type=System.EventArgs
----- stack frame 2 -----
MethodName=OnClick
Private=False
Public =False
 Parameter=e
 Type=System.EventArgs
----- stack frame 3 -----
MethodName=OnMouseUp
Private=False
Public =False
 Parameter=mevent
 Type=System.WinForms.MouseEventArgs
----- stack frame 4 -----
MethodName=WmMouseUp
Private=True
Public =False
 Parameter=m
 Type=System.WinForms.Message&
 Parameter=button
 Type=System.WinForms.MouseButtons
----- stack frame 5 -----
MethodName=WndProc
Private=False
Public =False
 Parameter=m
```

```
          Type=System.WinForms.Message&
          ————— stack frame 6 —————
          MethodName=WndProc
          Private=False
          Public =False
           Parameter=m
           Type=System.WinForms.Message&
          ————— stack frame 7 —————
          MethodName=WndProc
          Private=False
          Public =False
           Parameter=m
           Type=System.WinForms.Message&
          ————— stack frame 8 —————
          MethodName=WndProc
          Private=False
          Public =False
           Parameter=m
           Type=System.WinForms.Message&
          ————— stack frame 9 —————
          MethodName=OnMessage
          Private=False
          Public =True
           Parameter=m
           Type=System.WinForms.Message&
          ————— stack frame 10 —————
          MethodName=WndProc
          Private=False
          Public =False
           Parameter=m
           Type=System.WinForms.Message&
          ————— stack frame 11 —————
          MethodName=DebuggableCallback
          Private=True
          Public =False
           Parameter=hWnd
           Type=Int32
           Parameter=msg
           Type=Int32
           Parameter=wParam
           Type=Int32
           Parameter=lParam
           Type=Int32
          ————— stack frame 12 —————
          MethodName=DispatchMessageW
          Private=False
          Public =True
           Parameter=msg
```

```
Type=Microsoft.Win32.Interop.MSG&
------ stack frame 13 ------
MethodName=Microsoft.Win32.Interop.IMsoComponentManager.FPushMessageLoop
Private=True
Public =False
 Parameter=dwComponentID
 Type=Int32
 Parameter=reason
 Type=Int32
 Parameter=pvLoopData
 Type=Int32
------ stack frame 14 ------
MethodName=RunMessageLoop
Private=False
Public =False
 Parameter=reason
 Type=Int32
 Parameter=form
 Type=System.WinForms.Form
------ stack frame 15 ------
MethodName=Run
Private=False
Public =True
 Parameter=mainForm
 Type=System.WinForms.Form
------ stack frame 16 ------
MethodName=Main
Private=False
Public =True
------ stack frame 17 ------
MethodName=_main
Private=False
Public =True
 Parameter=_s
 Type=System.String[]
```

27   Writing Code for Your Code

 The commenting code can be found in the folder `prjCustomAttributes`.

Prior to VB .NET, the only means a developer had to document code was the use of comments. Commenting code is a widely varied art—each developer has their own style and technique for documentation. The blessing and the curse of comments is their free-form nature. While free-form comments allow developers to express themselves in whatever means they desire, the comments often fail in their overall purpose, which is to document the project at all levels.

I've worked in a number of development shops where the senior developers decided to implement a structured format for comments in critical areas, to introduce subroutines, for example. These structured comment blocks might contain a brief description of the routine, the original author, the date last modified, and possibly a change history. While the intentions of structured code commenting are noble, there are many problems with this method of code documentation. Most important, there's no way to police their use. If a lazy programmer decides he isn't going to use the structured comment headers, who's to stop him? Sure, someone can be paid to scour code for hours and make sure that each procedure has a comment, but that sounds like a waste of time and money. Plus, what happens when the code cop actually finds an uncommented routine? Who does she yell at? By definition, the code is undocumented, so there's no easy way to figure out who failed to add the comment block.

Visual Basic .NET attempts to aid in the code documentation effort through the use of *attributes*. Attributes are a type of class in the .NET Framework that you can create and "attach" to code elements—methods, events, properties, or even whole classes.

There are many predefined attributes built into the .NET Framework that help to describe characteristics of existing Framework elements. For example, the description that appears at the bottom of the Property Inspector in Visual Studio each time you select a property is an attribute of that property. The following illustration shows an example of this descriptive text:

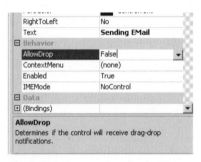

You are not limited to attributes that Microsoft thought you might need to describe your project. Because attributes are .NET Framework classes themselves, you can create and use your own. This is kind of like writing code for your code. Let's look at the beginning of a custom attribute:

```
<AttributeUsage(AttributeTargets.Class Or _
AttributeTargets.Method Or AttributeTargets.Constructor Or _
AttributeTargets.Property)> _
Public Class CodeDescriptor
    Inherits System.Attribute
```

```
Private FModifiedBy As String = "mjt"
Private FDate As Date
Private FDescription As String

Sub New(ByVal cName As String, ByVal dDate As String, ByVal cDesc As String)
    MyBase.New()

    FModifiedBy = cName
    Try
        FDate = CDate(dDate)
    Catch oEX As Exception
        FDate = Now
    End Try

    FDescription = cDesc
End Sub
```

This is a simple class called `CodeDescriptor` with three basic properties: a name (intended to be an author name), a last-modified date, and a description. The `CodeDescriptor` class inherits off base class `System.Attribute`. This class itself is declared with one of the built-in .NET Framework attributes, `AttributeUsage`. The declaration of this attribute describes where the new attribute can be used. In this case, you can use the new attribute on a class definition, a method, a constructor (a special type of method), or a property.

The constructor to the `CodeDescriptor` class merely takes default values for the three parameters and stores them in the private variables. Additional code (not shown here) is set up to make these three private variables accessible via properties.

Once the attribute is defined in this way, you can use it to describe code in your projects. The following is a simple class that uses the attribute to help describe it:

```
CodeDescriptor("mjt", "4/01/2001", _
"A normal label that defaults to Navy Forecolor")> _
Public Class BlueLabel
    Inherits Label

    <CodeDescriptor("mjt", "4/01/2001", "Base Constructor")> _
    Public Sub New()
        MyBase.New()
        Me.ForeColor = system.drawing.Color.Navy
    End Sub

End Class
```

Note the `CodeDescriptor` attribute passing in the author initials, the date, and some descriptive text. This attribute is used on both the class definition and the constructor for this new class.

Using Attributes for Documentation

So have you really improved anything? OK, you've defined a documenting attribute that your developers can attach to their code, but how do you force them to use it? You still have to police the use of your attribute. This is where the beauty of structured documentation kicks in: You can actually write code that tests for the presence or absence of a given attribute. Here is some code that does just that:

```
Public Shared Sub FindPropertiesMissingMe(ByVal _
t As Type)

Dim oAT As Attribute
Dim oPR As PropertyInfo
Dim bAtLeastOne As Boolean
Dim bFoundit As Boolean
Dim cLine As String

Console.WriteLine("")
Console.WriteLine("Class " & t.Name)
Console.WriteLine(" documenting the presence " & _
"of the CodeDescriptor Attribute:")
bAtLeastOne = False
For Each oPR In t.GetProperties()
    bFoundit = False
    For Each oAT In oPR.GetCustomAttributes(False)
        If TypeOf oAT Is CodeDescriptor Then _
        bFoundit = True
    Next
    cLine = oPR.Name
    If Not bFoundit Then
        cLine = cLine & " -MISSING"
    Else
        cLine = cLine & " -ok"
    End If
    Console.WriteLine(cLine)
Next
Console.WriteLine("End Class " & t.Name)

End Sub
```

First off, note that the FindPropertiesMissingMe method is declared as a shared method on the CodeDescriptor class. Shared methods are those called without requiring an instance of the class. This method is called as follows:

```
Dim t As type

t = Type.GetType("prjCustomAttributes.BookClass")
```

```
Call CodeDescriptor.FindPropertiesMissingMe(t)
```

Once called, the `FindPropertiesMissingMe` method uses reflection to hack into the type definition of the class that you pass in and look for the `CodeDescriptor` attribute on every property of that class. It then reports on its findings for every property to the console. The following shows the output of this method on a sample class where I used the attribute on almost all the properties:

```
Class BookClass
 documenting the presence of the CodeDescriptor Attribute:
Price -MISSING
Title -ok
Author -ok
ISBN -ok
End Class BookClass
```

Note that I forgot to add the attribute to the `Price` property, and my new method dutifully informs me of that. I've coded an attribute policeman!

In addition to reporting on the existence of an attribute, you can use the data within the attribute to automatically generate documentation for your code. I wrote a second method for my `CodeDescriptor` class that outputs the name, date, and description for all the `Code-Descriptor` attributes it finds in a class. Here is this new output:

```
Start Documentation, Class BookClass
BookClass       : mjt   05/02/2001 _
Storage for Book Detail Data

Documented Constructors
.ctor           : mjt   05/10/2001 Base Constructor
.ctor           : mjt   05/22/2001 Parameterized Constructor

Documented Properties
Title           : mjt   05/10/2001 Title of the book
ISBN            : mjt   05/10/2001 Publishers Book Code
Author          : mjt   05/10/2001 Author of the book

Documented Methods
(none)

End Documentation, Class BookClass
```

Imagine the possibilities now! You can create attributes to help you document your code, you can write code to help enforce their use in your entire software shop, and then you can write code to output the data within those attributes into a coherent, structured document, useful for code review or turning into superiors. Goodbye, comments!

28   My Code Can See Itself: Reflection

The reflection code can be found in the folder prjReflection.

I always wondered how the VB6 Object Browser was coded. It contained a list of all the objects available to my program, including ActiveX objects, as well as classes I had written myself. How did the Object Browser parse through all my code and display all of the available objects, along with their properties, events, and methods?

I still have no idea how they made this happen in Visual Basic 6, but Microsoft makes it all clear to me (and you) in the .NET Framework: A set of functionality collectively called *reflection* allows you to examine and describe classes in the .NET Framework.

Confused? Me too, at least at first. Who's writing code to describe other code? As you saw previously, some people are trying to automate and enforce the proper documentation of source code, but the guy who's in charge of writing the Object Browser for Visual Studio .NET is someone else. Since reflection is such a new topic, I thought it might be useful to try and use reflection to write something that looks like the Visual Studio .NET Object Browser. The end result of my endeavor can be seen in the following illustration:

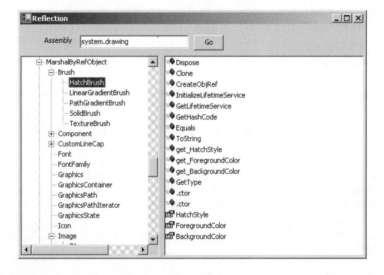

Getting Started

I decided (probably due to my unusually hard head) that my Object Browser was going to work a bit differently from the one in Visual Studio .NET. What I was really interested in seeing was the .NET Framework object hierarchy as a Treeview. I wanted to see the generic class Object as the root node of my Treeview and then have all the classes descend down from that. I kept the interface simple; I allow the user to type in an assembly name, and then I display all the classes in that assembly, as well as all the parent classes of those classes. After all, if I'm going to trace all the way back up to Object, I may need to travel outside the bounds of the entered assembly, since Object itself is in the system assembly.

Once the user supplies my program with an assembly, retrieving all of the types within it is done with the GetTypes method, as in the following code:

```
Sub FillTreeView(ByVal cDLL As String)

        Dim t As Type
        Dim oAS As System.Reflection.Assembly
        Dim oRoot As TreeNode
        Dim oNode As TreeNode
        Dim cTemp As String

        oHash.Clear()
        tvLeft.Nodes.Clear()
        tvLeft.Sorted = True

        Try
            oAS = System.Reflection.Assembly.Load(cDLL)
            For Each t In oAS.GetTypes()
                Call AddTypeToTreeView(t)
            Next

            tvLeft.Nodes(0).Expand()
        Catch oEx As Exception
            MsgBox(oEx.Message)
        End Try
    End Sub
```

This tiny little procedure is the base for extracting all of the type information out of the given assembly. The assembly's DLL name is passed in as the parameter. The Treeview tvLeft is cleared and set to display its nodes in sorted order. A HashTable named oHash is also cleared. (The purpose of the HashTable is explained later.) Then, the Assembly object is instantiated using the passed-in DLL name, and all of the types within it are iterated. For each type, a procedure named AddTypeToTreeview is called. The entire loop is enclosed in a Try…Except block to easily display any errors encountered when ripping through the types. (The concept of reflection was a new one to me, and it took me a little while to get up to speed while creating this project.)

Filling the Types *Treeview*

Imagine it's time now to add your first class to the `Treeview`. Say it's the `ToolboxBitmap-Attribute` class. (This is an actual class in the `System.Drawing` namespace.) To add this class to the proper place in the `Treeview`, you'll first have to locate the ancestor type for `Toolbox-BitmapAttribute` class, which happens to be the `Attribute` class. What if this class doesn't yet exist in the `Treeview`? (In this case, it won't—I already stated that the `ToolboxBitmap-Attribute` class is the first class you've attempted to put into the `Treeview` so far.) Before you can add the `ToolboxBitmapAttribute` class, you'll first have to add the `Attribute` class, which itself inherits from `Object`. Finally, since `Object` hasn't been added yet, you'll need to add that class to the `Treeview` first. Once `Object` is added, you can add `Attribute`, and then finally `ToolboxBitmapAttribute`.

What a mess, no? The basic premise here is to take the original class and loop upward through the object hierarchy, looking for a parent object that has already been added to the `Treeview`. If you find it, you can add your object to it as a child and move on. If you don't find the parent, then you need to mark and set aside that parent class to also add it to the `Treeview`, and keep moving upward. You are guaranteed to either get to the top of the `Object` hierarchy or to a parent class that has already been added to the `Treeview`. This rather nasty algorithm is embodied in the following procedure:

```
Private Sub AddTypeToTreeView(ByVal t As Type)

    Dim bDone As Boolean
    Dim oStack As New Stack()
    Dim aParent As TypeTreeNode
    Dim aNode As TypeTreeNode

    'loop upward from the passed in
    'class until you find the class
    'already in the hashtable
    bDone = (t Is Nothing)
    Do While Not bDone

        If oHash.Contains(t.FullName) Then
            'found, no more looping needed
            bDone = True
        Else
            'type not found, add it to the stack and _
            keep looping upward
            aNode = New TypeTreeNode(t)
            oStack.Push(aNode)

            t = t.BaseType
            bDone = (t Is Nothing)
```

```
        End If
Loop

'now, iterate the stack and add each node to the tree
Do While oStack.Count > 0
    aNode = CType(oStack.Pop, TypeTreeNode)
    t = aNode.Type

    If t.BaseType Is Nothing Then
        'is a root object
        tvLeft.Nodes.Add(aNode)
    Else
        'find the base type's node
        '(guaranteed to be there)
        'and add this node to it
        aParent = _
        CType(oHash.Item(t.BaseType.FullName), _
        TypeTreeNode)
        aParent.Nodes.Add(aNode)
    End If
    oHash.Add(t.FullName, aNode)
Loop

End Sub
```

Remember the HashTable named oHash that was cleared previously? That class contains a list of every type that has been added to the Treeview so far. It gives you a quick way to see if a given class already exists in the Treeview. The loop at the beginning of the procedure first checks if the given class is in the HashTable. If it is, then you're ready to add this class to the Treeview. If it is not in the HashTable, then a special Treeview node called a TypeTreeNode is created and pushed onto a Stack. Then, the ancestor class becomes the "current" class, and the loop is reiterated.

Once the loop is exited, the Stack represents all of the nodes that need to be added to the Treeview. They are removed in reverse order of their entry (which is what stacks are good at), and each type is added to the Treeview.

The TypeTreeNode bears some examination. This is just a standard TreeNode class with a Type property bolted onto it, so you can easily examine the Type for each node as it is clicked. That descendant class is shown here:

```
Class TypeTreeNode
    Inherits TreeNode

    Sub New(ByVal t As Type)
        MyBase.New()
        FType = t
```

```
        Me.Text = t.Name
    End Sub

    Private FType As Type
    Property Type() As Type
        Get
            Return FType
        End Get
        Set(ByVal Value As Type)
            FType = Value
        End Set
    End Property

End Class
```

Examining a Type

I wanted the right side of my Object Browser program to display the member information about each Type as it was clicked (properties, events, and methods). After stealing the little member icons used in the Object Browser with my handy screen capture program, I set out to create a procedure to fill a Listview with the member information for a given Type. That procedure is shown here:

```
Private Sub FillRightSide(ByVal t As Type)

    Dim mi As MemberInfo
    Dim lItem As ListViewItem
    Dim iImg As Integer

    lvRight.Items.Clear()

    For Each mi In t.GetMembers()

        Select Case mi.MemberType
            Case MemberTypes.Property, MemberTypes.Field
                iImg = 0
            Case MemberTypes.Event
                iImg = 1
            Case MemberTypes.Method, _
            MemberTypes.Constructor
                iImg = 2
            Case Else
                iImg = 0
        End Select
```

```
            lItem = lvRight.Items.Add(mi.Name)
            lItem.ImageIndex = iImg
            lItem.StateImageIndex = iImg
        Next
    End Sub
```

The GetMembers method is used to retrieve an array of MemberInfo objects for each member in the type. This simple loop iterates through each member and displays it, assigning it the appropriate ImageIndex based on whether it is a property, event, method, or constructor.

29   Programs Writing Programs: The CodeDOM

 The code-emitting example can be found in the folder prjCodeDOM.

If you're like me, you love writing code. You go to work early and write code, you skip lunch to write code, and then you come home, eat dinner, and hit the computer to write more code. OK, maybe you're not quite like me—good for you. There are some tasks in the code-writing process that can get tedious, however, and I just wish there was a way to automate them. For example, I always found adding properties to a VB6 class to be a pain. Here's an example VB6 property to show you what I mean:

```
Dim FCount as Integer
Property Let pCount(i as Integer)
    FCount = i
End Property
Property Get pCount as Integer
    pCount = FCount
End Property
```

What a pain, right? I count six instances of the word pCount or FCount, and four occurrences of the word Property. Granted, VB .NET improves on the syntax for properties, but even so, how many property definitions do you think you'll write in the next 12 months or so?

Actually, come to think of it, sometimes the entire act of creating a class seems a bit tedious, especially if you're a database programmer like I am. I can't begin to imagine how many times I've printed out a list of columns in a SQL Server table and started writing a class to encapsulate some or all of those columns—mapping them to properties in my new class.

I always tell my end-user community, "If you find you're doing something tedious on a PC, then you're probably doing it wrong." In other words, if someone is typing numbers from a PC-generated report into a spreadsheet, then there's probably some way a developer could automate that process for that user. The same rule applies to code development—most tedious, often-occurring tasks can probably be automated.

The .NET Framework includes functionality that allows you to write programs that emit runnable code in any .NET language. This functionality is collectively called the CodeDOM, or Code Document Object Model. The CodeDOM describes a source code document using a collection of .NET Framework classes. These classes allow you to automatically generated working .NET code.

Writing Code from Table Structures

The example project, prjCodeDOM, displays one possible way of using the CodeDOM to eliminate the tedious task of encapsulating a row in SQL Server table as a business class. The first part of the program loads all of the tables and views from the Northwind database into a Listbox:

```
Private Sub Form1_Load(ByVal sender As System.Object, _
    ByVal e As System.EventArgs) Handles MyBase.Load

    Dim SQL As String

    SQL = "select Name from dbo.sysobjects "
    SQL &= " where OBJECTPROPERTY(id, N'IsView') = 1 "
    SQL &= " or OBJECTPROPERTY(id, N'IsUserTable') = 1"

    Dim aDA As New SqlDataAdapter(SQL, CONNECTIONSTRING)
    Dim aDS As New DataSet()
    aDA.Fill(aDS, "Sysobjects")
    Dim aDV As New DataView(aDS.Tables("SysObjects"))

    lbTables.DataSource = aDV
    lbTables.DisplayMember = "Name"

End Sub
```

This procedure gets all of the tables and view names by querying the SQL Server system table named sysobjects. The results of this query are loaded into a DataSet, and then attached to the Listbox via a DataView. You can see the filled Listbox in the following illustration:

When a `Listbox` item is clicked, the `EmitCode` procedure is called. The `EmitCode` procedure uses various classes built into the CodeDOM to generate a class that matches the selected table, mapping table columns to properties:

```
Dim oProvider As CodeDomProvider

'set up the code generator
If rbVB.Checked Then
    oProvider = New VBCodeProvider()
Else
    oProvider = New CSharpCodeProvider()
End If

    Dim oGen As ICodeGenerator = oProvider.CreateGenerator()
```

The code generator setup starts with a `CodeDomProvider` class. Note that this class can either be a `CsharpProvider` or a `VBCodeProvider`, based on the setting of a radio button in the program. The provider then calls `CreateGenerator`, which instantiates an `ICodeGenerator` instance. This is the class that generates the code for your dynamically generated class.

The code that generates your class uses many of the elements of the CodeDOM namespace, as listed in the following table:

CodeDOM Class	Responsible For
CodeCommentStatement	Comments in the code.
CodeNamespace	The namespace within which the class is declared.
CodeNamespaceImport	The Imports statement at the top of the source document.
CodeTypeDeclaration	The class definition itself.
CodeMemberField	The private variable that stores the value of each property.
CodeMemberProperty	The property that maps to each table column.
CodeTypeReference	A variable type, like String or Integer. This is the type of both the private member and the property that make up each column.

The program loops through all of the fields in the table, mapping each to a property in the class. The type of the property is determined from the SQL data type of the column to which it corresponds.

Once all of the class elements are defined, the magic line that generates the code is as follows:

```
oGen.GenerateCodeFromNamespace(oNS, tOut, Nothing)
```

The namespace oNS is of type CodeNameSpace. The variable tOut is a StringWriter that was used in all of the class-generation code in the preceding code example. Once this line is executed, the StringWriter contains the source code for your class. The end of the procedure simply copies this text into a Textbox for display. An example of the generated class for the Northwind view [Category Sales for 1997] is as follows:

```
'_____
'    class CategorySalesfor1997
'    generated 12/22/2001 4:53:37 PM
'_____
'

Imports System
Imports System.Data

Namespace MyNameSpace

    Public Class CategorySalesfor1997
        Inherits [Object]

        Private FCategoryName As String

        Private FCategorySales As Single

        Public Property CategoryName As String
            Get
                Return FCategoryName
            End Get
            Set
                FCategoryName = Value
            End Set
        End Property

        Public Property CategorySales As Single
            Get
                Return FCategorySales
            End Get
            Set
                FCategorySales = Value
            End Set
        End Property
    End Class
End Namespace
```

You can probably imagine all of the cool utilities you can write now that you can generate code on the fly. Once you master this task, you can read further into the CodeDOM and learn how to actually compile and run the generated code dynamically. It shouldn't be too hard to extend this database-to-class example to actually compile the generated name-space and create a custom collection of the class based on rows from the corresponding table.

30   Discovering the New Diagnostic Classes

 The diagnostic code can be found in the folder `prjDiagnostics`.

Visual Basic .NET provides several robust diagnostic classes that make it much easier to track down bugs in your applications, whether the bugs show up during development or after installation on the end user's machine.

Sending Output to the Debug Window

The `Debug` object should be familiar to VB6 veterans, but it has undergone some enhancements in VB .NET. Instead of a single `Print` method to write output to the immediate window (now called the *Output window*), you have a choice of several methods:

Method Name	Notes
WriteLine	Writes the specified output to the Output window, followed by a linefeed.
WriteLineIf	If passed-in condition is true, writes the specified output to the Output window, followed by a linefeed.
Write	Writes the specified output to the Output window.
WriteIf	If passed-in condition is true, writes the specified output to the Output window.

In addition, the properties `IndentSize` and `Indent` allow further formatting of the text in the Output window. `IndentSize` refers to the number of characters for which an indent level consists. By increasing and decreasing the `Indent` property, you can control the output formatting.

For the experienced VB programmer, your old friend the `Assert` method is back. The `Assert` method allows you to test a condition and display a message if that condition is not true. This functionality is sort of the opposite of `WriteLineIf`, but the program stops execution entirely if the assertion (the condition parameter of the `Assert` method) fails. Many programs use this to test that a variable falls within a certain range or that an object is not null before moving on to processing that relies on the value of that variable.

The Debug methods and properties just described are demonstrated in the following code (which can be found in the example project). This procedure initializes three integer variables to random values, and then displays their values in the Debug window:

```
Private Sub cbDebug_Click(ByVal sender As Object, ByVal e As _
System.EventArgs) Handles cbDebug.Click

    Dim oRand As New Random()
    Dim i, j, k As Integer

    i = oRand.Next(0, 100)
    j = oRand.Next(0, 100)
    k = oRand.Next(0, 100)

    Debug.IndentSize = 5
    Call Debug.WriteLine("-- about to " & _
    "start debugging output --")
    Debug.Indent()
    Call Debug.WriteLine("i=" & i)
    Call Debug.WriteLine("j=" & j)
    Call Debug.WriteLine("k=" & k)
    Debug.Indent()
    Call Debug.WriteLine(oRand)
    'can write objects to debug window, not just _
    simple types
    Debug.Unindent()
    Debug.Unindent()
    Call Debug.WriteLine("-- debugging output completed _
    --")

    Call Debug.Assert(i <= 90, "variable i is over 90")
    Call Debug.WriteLineIf(j > 50, "variable j is over 50")
End Sub
```

NOTE   The Trace class is interchangeable with the Debug class. The methods and usage are identical. Microsoft recommends that you compile out the Debug methods from your final, production application compiles, but leave the Trace methods in for post-delivery diagnostic/debugging needs.

Switching Debug Output On and Off

A BooleanSwitch is a simple class that allows for the control of Debug output based on the value of an environment variable or a Registry setting. This is useful in a production environment. You can write code that by default would not create Trace or Debug output, but when a simple configuration file setting is flipped, your application creates Debug output that might help you track down a bug. For example, this Debug output might take the form of text file logs that could be e-mailed from the customer site to your office.

Each BooleanSwitch that you want to use has a default name that distinguishes itself from other switches. If the name you choose is MySwitch, for example, then creating a file named app.config with the following structure would set up that switch:

```
<configuration>
   <system.diagnostics>
      <switches>
         <add name="MySwitch" value="1" />
      </switches>
   </system.diagnostics>
</configuration>
```

Once properly set up as shown, the switch value can be tested and used with this code:

```
Protected Sub cbBooleanSwitch_Click(ByVal sender As Object, _
ByVal e As System.EventArgs)

CONST BSWITCHNAME = "MySwitch"

Dim oSwitch As New BooleanSwitch(BSWITCHNAME, _
"BooleanSwitch Demo")

If oSwitch.Enabled Then
    put debugging output code here>
End If

End Sub
```

Setting Different Levels of Debug Output

The TraceSwitch class is very similar to the BooleanSwitch class, except that it provides multiple levels for Debug output, instead of just on or off. The TraceSwitch is set up in the same way that the BooleanSwitch is, using the same app.config file. Instead of setting to just 0 or 1, however, you can set the TraceSwitch value to 0–4. The meaning of each value is as follows:

Switch Value	Meaning
0	Off
1	Info
2	Warning
3	Error
4	Verbose

The exact meaning of these terms is up to the programmer. You must decide what messages you are going to put into the Info section, the Warning section, and so on.

What this allows you to do is create short, simple trace logs of your program (perhaps that list only the procedure names as they're called), or get as verbose as you need (logging every value of every variable, if necessary). Then, depending on the problem that you're trying to uncover, you can set the appropriate Registry setting for the TraceSwitch and produce the desired Debug output.

A simple TraceSwitch example is given in the example code. To use it, make sure the app.config file contains the TestTraceSwitch setting as shown here, and then click the TraceSwitch button to see the Debug output:

```
<configuration>
    <system.diagnostics>
        <switches>
            <add name="TestTraceSwitch" value="2" />
        </switches>
    </system.diagnostics>
</configuration>

Protected Sub cbTraceSwitch_Click(ByVal sender As Object, ByVal _
e As System.EventArgs)

Const TSWITCHNAME As String = "TestTraceSwitch"
Dim oSwitch As New TraceSwitch(TSWITCHNAME, TSWITCHNAME)

    If oSwitch.TraceInfo Then debug.WriteLine _
    ("info messages enabled")
    If oSwitch.TraceWarning Then _
    debug.WriteLine("warning messages enabled")
    If oSwitch.TraceError Then _
    debug.WriteLine("error messages enabled")
    If oSwitch.TraceVerbose Then _
    debug.WriteLine("verbose messages enabled")
End Sub
```

Customizing Trace Output

A TraceListener is a class that directs Debug output to a location: the Output window, a text file, or even the Windows NT event log. By default, Debug and Trace output is directed to the Output window. This functionality is encapsulated in the DefaultTraceListener class. Because you're living in Object-Oriented Land now, you can create descendants of the DefaultTraceListener class that will do your own evil bidding.

Like what? A simple example might be to output a time stamp along with any message you might be sending to the Debug window. You might imagine that adding this time stamp to every `Debug.Writeline` statement in your application might take a while. A much more efficient way of doing this is to create a custom listener that adds the time stamp, and then tell the `Debug` class to use that listener instead of the default listener. The code that follows is an example listener class that adds a time stamp to the `Debug` output:

```
Class TimeStampTraceListener
        Inherits DefaultTraceListener

        'adds the current time stamp
        'to the message about to be output as a trace
        Private Function FormatMessage(ByVal s As String) _
        As String

            Dim cMsg As String

            cMsg = Format(now, "hh:mm") & ": "
            cMsg = cMsg & s

            Return cMsg

        End Function

        Public Overrides Sub WriteLine(ByVal s As String)
            MyBase.WriteLine(s)
        End Sub

        Public Overrides Sub Write(ByVal s As String)
            MyBase.Write(FormatMessage(s))
        End Sub

    End Class
```

To write your own listener, you must inherit off the `DefaultTraceListener` class and override the `Write` and `WriteLine` methods. The previous class does exactly this. The `Write` method slaps a time stamp onto the desired output, and then calls the respective ancestor method to get the output to the appropriate place. The `WriteLine` method does nothing new (because `WriteLine` in turns calls `Write`, which handles the time stamp).

To use this new listener, you would perform something like the following:

```
Trace.Listeners.Clear()
Trace.Listeners.Add(New TimeStampTraceListener())
```

The `Clear` method is important because it removes all listeners that are currently assigned to the `Trace` (or `Debug`) class. After setting up the `TimeStampTraceListener`, the output after calling `Trace.WriteLine("test message")` would look something like this:

```
10:34: test message
```

One of the interesting things about listeners is that you can have more than one listener running at the same time. The example program creates a second listener that adds the name of the calling procedure to the Debug output. (I'm sure many of you would agree with me that this is indeed a useful feature!) The sample program adds an instance of this class (called the MethodNameTraceListener) and an instance of the TimeStampTraceListener to the Trace object. The sample output after calling Trace.WriteLine("test message") looks like the following:

```
10:55: test message
WriteLine: cbTraceListener_Click: test message
```

Because there are two listeners on the Trace object, two lines are written for every Trace.WriteLine call.

Outputting Trace Data to Text

Another useful debugging function is to direct the output of the TraceListeners to a text file. This is done using the class TextWriterTraceListener. A simple example of using this class follows:

```
Protected Sub cbTraceText_Click(ByVal sender As Object, _
ByVal e As System.EventArgs)

    Dim i As Integer
    Dim fOut As Stream = _
    file.Create("c:\TextTraceOutput.txt")
    Dim oTextListener As New TextWriterTraceListener(fOut)

    Trace.Listeners.Clear()
    Trace.Listeners.Add(oTextListener)
    For i = 1 To 10
        Trace.WriteLineIf(i Mod 2 = 0, _
        "using WriteLineIf to write Even loop iteration _
        (" & i & ")")
        Trace.WriteLineIf(i Mod 2 = 1, _
        "using WriteLineIf to write Odd  loop iteration _
        (" & i & ")")
    Next
End Sub
```

The parameter of the TextWriterTraceListener is a Stream, which is defined in the preceding line. This stream creates a new text file, named c:\TextTraceOutput.TXT in this example. Then, the TextWriterTraceListener is added as the sole listener on the Trace object. Finally, a simple loop is executed and Trace lines are written to the text file, using WriteLineIf to alternately write an "is even" or "is odd" message.

Automatically Removing Debug Code

VB .NET has a new feature that allows you to define a conditional attribute on a procedure. This allows you to define compilation constants in your application that can prevent subroutines from being included in your application. Here is a trivial example:

```
Private Sub <Conditional("DEBUG")> MethodRunsOnlyIfDebugSet(ByVal cMsg As
    ➡String)
    Debug.WriteLine(cMsg)
End Sub

Protected Sub cbConditional_Click(ByVal sender As Object, ByVal e As System.
    ➡EventArgs)
    Call MethodRunsOnlyIfDebugSet("test message")
End Sub
```

The first sub, MethodRunsOnlyIfDebugSet, is defined with the Conditional attribute. This states that if the DEBUG constant is set, then the compiler should include this procedure in the application. If the DEBUG is not set, then this entire procedure (and all calls to it) should be removed from the compilation altogether.

The benefit to this setup is that if you use the conditional method, you don't have to make any decisions when writing code. You can simply call this method whenever you want to display some Debug code, but if (when) the DEBUG constant gets removed in the production compilation of the application, all of the Debug code is automatically removed from the final compilation.

NOTE   To set or clear the DEBUG and/or TRACE constants in your project, right-click your project name in the Solution Explorer, select Properties from the menu, and click Build under Configuration Properties in the dialog box. There, you will see the DEBUG and TRACE check boxes under Conditional Compilation Constants.

31   Logging Events the Easy Way

 The event-logging code can be found in the folder prjEventLogging.

Microsoft left Windows NT/2000 programmers with a built-in operating system tool for logging program operation: the NT event logs. The event logs can be used to log occurrences from the mundane to the catastrophic.

There are three built-in event logs: the Application, System, and Security event logs. The logs are identical except for the names—you can actually write any event in any of the logs, but obviously, you should keep the naming convention consistent to allow your users to more readily find the events you're logging. In addition, you can create your own event logs.

Event logging is important enough that you'd expect that the .NET Framework would contain support for it—and you'd be right. There is an EventLog class in the System .Diagnostics namespace that handles all NT event-logging support. All event-logging functions are done by adding an EventLog instance to your project and then setting the appropriate properties for the object at either runtime or design time. The most important property to set is the Log property, which tells the object in which event log it will perform its work.

Writing to an Event Log

Writing to an event log is done with the WriteEntry method. The second parameter in the following code specifies whether the entry you are writing is a Warning, Error, Information, Successful Audit, or Failed Audit type of entry. In this example, two entries are written to the Application event log:

```
'writes a few test entries.
Private Sub cbWrite_Click(ByVal sender As System.Object, _
ByVal e As System.EventArgs) Handles cbWrite.Click

    Call oEventLogIO.WriteEntry("here is a test Info " & _
    "message to the Application Log", _
        System.Diagnostics.EventLogEntryType.Information)

    Call oEventLogIO.WriteEntry("here is a test " & _
    "Warning message to the Application Log", _
        System.Diagnostics.EventLogEntryType.Warning)

    End Sub
```

Reading from an Event Log

The EventLog class has a property named Item that represents an array of EventLogEntry objects. Each EventLogEntry object contains all the information about a single entry in the given log. The following code reads the 10 most recent entries in the array and displays some information about them in a Listbox named lbEventLog:

```
Protected Sub cbRead_Click(ByVal sender As Object, ByVal e _
As System.EventArgs) Handles cbRead.Click

    Dim i As Integer
    Dim iCtr As Integer
    Dim oE As EventLogEntry
    Dim cMsg As String
```

```
iCtr = oEventLogIO.Entries.Count
For i = 0 To 9
    oE = oEventLogIO.Entries.Item(iCtr - 1 - i)
    cMsg = oE.TimeGenerated.ToString & " "
    cMsg = cMsg & oE.Message

    Call lbEventLog.Items.Add(cMsg)
Next

End Sub
```

Note that the most recent entries are at the end of the Item array, so you have to read backward to get the 10 most recent entries.

Monitoring an Event Log for Changes

Setting the property monitoring on the EventLog instance to True creates an object that fires an event whenever an entry is written to the given event log. (The event fires when any program writes to the log, not just your own program.) A simple example of the event fired is shown here:

```
Private Sub oEventLogMonitor_EntryWritten(ByVal sender As _
System.Object, ByVal e As_
System.Diagnostics.EntryWrittenEventArgs) Handles oEventLogMonitor.EntryWritten
    lbStatus.Text = _
    "monitor detected event log entry written, " & Now
End Sub
```

This code writes a simple message to a label control. The System.Diagnostics.Event-LogEvent parameter on the procedure gives you full access to the EventLogEntry object that encapsulates the log entry.

Using a Custom Event Log

If you wish, you can use the NT event log engine, but write to your own log. The following code demonstrates creating an event log named DotNetTest, after first checking if that log already exists. Once created, the source on the EventLog object is set to this new log, and an entry is written:

```
Protected Sub cbCustom_Click(ByVal sender As Object, ByVal e As _
System.EventArgs) Handles cbCustom.Click

    Dim oEVCustom As New EventLog()
```

```
oEVCustom.Source = "DotNetTest"
oEVCustom.Log = "DotNetTestLog"
oEVCustom.WriteEntry("test Event log entry.")

lbStatus.Text = "Custom Event Log created. Go into " & _
"Event Viewer to see the new log"
```

End Sub

The following illustration shows the new event log in the Windows 2000 Event Viewer:

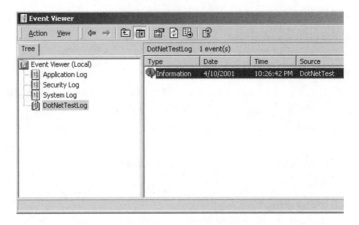

To delete a custom event log, simply call the `Delete` method on the `EventLog` object.

32   Monitoring Your Application's Performance

 The Performance Monitor code can be found in the folder `prjPerformanceCounters`.

The Windows NT/2000 platform has some wonderful performance-monitoring tools built right into the operating system. Most people think of the Performance Monitor as the program used to query and log system performance results such as processor utilization, hard disk performance, thread utilization, and so on. With the introduction of the .NET Framework, however, programmers have access to the same operating system performance tools that can be built right into their applications.

There are hundreds of individual performance counters in the Windows NT operating system. I counted exactly 700 on my Windows 2000 system, but this number can probably go up and down depending on what services and applications are installed on a given computer. This large number of individual counters is grouped into categories for easier lookup. When I see anything grouped into categories and I want to write a program to display them, I think Treeview. (I'm addicted to the Treeview control, I admit it.) The following subroutine loads all of the available performance counters, grouped by their category, into a Treeview named tvCounters:

```
Sub FillCategories()

    Dim aCat As PerformanceCounterCategory
    Dim oCounter As PerformanceCounter
    Dim i As Integer
    Dim tnRoot As TreeNode
    Dim tnParent As TreeNode
    Dim tnNode As TreeNode
    Dim cInstance As String

    tnRoot = tvCounters.Nodes.Add("Performance Counters")

    For Each aCat In PerformanceCounterCategory.GetCategories
        tnParent = tnRoot.Nodes.Add(aCat.CategoryName)
        If aCat.GetInstanceNames.GetLength(0) = 0 Then
            cInstance = ""
        Else
            cInstance = aCat.GetInstanceNames(0)
        End If

        For Each oCounter In aCat.GetCounters(cInstance)
            tnNode = tnParent.Nodes.Add(oCounter.CounterName)
        Next
    Next
    tnRoot.Expand()
End Sub
```

There's quite a bit to cover in this relatively small block of code. First, a root node is added to the Treeview. Then, the available performance counter categories are iterated by using the method GetCategories on the static object (no need to instantiate) named PerformanceCounterCategory. For each category, a node named tnParent is added to the Treeview as a child of the root node. Then, for each category, the available counters in this category are also iterated, with a node added for each. You can see a portion of the results in this illustration:

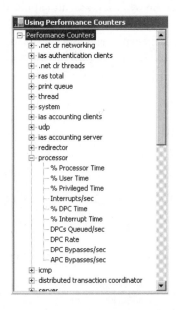

Once the Treeview was filled, I wanted to provide users with feedback about each counter and each category as they clicked them. There is built-in help text for both counters and categories, and providing this help as feedback was a simple matter of responding to the Treeview's AfterSelect event, as in the following code:

```
Private Sub tvCounters_AfterSelect(ByVal sender As _
System.Object, ByVal e As _
System.Windows.Forms.TreeViewEventArgs) Handles _
tvCounters.AfterSelect

    Dim cCatName As String
    Dim cCntName As String
    Dim oCategory As PerformanceCounterCategory
    Dim oCounter As PerformanceCounter
    Dim aList As String()

    cbCheck.Enabled = False
    If e.Node.Parent Is Nothing Then Exit Sub 'root

    'is a category node
    If e.Node.Parent.Text = "Performance Counters" Then
```

```
          cCatName = e.Node.Text
          oCategory = New _
          PerformanceCounterCategory(cCatName)
          lbHelp.Text = oCategory.CategoryHelp

    Else

       Try

             cCatName = e.Node.Parent.Text
             cCntName = e.Node.Text
             oCounter = New _
             PerformanceCounter(cCatName, cCntName)
             lbHelp.Text = oCounter.CounterHelp

       Catch oEX As Exception
             lbHelp.Text = _
             "Error reading Performance Counter"
       End Try

    End If

 End Sub
```

This code is only the portion of the AfterSelect event in the final project that deals with retrieving the help text for either the counter or category help text. Note that I determine whether the user clicked a counter or category by examining the caption of the parent node in the Treeview. If the parent node's caption is "Performance Counters," then I assume that this is a category. If the parent node's caption is anything else, I assume that the clicked node is a counter. Once I determine if a counter or category node was clicked, I instantiate the respective object instance and retrieve the property value that represents the help text (CounterHelp for the PerformanceCounter class, CategoryHelp for the PerformanceCounter-Category class).

Retrieving Performance Counter Instances

It would seem at first glance that once you identify a performance counter on the system, you could start it up and read some values. However, there is one more important concept to consider: the concept of instances. A performance counter might have multiple instances on a single computer. For example, suppose you want to monitor processor performance on a high-end, four-processor server. The logical question to ask is which of the four processors do you want to monitor? Or, if you want to monitor the relative processor time taken by each running thread on the system, you would first have to get a list of all available threads. These are known as *instances* of each counter.

The instances are actually defined at the category level, not at the individual counter level. For example, all the performance counters under the Threads category deal with the same instances. The remainder of the AfterSelect event code deals with retrieving the instances from the currently selected category and filling a Listbox with these instance names:

```
cCatName = e.Node.Parent.Text
cCntName = e.Node.Text
oCounter = New PerformanceCounter(cCatName, cCntName)
lbHelp.Text = oCounter.CounterHelp

oCategory = New PerformanceCounterCategory(cCatName)
aList = oCategory.GetInstanceNames
lbInstance.DataSource = aList
cbCheck.Enabled = True

If lbInstance.Items.Count > 0 Then
    lbInstance.SelectedIndex = 0
End If
```

The available instances of the given category are placed into an array named aList. The statement lbInstance.DataSource = aList populates the Listbox named lbInstance with the contents of this array. (The array will be empty if the current category has only a single instance.) Finally, if the Listbox has been filled, the first item is selected.

Querying the Performance Counter

With the addition of instances, you finally have all the information needed to actually query a performance counter value. The following code, executed when a button is clicked, retrieves the currently selected performance counter value in the application:

```
Protected Sub cbCheck_Click(ByVal sender As Object, ByVal e As System.EventArgs)

    Dim cCatName As String
    Dim cCntName As String
    Dim oCounter As PerformanceCounter
    Dim tnNode As TreeNode
    Dim cInstance As String = ""
    Dim r As Single

    tnNode = tvCounters.SelectedNode
    cCntName = tnNode.text
    cCatName = tnNode.Parent.text

    If lbInstance.SelectedIndex > -1 Then
        cInstance = lbInstance.SelectedItem.ToString
    End If
```

```
Try
    oCounter = New _
    PerformanceCounter(cCatName, cCntName, cInstance)
    r = oCounter.RawValue()
    lbValue.text = "Value = " & r.ToString
    lbRecordedAt.Text = _
    "Recorded At: " & Format(Now, "dd:hh:ss")

Catch oEX As Exception
    lbHelp.Text = "Error Retrieving Performance information"
End Try
End Sub
```

There is nothing too fancy in this code. Using the Treeview and the instance's Listbox, the category name, counter name, and instance name are retrieved and stored into string variables (the instance name might be an empty string). A PerformanceCounter variable is instantiated using these string names, and a label control is filled by calling the RawValue method off this variable. I also filled a second label with the current time, which makes it easier to verify that the button is a working event if the performance counter value is unchanged from button click to button click.

There are multiple ways to query a performance counter for data. Using the RawValue method as just shown is the simplest technique. You can also call the NextValue method, which turns the raw readings into a best-fit line and then returns a point on that line. Finally, you can use the NextSample method, which allows you to take two or more samples over time and then compare them or perform calculations on them. See the section in the Microsoft Framework help entitled "Performance Counter Value Retrieval" for detailed information on getting the most out of your performance counter readings.

33   Middle Management

The system management example can be found in the folder prjSystemManagement.

The Systems.Management namespace provides a .NET implementation to the WMI (Windows Management Instrumentation) API. This set of functions gives you access to management information such as available disks and disk space, event log information, running processes, low-level hardware like the cooling fan or SCSI ports, and network protocols. Literally hundreds of WMI classes are available for querying.

The *ManagementObject* and *ManagementObjectSearcher*

The ManagementObject and ManagementObjectSearcher classes provide the ability to look for and retrieve WMI objects on your system. The Searcher class uses a SQL-like interface for performing its queries. The following code sets up a `ManagementObjectSearcher` instance to find all of the event log entries that have a source of `cdrom`:

```
Dim oMOS As New ManagementObjectSearcher()
Dim oMO As ManagementObject
Dim SQL as string

Cursor = Cursors.WaitCursor
Try
    SQL = "select * from Win32_NTLogEvent "
    SQL &= "where SourceName = 'cdrom'"

    oMOS.Query.QueryString = SQL

    For Each oMO In oMOS.Get
        (Do something with each oMO here)
    Next
Finally
    Cursor = cursors.default
End Try
```

Each object that is returned is of the `ManagementObject` class. You can learn most about the objects by scanning through the Properties collection on each object returned. The sample code loads a few of these properties into a `Listview`, as seen in the following illustration. It looks from the event log entries that I was trying to read a bad compact disc:

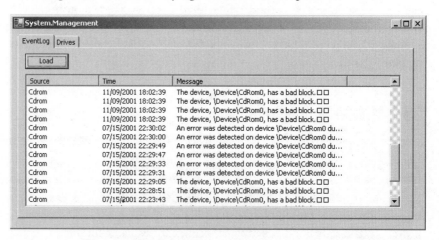

The WMI interface is absolutely enormous in all of the management information it can provide. Most of the querying is handled in a similar method to the preceding example; it simply becomes a matter of learning the different WMI objects available so that you can construct your queries. More advanced WMI functionality includes hooking into management events (such as receiving an event as .NET classes get created and/or destroyed), or retrieving WMI objects asynchronously (good for working across WANs, for example).

34   Braving the Basics of GDI+

 The GDI+ code can be found in the folder `prjBasicGDIPlus`.

I've always been drawn to the subject of computer graphics. The very thought of creating animated pixels on a computer screen was one of the primary things that drew me into the computer field. I remember writing a program on my very first PC—an Apple 2c. (I'm dating myself now, aren't I? Oh well.) The program recreated the cover for Pink Floyd's album *The Wall*. (More self-dating—I said *album*, as opposed to CD.) The program plotted the basic brick outline and then the album logo using nothing but the `PSET` command (plot a single pixel) and about a zillion loops. I was really proud of that program; it looked just like the album cover. (To me, anyway—I was only 15.)

I'm still a sucker for computer graphics at all levels—from state-of-the-art movie effects like *The Matrix* to the ever-changing standards in the world of PC game programming. Unfortunately, my math skills never caught up with my love of computer graphics, so I could never quite cut the mustard programming for id Software or a similar company.

You're not going to mistake me for a graphics-programming guru when you look at the GDI sample program on the CD, either. Its main purpose is to demonstrate some of the graphics classes and methods in the .NET Framework. The graphics classes in VB .NET are collectively called GDI+, which is apparently an improvement over the "old" GDI API found in regular Win32 programming. (Hey, the name ends in a "+", so it must be better, right?) The graphics output produced by the sample program is rather simple, but it should give you an idea of how to start creating graphics for your applications.

The *Graphics* Class

OK, you're ready to draw. So where exactly do you draw? Usually, you need an object instantiated from the `Graphics` class to do your drawing. A `Graphics` object represents a drawing surface (an electronic piece of paper, if you will).

NOTE   If you have experience with any graphics programming in the pre-VB .NET world of the Win32 API, then it makes sense to tell you that the `Graphics` object is an encapsulation of a Windows device context. If you don't have such prior experience, then never mind...

If you plan on drawing directly onto a control, you can get at the drawing surface associated with that control by writing your drawing code in the `Paint` method of the control:

```
Protected Sub pnDraw_Paint(ByVal sender As Object, ByVal e As_
    System.WinForms.PaintEventArgs)

    Dim gr as Graphics

    gr = e.Graphics

    (do stuff with gr here)

End Sub
```

The `Paint` event passes in the `Graphics` object associated with the control as a component of the second parameter, which allows you to draw all over the control. The drawing is more or less permanent, meaning that if you were to cover up your application with another window and then Alt+Tab back over to it, a new `Paint` event would get automatically fired, allowing your custom drawing code to be re-executed. In addition, you can force a firing of the `Paint` event by calling the `Invalidate` method on the control you wish to repaint.

Good Penmanship

So you have your drawing surface; now you need an instrument or two to draw with. If you want to draw lines and curves, the first class with which you'll need to become familiar is the `Pen` class. A Pen object contains all of the properties necessary to draw a line in a certain width, color, and style (dotted, dashed, and so on). There are two ways to instantiate a `Pen` object. The first is to use the `New` operator as you would for any other object, passing in the desired color of the pen as the first parameter:

```
Dim p As New Pen(Color.Red)
```

This method can be used to create pens of any color. However, there is a built-in collection object named `Pens` that contains several dozen colored pens, already predefined. To use a pen in this collection, you can do something like the following:

```
Dim p as Pen = Pens.Red
```

You can see all the colors available in the `Pens` collection using the Intellisense feature in Visual Studio.

Now that you can define a pen and you have access to a graphics class, you can draw a line on a control.

```
Private Sub pnDraw_Paint(ByVal sender As Object, ByVal e As_
    System.Windows.Forms.PaintEventArgs) Handles pnDraw.Paint

    Dim p as Pen = Pens.Red
    e.Graphics.DrawLine(p, 0,0, e.ClipRectangle.Width,  e.ClipRectangle.Height)

End Sub
```

Here, you define a red pen and pass it, along with four integers, to the DrawLine method on the Graphics class. The four integers give the starting point and the ending point of the line you want to draw (start left, start top, end left, end top, respectively). The e.ClipRectangle property gives you access to the width and height of the control upon which you're drawing, so the DrawLine method in the preceding code draws a diagonal line from the upper-left corner to the lower-right corner of the control, using the pen color set in Pen variable p.

Brushes

Brushes are for filling in enclosed areas, like the interior of rectangles or circles. The Brush class itself is abstract, meaning you cannot inherit directly from it. Instead, you create an instance of one of its ancestors, like the SolidBrush class:

```
Dim b As New SolidBrush(Colors.Blue)
```

The SolidBrush class can be used to create brushes of any color. However, like the Pens collection, there is a built-in collection object named Brushes that contains several dozen colored brushes, already predefined. To use a brush in this collection, you can do something like the following:

```
Private Sub pnDraw_Paint(ByVal sender As Object, ByVal e As_
    System.Windows.Forms.PaintEventArgs) Handles pnDraw.Paint

    Dim b as Brush = Brushes.Green
    e.Graphics.FillRectangle(b, e.ClipRectangle)
End Sub
```

This Paint event paints the control green. Of course, setting a control to look green can be more easily done using the already-supplied BackColor property, so it's time I showed you some more sophisticated drawing methods for scribbling on your controls.

Graphics Class Methods

There are a few dozen methods on the Graphics class that can be used to draw all different shapes, lines, and curves. The sample program in this section goes through several of them.

Listed here is a summary of the methods in the sample program. Almost all of these methods can be called with multiple parameter lists:

DrawArc   Draws part of an ellipse. Passed in are a pen, the parameters to define the ellipse, and the starting and ending angle value for the arc, specified in degrees.

DrawBezier   Draws a Bezier curve (pictured in the following illustration), which is a curve that is generated from a set of control points. The DrawBezier method accepts a pen and the list of control points as its parameters.

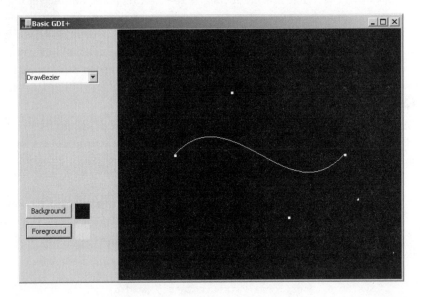

DrawLine   Draws a straight line. Accepts a pen and four values that represent the starting *x, y* and ending *x, y* coordinates of the line. The example program draws several lines in a grid pattern.

FillEllipse   Draws a filled ellipse. The ellipse is defined by specifying a rectangle, inside which the ellipse is drawn.

DrawString   Draws text onto the surface. A Font object, a brush, and either a starting point or an enclosing rectangle are specified.

FillPie   Draws a pie, which is like a filled-in arc. This method draws one pie slice out of an ellipse. An enclosing rectangle is passed in, as well as the starting and ending angles.

FillPolygon   Draws a polygon (pictured in the following illustration), which is defined by a set of points. The method automatically connects the first point specified to the last point.

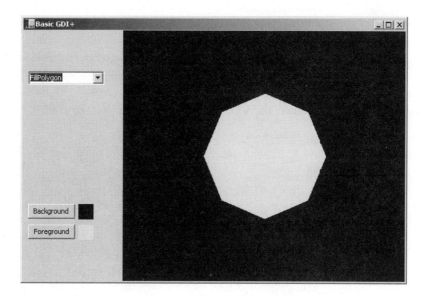

FillRectangle   Fills a rectangle with the passed-in brush.

TransparentBrush   Not a method of the Graphics class, this is instead an example of creating a brush with a transparent color. A transparent brush can be defined as follows:

```
Dim bTrans As New SolidBrush(Color.FromARGB(192, Color.Red))
```

The FromARGB method accepts a color parameter and an alpha, or transparent value, from 0 to 255. This example creates a 75 percent transparent brush. The example program draws an ellipse using this brush over some text. As expected, the text shows plainly through the ellipse.

NOTE   In general, the methods that start with Draw accept a pen as a parameter and draw the outline of a shape, line, or curve. The methods that begin with Fill accept a brush as a parameter and output a filled shape.

35   Advanced GDI+: The *GraphicsPath* and *Transform* Objects

The Advanced GDI+ code can be found in the folder prjAdvancedGDIPlus.

The preceding section discussed the Pen, Brush, and Graphics classes. These classes correspond to similar classes in the pre-VB .NET, Win32 API world. (The Graphics class is an encapsulation of the device context, which may not have been apparent, because it was renamed to a more descriptive name.) The *plus* in GDI+, however, refers to a number of new features that were not part of any previous API but are extremely useful in graphics programming—so useful, in fact, that most graphics programmers have been reinventing the wheel for each one of their programs. I'll use these features to create a simple Sprite class, which can be plugged in to create the scene shown in the following illustration:

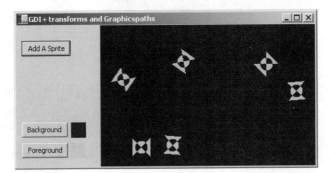

The *GraphicsPath*

The GraphicsPath class is a somewhat abstract but extremely powerful feature built into the .NET Framework. A GraphicsPath allows you to define complex drawing objects by connecting lines, curves, polygons, text, and virtually any other drawing element together. Once your GraphicsPath is defined in this way, you can treat it as a single object. Here is a chunk of code that sets up a simple little shape into a GraphicsPath object instance:

```
Private Sub SetupGraphicsPath()

    gp = New GraphicsPath()

    gp.AddLine(0, 20, 40, 20)
    gp.AddLine(20, 0, 20, 40)
    gp.AddEllipse(New Rectangle(10, 10, 20, 20))

    gpSave = New GraphicsPath()
    gpSave = CType(gp.Clone, GraphicsPath)

End Sub
```

My original intent when defining this object was to create a circle with two lines going through it, but the end result was even cooler than that idea, so I kept it. The preceding code draws a horizontal and a vertical line through the center of a circle. The two lines extend out past the circle.

The last two lines of code in the `SetupGraphicsPath` sub create a copy of the defined `GraphicsPath` using the `Clone` method. The reason I need to save this copy will become clear as I further explain my `Sprite` class.

To draw a `GraphicsPath` on a `Graphics` object, you can use the `DrawPath` or the `FillPath` method. The following code draws the `GraphicsPath` variable gp onto the `Graphics` object gWorld using a blue brush object as the fill color:

```
Public Sub DrawFrame(ByVal gWorld As Graphics, ByVal nWidth _
As Integer, ByVal nHeight As Integer)

    Dim bColor As New SolidBrush(Color.Blue)

    gWorld.FillPath(bColor, gp)

End Sub
```

Do You Know What the Matrix Is (Neo)?

Take note that the `GraphicsPath` object just discussed is defined in a small coordinate space—the entire object fits into a rectangle from (0,0) to (40,40) in the screen. My eventual goal is to take this little object and move it all across a painted area. Furthermore, it would be cool if I could rotate it around like it was spinning. Both of these operations can be accomplished though the use of the `Matrix` class. A matrix is a set of numbers arranged in rows and columns. Matrices are most useful in describing movement of objects through coordinate systems (both 2D and 3D coordinate systems)—movement such as rotations, translations, scaling, and something called *shear*. The purpose of this text is not to give a full background on matrix mathematics, so I don't want to get into the gory mathematical details. Instead, I'll just show you the `Matrix` class and how to use it to perform simple movements.

To create a rotation matrix that spins an object around, you can do something like the following:

```
Dim mR As Matrix = New Matrix(1, 0, 0, 1, 0, 0)
mR.RotateAt(FRotationAngle, New PointF(20, 20))
```

The first line instantiates a member of the `Matrix` class and initializes it to what's known as an *identity matrix*. An identity matrix performs no movement if it's used on an object. The `RotateAt` method is then called on the `Matrix`. The first parameter specifies the angle of rotation, and the second parameter specifies the 2D point around which the rotation takes place. I chose a rotation point of (20,20) because that represents the center of my 40×40 sprite. Once the rotation matrix is set up in this fashion, I can perform the `Transform` method on the intended `GraphicsPath` object and pass the `Matrix` object in as the sole parameter, as shown here:

```
gp.Transform(mR)
```

This rotates the `GraphicsPath` object as specified in the matrix. To translate (move) a `GraphicsPath` object to a new set of coordinates, you can perform an operation similar to this:

```
Dim mT As Matrix = New Matrix(1, 0, 0, 1, 0, 0)

mT.Translate(X, Y)
gp.Transform(mT)
```

This code sets up an identity matrix, translates the coordinates to position (X, Y), and then moves the `GraphicsPath` object gp to those coordinates by using the `Transform` method.

NOTE   The order that `Matrix` transformations are performed is important. Rotating an object and then translating it yields a much different result than translating first and then rotating. You have to be careful to perform your translations in the correct order to get the intended final position of your objects.

Putting it Together: The *SimpleSprite* Class

Thanks to the magic of object-oriented programming, I now have enough background information to construct a fully contained `Sprite` class, which is reproduced here in its entirety:

```
Imports System.Windows.Forms
Imports System.Drawing
Imports System.Drawing.Drawing2D

Public Class SimpleSprite

    Private FWidth As Integer = 40 'my size
    Private FHeight As Integer = 40

    Private FPosition As New Point(0, 0) 'position of sprite
    Private FVelocity As New Point(0, 0) 'how fast it moves per frame
    Private FRotationAngle As Integer = 0
    Private FRotatationDirection As Integer = 5

    Private FColor As Color
    Private gp As GraphicsPath
    Private gpSave As GraphicsPath

    Public Sub New(ByVal aColor As Color)
        MyBase.new()

        FColor = aColor

        Dim oRand As New Random()
```

```
        Do While FVelocity.X = 0
            FVelocity.X = oRand.Next(-5, 5)
        Loop
        Do While FVelocity.Y = 0
            FVelocity.Y = oRand.Next(-5, 5)
        Loop

        Call SetupGraphicsPath()

    End Sub

    Property Color() As Color
        Get
            Return FColor
        End Get
        Set
            FColor = Value
        End Set
    End Property

    Private Sub SetupGraphicsPath()

        gp = New GraphicsPath()

        gp.AddLine(0, 20, 40, 20)
        gp.AddLine(20, 0, 20, 40)
        gp.AddEllipse(New Rectangle(10, 10, 20, 20))

        gpSave = New GraphicsPath()
        gpSave = CType(gp.Clone, GraphicsPath)

    End Sub

    Public Sub RandomPosition(ByVal aWorldSize As Size)

        Dim oRand As New Random()
        FPosition.X = oRand.Next(0, aWorldSize.Width)
        FPosition.Y = oRand.Next(0, aWorldSize.Height)

    End Sub

    Public Sub DrawFrame(ByVal gWorld As Graphics, ByVal _
    nWidth As Integer, ByVal nHeight As Integer)

        Dim oRand As New random()
        Dim mT As Matrix = New Matrix(1, 0, 0, 1, 0, 0)
        Dim mR As Matrix = New Matrix(1, 0, 0, 1, 0, 0)
```

```vb
Dim bBounced As Boolean = False

Dim bColor As New SolidBrush(FColor)

mR.RotateAt(FRotationAngle, New PointF(20, 20))
gp.Transform(mR)

mT.Translate(FPosition.X, FPosition.Y)
gp.Transform(mT)

gWorld.FillPath(bColor, gp)

'reset the graphicspath
gp = CType(gpSave.Clone, GraphicsPath)

'move the sprite
FPosition.X += FVelocity.X
FPosition.Y += FVelocity.Y

'if reaches edge of world, 'bounce'
If FPosition.X > nWidth - FWidth Then
    FPosition.X = nWidth - FWidth
    FVelocity.X = -FVelocity.X
    bBounced = True
End If
If FPosition.X < 0 Then
    FPosition.X = 0
    FVelocity.X = -FVelocity.X
    bBounced = True
End If


'same for y
If FPosition.Y > nHeight - FHeight Then
    FPosition.Y = nHeight - FHeight
    FVelocity.Y = -FVelocity.Y
    bBounced = True
End If
If FPosition.Y < 0 Then
    FPosition.Y = 0
    FVelocity.Y = -FVelocity.Y
    bBounced = True
End If

'50-50 chance that the spin direction
'will change after a bounce
If bBounced And oRand.Next(0, 100) Mod 2 = 0 Then
    FRotatationDirection = -FRotatationDirection
End If
```

```
            FRotationAngle = FRotationAngle + FRotatationDirection
            If FRotationAngle > 360 _
            Then FRotationAngle = (FRotationAngle Mod 360)
            If FRotationAngle < 0 _
            Then FRotationAngle = FRotationAngle + 360
        End Sub

    End Class
```

The `SimpleSprite` class contains all the information about a single object, including its color, its position in the world, the speed at which it's moving, and its rotation speed and direction. When the object is instantiated, the `SetupGraphicsPath` method is called (described earlier), which defines the shape of the object. In addition, the velocity of the object is defined by setting the values in a `Point` structure to a random number between −5 and +5.

All of the drawing work happens in the `DrawFrame` method. A `Graphics` object is passed into this method, along with the width and height of the surface. Drawing is done by setting up matrices as described previously and performing the rotation and translation necessary to place this object into the world. Then the sprite is drawn onto the `Graphics` object using the `GraphicsPath.FillPath` method.

After the drawing is done, several housecleaning steps are performed. First, the `Graphics-Path` object is set back to its original state by cloning the `gpSave` variable. (Recall that I created `gpSave` by cloning my original `GraphicsPath` variable.) This is a quick way to reset all of the rotation and translation matrices back to an identity state. If I did not do this, further rotations and translations would be appended to the existing ones. My code is written to always start from "square one," apply the appropriate rotation, and finally to move the object to its final place in the world. Next, the position of the object is updated, and checks against the boundary of the world are performed to see if I need to make the object bounce off one of the edges. Finally, I update this object's rotation. As an added feature, I added some code that switches the object's rotation direction after it bounces, but this rotation direction switch happens only 50 percent of the time for some variety.

Using the *SimpleSprite* Class

The sample project in this section uses an `ArrayList` collection to keep track of any number of `SimpleSprite` object instances; press the Add a Sprite button to add another one to the list. A timer variable is instantiated to draw the world in an endless loop. The drawing of the world is handled with the following few lines of code:

```
    Private Sub DrawTheWorld()

        Dim oSprite As SimpleSprite
```

```
Dim g As Graphics
g = pnDraw.CreateGraphics
Try
    g.FillRectangle(New SolidBrush _
    (pnBackColor.BackColor), pnDraw.ClientRectangle)

    'draw each sprite in the list
    For Each oSprite In aSpriteList
        oSprite.Color = pnForeColor.BackColor
        Call oSprite.DrawFrame(g, pnDraw.Width, _
        pnDraw.Height)
    Next

Finally
    g.Dispose()
End Try
End Sub
```

In this code, a `Graphics` class is created from the `Panel` control on the form. The entire panel is rendered in the currently selected background color. Then, for each `SimpleSprite` object defined in the `ArrayList`, the color is reset, and the sprite is drawn using the `DrawFrame` method I've already discussed.

NOTE   The preceding scene-rendering code is so simple and short because all the work is done inside the `SimpleSprite` class, as it should be. *Encapsulation*, or hiding implementation details inside a black box, is one of the primary features of object-oriented programming. Imagine how useful it would be to download an Open Source version of the `SimpleSprite` class and not have to worry about all the implementation details of how to draw the sprite to your graphics object. Simply call the `DrawFrame` method and it's done! Another big feature of object-oriented programming is *polymorphism*, meaning the ability to create child classes easily off ancestor classes. You can make the `SimpleSprite` class an ancestor class and use it as a base to create dozens of different-shaped sprites with only a little extra work—simply by overriding the `SetupGraphicsPath` method. This would give you a great starting point for a great 2D, Space Invaders–like shooter.

36   Something About Screensavers

 The screensaver code can be found in the folder `prjScreenSaver`.

I decided to put together many of the graphics concepts I just discussed and come up with a basic `Screensaver` class that can be extended and reused. The `ScreenSaver` class will be responsible for managing a list of `Sprite` objects created from a class similar to the `Simple-Sprite` I created earlier. The class will also manage a few bitmaps needed to perform its drawing. When I'm done, I'll have the colorful screensaver shown in the following illustration.

(I know, the picture is in black and white; you'll have to run the program yourself to see the colors—or just trust me.)

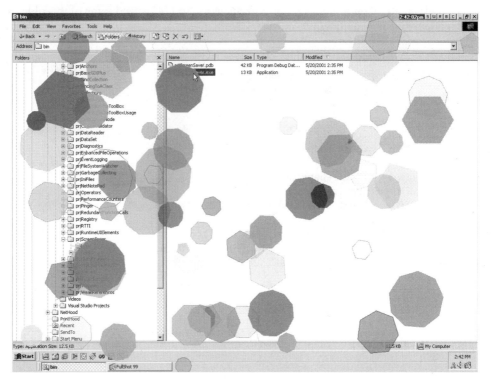

Screensaver Basics

Writing screensavers for Windows is much easier than many programmers anticipate. The trick is that the SCR file that goes into the Windows folder is just an EXE file that's been renamed with an SCR extension. Windows will call the EXE with one of two commandline parameters: /s or /r. If the passed-in command- line parameter is /s, you should run the setup dialog for your screensaver. If the command line is /r, then you should actually run the screensaver.

Screen Capture

Many screensavers appear to be drawing their effects right over the top of your word processor, e-mail program, or whatever applications you happened to have open when the screensaver kicks in. In truth, this is a cleverly disguised trick. Most screensavers perform this trick by grabbing an image of the screen, copying it onto a bitmap, and then drawing on that bitmap.

In the Win32 environment, there were several API-based methods for grabbing the Desktop window handle for the purpose of treating it like a bitmap. Unfortunately, I couldn't find a similar method built into the .NET Framework, so I borrowed some of this older Win32 API code to get the job done:

```
Protected Sub CaptureScreen()

    Dim hSDC, hMDC As Integer
    Dim hBMP, hBMPOld As Integer
    Dim r As Integer

    hSDC = CreateDC("DISPLAY", "", "", "")
    hMDC = CreateCompatibleDC(hSDC)

    FW = GetDeviceCaps(hSDC, 8)
    FH = GetDeviceCaps(hSDC, 10)
    hBMP = CreateCompatibleBitmap(hSDC, FW, FH)

    hBMPOld = SelectObject(hMDC, hBMP)
    r = BitBlt(hMDC, 0, 0, FW, FH, hSDC, 0, 0, 13369376)
    hBMP = SelectObject(hMDC, hBMPOld)

    r = DeleteDC(hSDC)
    r = DeleteDC(hMDC)

    oBackground = Image.FromHbitmap(New IntPtr(hBMP))
    DeleteObject(hBMP)

End Sub
```

The end result of this procedure is to store the image of the Windows Desktop in the bitmap object named oBackground. It does this by creating a device context for the display device, then creating a bitmap, and finally copying the image of the display into this bitmap. Note that because I've resorted to using "old-style" API calls in this procedure, I have to take better care of cleaning up my resources with the appropriate DeleteDC and Delete-Object calls. The VB .NET garbage collector doesn't keep track of Windows resources like those created in this procedure.

The *SaverSprite*

I decided to make a few modifications to the SimpleSprite class used in the earlier example program, and the result of those modifications is the SaverSprite class. Since the two classes are so similar, I don't want to waste time explaining this new class from the ground up. I will, however, point out the key differences in this new class.

Shape of object   The sprites in the screensaver still use a GraphicsPath to control their shape, but they are all defined as regular polygons of between 5 and 12 sides. See the SetupGraphicsPath method to see how the polygon was specified. The radius of each sprite is also a random value.

Update and draw code is split up into two procedures   The original class had the code to update the object position in the same procedure as the code to draw the sprite. Since these are really two distinct jobs, I decided to break them into two procedures named UpdatePosition and DrawFrame.

Random colors   Each sprite has a random inner and outer color. Both colors are defined with a random transparency as well, giving a very colorful final effect.

The *ScreenSaver* Class

The ScreenSaver class itself contains both the ArrayList that holds the SaverSprite objects and the screen capture code described previously. All that's really left to explain is how the class renders its image onto a form. The main method call is named Tick, shown here:

```
Public Sub Tick(ByVal f As form)

    Dim g As Graphics
    Dim oWork As Bitmap

    FTicks += 1

    'copy the background bitmap to a work bitmap
    oWork = CType(oBackground.Clone, Bitmap)
    Try
        'draw stuff on the work bitmap
        Call DrawSaver(oWork)

        g = Graphics.FromHWND(f.Handle)
        Try
            g.DrawImageUnscaled(oWork, 0, 0)
        Finally
            g.Dispose()
        End Try
    Finally
        oWork.Dispose()
    End Try

End Sub
```

The Tick method executes every time the screensaver is redrawn. The first thing it does is to create a work bitmap named oWork, cloned from the background bitmap. Then the

DrawSaver method is called, which is the code that renders the polygons onto the work bitmap. Finally, the work bitmap's image is copied onto the passed-in form using the DrawImageUnscaled method, and cleanup is performed.

The DrawSaver method, the code that renders the sprites, is as follows:

```
Protected Sub DrawSaver(ByVal oBitmap As Bitmap)

    Dim gr As Graphics
    Dim oSprite As SaverSprite

    gr = Graphics.FromImage(oBitmap)
    Try
        For Each oSprite In aSpriteList
            oSprite.UpdatePosition(New Size(FW, FH))
            oSprite.DrawFrame(gr)
        Next
    Finally
        gr.Dispose()
    End Try

End Sub
```

This code simply iterates through the ArrayList and calls the position update and draw methods of each sprite therein.

One can see how easily extendible both the ScreenSaver and SaverSprite class objects are. You can override the SetupGraphicsPath method on the SaverSprite to create objects of all different shapes. Likewise, you can make screensavers that do any type of drawing by overriding the InitializeSaver and DrawSaver methods. Using inheritance in this way can save you an extraordinary amount of work in the long run. Suppose you decide to write an entire series of screensavers to sell, enter in a graphics contest, or put on your website as Open Source freeware. Having base screensaver foundation classes prevents you from having to rewrite (or even copy/paste) code from old projects into new ones. Simply inherit off the base classes and all the existing functionality is available in your new class for free.

37 Having a Dialog with your Users

 The new operator code can be found in the folder prjDialogs.

Windows provides a basic set of dialog boxes for common functions like selecting files, colors, and fonts. Formerly available to VB programmers via ActiveX controls, you now have access to these controls as .NET Framework classes. This section demonstrates the basic dialog boxes and the important members of each. The sample program in this section is the beginning of a functional word processor using the RichTextBox control.

The *OpenFileDialog*

The OpenFileDialog allows the user to select a file from any permanent disk resource (hard drive, network drive, floppy disk, etc.). You've probably used the OpenFileDialog in almost every Windows program you've ever used, so the look of the dialog box should be pretty familiar:

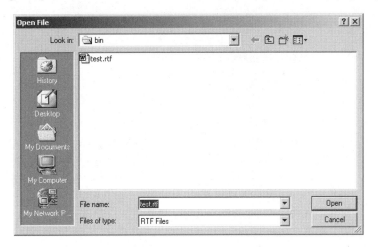

There are two ways to use an OpenFileDialog in your application. The first way is the visual way. To do this, you locate the OpenFileDialog on the toolbar and double-click. You'll see an instance of the OpenFileDialog control created in the non-visual component area of the form designer, as in the following illustration:

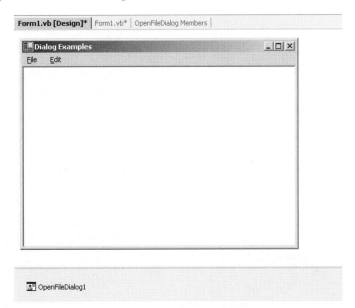

By setting up the dialog box this way, you can click the instance in nonvisual component area of the form designer in order to edit the properties of the dialog box at design time, just as you would edit the design-time properties of any other control.

The second way to use an OpenFileDialog in an application is to create an instance of it directly, as you would any other nonvisual class like a HashTable or a FileInfo class:

```
Dim o As New OpenFileDialog()

o.Filter = "RTF Files|*.rtf|All Files|*.*"
If o.ShowDialog() = DialogResult.OK Then
    <do some stuff>
End If
```

The preceding code demonstrates how to display the OpenFileDialog using the ShowDialog method. This method returns a parameter indicating what action was taken by the user, usually DialogResult.OK or DialogResult.Cancel. This is a much easier method than determining how VB6 common dialog boxes were closed; in that case, the best way was to set up an error trap and set the dialog box to generate an error when it was closed via the Cancel button.

Here some additional useful members of the OpenFileDialog class:

Member Name	Member Type	Description
Multiselect	Property	When true, allows user to multi-select files using Ctrl and Shift.
CheckFileExists	Property	When true, returns an error message if the user types in a filename that doesn't exist in the current folder. (This member is useful when you're trying to prompt the user to open an existing file, rather than create a new one.)
Filename/Filenames	Property	A string (or string array) of the file or files selected by the user.
InitialDirectory	Property	Specifies which folder the dialog box displays when it is first displayed.
Filter	Property	Specifies which types of files (by extension) will be shown in the dialog box. The format of this string is $t|e$, where t is a text description and e is a filename extension. Multiple filters can be specified in the string; they should be separated by the pipe (|) symbol.

Member Name	Member Type	Description
FileOk	Event	Allows you to perform some type of custom checking when the OK button is clicked and cancel the selection of that file; perhaps you want to prevent the user from opening up the application's own log file, for example.

The sample program displays the OpenFileDialog and loads the selected rich text format (RTF) file into a RichTextBox control using the following routine:

```
Private Sub mOpen_Click(ByVal sender As System.Object, _
    ByVal e As System.EventArgs) Handles mOpen.Click

    If OpenFileDialog1.ShowDialog() = DialogResult.OK Then
        pFileName = OpenFileDialog1.FileName
        rtb.LoadFile(pFileName)
    End If
End Sub
```

The *SaveFileDialog*

The SaveFileDialog looks exactly like the OpenFileDialog, but it is intended for use when your user is writing files to disk, as opposed to opening files. Because of this, it contains some specific members:

Member Name	Member Type	Description
CreatePrompt	Property	When true, prompts the user when he enters a filename that does not yet exist.
OverwritePrompt	Property	When true, prompts the user when he enters a file that already exists ("Are you sure you want to overwrite this file?").

You use the SaveFileDialog in exactly the same way as the OpenFileDialog, by calling the ShowDialog method and checking that the result is DialogResult.OK. Once you've established this, you can check the Filename property to see what file the user selected, and then write whatever data you wish to that file. Here is the save code in the sample program:

```
Private Sub mSave_Click(ByVal sender As System.Object, _
    ByVal e As System.EventArgs) Handles mSave.Click

    If SaveFileDialog1.ShowDialog() = DialogResult.OK Then
        pFileName = SaveFileDialog1.FileName
        rtb.SaveFile(pFileName)
    End If

End Sub
```

The *FontDialog*

Obviously enough, the FontDialog allows the user to select one of the fonts that he currently has installed on his system.

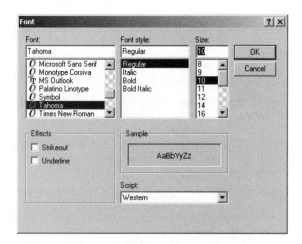

The FontDialog can be customized in several different ways by manipulating various properties. Here are the properties that customize the options on the dialog box displayed, as well as the range of fonts that will be displayed:

Member Name	Description
AllowScriptChange	When true, allows the user to manipulate the script Combobox on the dialog box to change the script of the selected font.
AllowVectorFonts	When true, displays vector fonts as well as standard (TrueType) fonts.
AllowVerticalFonts	When true, displays vertical as well as horizontal fonts.
FixedPitchOnly	When true, displays only fixed-pitch fonts (like Courier New).
MinSize/MaxSize	Sets the minimum and maximum point size displayed in the dialog box.
ShowApply	When true, dialog box contains an Apply button.
ShowColor	When true, dialog box contains a color selector Combobox.
ShowEffects	When true, displays check boxes for strikethrough and underline effects.
ShowHelp	When true, dialog box contains a Help button.

The sample code displays the dialog box and then applies the selected font to the currently selected text in the `RichTextBox`:

```
If FontDialog1.ShowDialog = DialogResult.OK Then
    rtb.SelectionFont = FontDialog1.Font
End If
```

The *ColorDialog*

The `ColorDialog` allows the user to choose a color. (Can't get much more concise than that, huh?)

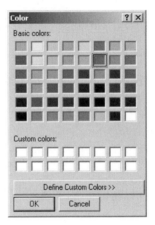

As with the others, the `ColorDialog` can be customized in several ways via the state of its properties. Here are the properties that can change the appearance and function of a `Color-Dialog`:

Member Name	Description
`AllowFullOpen`	When true, allows the user to open the Custom Colors portion of the dialog box.
`CustomColors`	Allows the user to set or return the custom colors displayed. This lets the user save a list of custom colors specific to their program and display them in the color dialog box.
`FullOpen`	When true, the `ColorDialog` opens up with the Custom Color portion displayed.
`ShowHelp`	When true, dialog box contains a Help button.
`SolidColorOnly`	When true, user can select only solid (non-dithered) colors.

PART III

OOP Techniques

- OOP development techniques

- Encapsulation, inheritance, and polymorphism

- Adding UI controls to the VB toolbox

- Inheritance and descendant classes

- Code interfaces

- Reading and writing INI files

- Serializing/deserializing objects

- Adding controls to the Toolbox

- Object graph serialization

- Using garbage collection

- Using the Get and Set accessor methods to set up properties

- Sharing code using the global assembly cache

38   Embracing Object-Oriented Programming

 The OOP code can be found in the folder prjCustomValidator.

Successful object-oriented programming (affectionately called OOP) requires new strategies for tackling problems and organizing code. Let's take a simple task and solve it using a traditional VB6 method, and then tackle the same problem in an object-oriented framework to see the differences between the two methods.

The simple task you're going to perform using both methods is implementing an algorithm to validate user-entered credit card numbers. You'll use an implementation of the well-known LUHN algorithm to perform the actual determination of whether a card number is accurate. The details of that algorithm are not important to this programming exercise and therefore will not be included here. Suffice to say that you have a ready-to-drop-in function named CheckCCNumber with the following signature:

```
Function CheckCCNumber(ByVal cCCNo As String) As Boolean
```

This function returns True if the passed-in string is a valid credit card number. Assume that the routine can handle the removal of spaces in the number. How would you use such a function in a Visual Basic program? The most likely situation that comes to mind is "attaching" the validation function to a Textbox. In this scenario, the user enters the credit card number into the Textbox, the validation function is performed, and some action is taken based on the result of the validation function.

Method 1: Non-OOP

The traditional *procedural-programming* (non-OOP) method of accomplishing this task would be to use the LostFocus event of the Textbox as the point at which to call the validation function. A typical VB6 code snippet might look like this:

```
Private Sub tbCredCard_LostFocus()
    If Not CheckCCNumber(tbCredCard.Text) then
        Call MsgBox("Invalid Credit Card Entered")
    End If
End Sub
```

So, is anything "wrong" with this method of coding? Technically, no. Linking up a Textbox to a validation function in this way works perfectly well. However, some potentially difficult situations arise out of coding in this style:

Cut-and-paste nightmare for multiple controls   Suppose your application consists of multiple forms, and many of these forms are going to require a Textbox that performs credit card validation. In this situation, the three-line If statement in the preceding code example will have to be repeated in the LostFocus event of each one of these Textbox objects. Furthermore, the parameter of the validation function will have to be changed to match the Textbox upon which the check is to be performed. It is easily conceivable that a programmer might paste the code into each new Textbox LostFocus event that requires credit card validation but forget to change the parameter. (I know. I've made this exact error on more than one occasion.) This would lead to a strange bug where the validation was seemingly not being performed at the right time on the right data.

Furthermore, having all of this duplicate code in multiple controls becomes problematic if you decide to change the error action of the validation. (For example, you decide to change the text of the error message in the MsgBox command.) To accomplish this, you will have to hunt down every instance of the validation code in your application and change the text accordingly. If you miss one, your application will look or act different from form to form, which is one sign of an unprofessional-looking application.

Difficult to document for other programmers   If multiple developers are developing this application, how and where do you put the appropriate comments to document the behavior and linkage of the Textbox and the validation function? You should document the function itself, as well as the call to the function (the LostFocus event). Again, if multiple Textbox objects are being used throughout the application, comments are being duplicated throughout the application.

Location of the validation function   The validation function will probably be placed into a common functions library of one sort or another. I've seen dozens of libraries of this type in different group programming environments in which I've worked, and they're not pretty. Usually, an application's common functions library is one or more module packs with dozens (if not hundreds) of completely unrelated functions. You might have the credit card validation function right next to the code that loads the 50 states into an array, right next to the code that generates sine and cosine tables, right above the code that converts long filenames to DOS 8.3 format. How does anyone find anything in these huge libraries? The answer, without having an intimate, experienced knowledge of the library, is that one does *not* find anything in them. Nothing short of months of experience and asking other developers questions gets the new developer up to speed on all the common tasks available to him.

Method 2: OOPs Away!

Now it's time to make all of the problems just listed vanish with a wave of my magic OOP wand. In the object-oriented world, an experienced programmer might immediately think to explicitly link the Textbox control and the credit card validation code into a single, all-new, special function called Textbox. The code for this type of Textbox is as follows:

```
Imports System.Drawing
Imports System.Windows.Forms
```

```
Imports System.Text

Public Class CreditCardValidatorTextBox
    Inherits TextBox

    Private FBadCreditCardColor As Color

    Sub New()
        MyBase.New()
        FBadCreditCardColor = color.Red
    End Sub
    Property BadCreditCardColor() As Color
        Get
            Return FBadCreditCardColor
        End Get

        Set
            FBadCreditCardColor = Value
            'refresh the control if it has contents
            If len(Me.Text) > 0 Then Call Refresh()
        End Set
    End Property

    Protected Overrides Sub OnGotFocus(ByVal e _
    As System.EventArgs)
        Me.ForeColor = color.Black
        Me.SelectAll()
        Call MyBase.OnGotFocus(e)
    End Sub

    Protected Overrides Sub OnLostFocus(ByVal e _
    As System.EventArgs)
        If Not CheckCCNumber(Me.Text) Then
            Me.ForeColor = FBadCreditCardColor
            Call refresh()
        End If

        Call MyBase.OnlostFocus(e)
    End Sub

 Private Function CheckCCNumber(ByVal cCCNo _
 As String) As Boolean
(details of this function omitted, see code for how to validate a credit card)
    End Function
End Class
```

The new object is inherited off a basic Textbox control. The check for the validation happens in the OnLostFocus method. The purpose of this method is to have a "normal" Visual Basic routine that is responsible for calling the LostFocus event of each individual control.

NOTE   You wouldn't want to call the validation code in the actual LostFocus event in the control definition because you would be "stealing" the event from the programmers who actually use your control. Instead, any LostFocus code that you need to write when your control loses focus should be called in the OnLostFocus method. Most of the control events have partner methods for the same purpose. However, make sure to call the ancestor method by issuing MyBase.OnLost-Focus(e), or the users of your control will still not be able to have their own LostFocus events.

In the control in the preceding example, if the validation fails, the text of the control is changed to a different color. To make even further use of object-oriented programming, I've made this extra color a property of my new control, which means the programmer can change it to match the color scheme in their application.

The OnGotFocus event is responsible for putting the text back to black when the user enters the control, just so the user isn't forced to edit red text. As a convenience, the current text in the control is selected when the user gives the control focus.

Let's see how this object-oriented design addresses the problems listed in the prior, non-OOP example.

Cut-and-paste nightmare for multiple controls   The cut-and-paste nightmare is gone because the Textbox and its validation code have been put together into one place in the code. No programmer-required linkage has to be done between the control and the validation. This is one of the primary benefits of OOP: the ability to group code (the validation function) and data (the Textbox and the text within it) into a single place within the code.

If the author decides to change the fail action of the validation, this is easily changed in one place. If the author desires a choice of multiple failure actions, these are again all coded into the same control, with a property to determine which action to take. (Or, fancier yet, the programmer could create further subclasses off this class that behave differently upon failure.)

Difficult to document for other programmers   Documentation is quite easy in the OOP world. The author of the control documents the source of the control itself. When the control is used on a form, no additional coding is required. The programmer studying the application sees that a control class named CreditCardValidatorTextBox was used on a certain form and can search the code for the definition of that class.

Location of the validation function   Again, the code and the data are all together, so the problem of huge modules of disparate functions often goes away automatically in the OOP world. The sine and cosine functions are often hidden away in their own class, the state loader has a class of its own, and the credit card validator is separated from each of those.

This simple example demonstrates how some of the failures of the procedural-based programming style have been addressed through the use of object-oriented programming methods. Admittedly, there is a learning curve when moving into the object-oriented world, but once that curve has been overcome, you'll find yourself solving all of your new programming challenges using these methods. The goal is to get yourself "thinking OOP" as new projects come your way.

39   Encapsulation Fascination

The encapsulation example can be found in the folder `prjOOPFundamentals`.

One of the primary concepts that define object-oriented programming is called *encapsulation*. This concept describes a method of grouping together data elements and the code that acts on those elements.

Encapsulation is not necessarily a new concept to the Visual Basic developer. VB6 classes gave you the means to encapsulate objects and data into a single place. However, pre-VB .NET classes were not introduced until VB version 4, so many of the old-school VB programmers who did not start by using them may have eschewed them altogether. Nothing in VB versions 6 and earlier forced you to use classes.

VB .NET, as you might guess, is a whole different animal. Everything, and I mean *everything*, is encapsulated into a class in the .NET world. This pretty much forces you to think in object-oriented terms as you develop your software. And this means that the encapsulation of data and code into classes is something with which you'll need to become expertly familiar. Don't get intimidated by this, though. Most developers find that once they've retrained themselves to think in object-oriented terms, they can't figure out how they wrote code by *not* thinking along these lines.

To demonstrate the components of object-oriented design, I've developed the rough framework for a little VB .NET game. The game will consist of a bunch of "somethings" that exist in the game world and interact with each other.

When developing in an OOP language, the goal is to abstract the program into appropriate classes, or objects. In this little game example, it's probably pretty clear that we're going to want each of the little "somethings" in the game world to be instances of a class. I've named that class `WorldEntity`. Here's the definition of the `WorldEntity` class:

```
Class WorldEntity

    Property Location() As Point
    Property Color() As Color
    Property HitPoints() As Integer
    ReadOnly Property IsDead() As Boolean

    Public Function DistanceFrom(ByVal p As Point) As Single
    Public Overridable Sub Damage(ByVal nAmt As Integer)
Public Overridable Sub Draw(ByVal g As Graphics)

End Class
```

A `WorldEntity` class is defined by its location in the world, the color with which it will be drawn, a number of *hit points* (an integer value that determines the health of the object), and a read-only Boolean property that determines whether the object is "dead" or not. There are also two methods in this class; the `DistanceFrom` method determines how far away the `WorldEntity` is from a point, and the `Damage` method administers some form of damage to the object.

A critical feature to encapsulation is *data hiding*, which means that any users of this class need not understand any of the implementation details of this class—you only need understand what each property and method does at a conceptual level. This means that you really need to understand nothing more than the preceding class definition in order to use this class in your own game applications.

Another important advantage of data hiding is that the developers of the class can change the underlying implementation of the properties and methods, and be confident that they are not "breaking" parts of the code outside the class they are changing. As long as the conceptual idea behind each property or method member is not broken, the developers are free to implement each member as they wish.

NOTE   The properties, events, and methods of a class are collectively called the *members* of the class.

Encapsulating the `WorldEntity` classes into their own class is pretty much a no-brainer. What might seem less obvious, however, is that the game world itself is a good candidate for a new class. Here is the interface of the world class, called `TheWorld`:

```
Class TheWorld
```

```
Public Sub New()
Public Sub AddWorldEntity(ByVal o As WorldEntity)
Public Sub Draw(ByVal g As Graphics)
Public Function ClickedOnEntity(ByVal p As Point) As WorldEntity
Public Function NumEntities() As Integer
```

```
End Class
```

Again, the users of this class need understand nothing about how these members are implemented "under the hood." You only need to understand what each member is supposed to do. For the sake of seeing data hiding in action, however, let's open up the hood of these two classes to see what's going on.

WorldEntity Class Details

The Location, Color, and HitPoints properties on the WorldEntity class work the same way. They use a private variable to store their information internally, and they expose the data in that variable via a property. Here is the code that sets up the Location property:

```
Private FLocation As Point
Property Location() As Point
Get
    Return FLocation
End Get
Set(ByVal Value As Point)
    FLocation = Value
End Set
End Property
```

This might seem like an awful lot of code to set up a single property in a class. Why not simply replace the private FLocation variable with a public variable named Location and be done with it? The truth is, making this replacement would deal in less code, but using the Get and Set subroutines against a true property helps us further encapsulate game logic later. For example, now examine the code that sets up the HitPoints property:

```
Private FHitPoints As Integer
Property HitPoints() As Integer
    Get
        Return FHitPoints
    End Get
    Set(ByVal Value As Integer)
        FHitPoints = Value
        If FHitPoints < 0 Then FHitPoints = 0
    End Set
End Property
```

This code is almost identical to the code for the Location property, with one important difference. In the Set procedure of the HitPoints property, a check is performed to see if the HitPoints value has dropped below 0. If it has, it is restored back up to 0. This important piece of "business logic" (more appropriately thought of as "game logic" in this context) is placed in the most appropriate place—in the code that establishes the HitPoints property. This means that any time a WorldEntity has its HitPoints changed by any means (combat, accident, poison, healing, magic, etc.), the "below 0 disallow" logic will be executed. This is a perfect example of encapsulating logic inside the class and hiding implementation details from the user of the class.

Let's examine the Draw method on the WorldEntity class:

```
TODO: ellipse just placeholder for now, _
      will switch to actual graphics later
Public Overridable Sub Draw(ByVal g As Graphics)
      Dim r As Rectangle

      r = New Rectangle(Location.X - 2, Location.Y - 2, 8, 8)
      Call g.FillEllipse(New SolidBrush(Color), r)
End Sub
```

Note the initial comment stating the intent to come back to this code and replace the simplistic ellipse representation of each object with a more respectable graphic later. The fact that the Draw method is encapsulated inside the WorldEntity class makes it extremely easy for me to replace this code when I choose to do so. I can replace the three-line ellipse drawer with any type of sophisticated drawing code that I want, and be sure that I don't break any other part of my game program (so long as I leave the actual method name and parameter list the same).

TheWorld Class Details

The class TheWorld is smaller than the entity class in this early game engine, so let's examine the code in its entirety:

```
Class TheWorld
    Private FEntities As Collection

    Public Sub New()
        MyBase.new()
        FEntities = New Collection()
    End Sub

    'TODO: collision detection?
    Public Sub AddWorldEntity(ByVal o As WorldEntity)
        FEntities.Add(o)
```

```
End Sub

Public Sub Draw(ByVal g As Graphics)

    Dim o As WorldEntity
    Dim r As Rectangle

    g.FillRectangle(New SolidBrush(Color.Black), g.ClipBounds)

    For Each o In FEntities
        o.Draw(g)
    Next

End Sub

Public Function ClickedOnEntity(ByVal p As Point) As WorldEntity

    Dim o As WorldEntity

    For Each o In FEntities
        If o.DistanceFrom(p) < 8 Then
            Return o
        End If
    Next
    Return Nothing
End Function

Public Function NumEntities() As Integer
    Return FEntities.Count
End Function

End Class
```

The WorldEntity objects that make up the world are kept in a standard Collection object. This makes the AddWorldEntity method extremely easy to implement—I just add the object instance to the collection. Note that the FEntities collection is not directly exposed to the outside world (it is declared private). Because this collection is hidden, I don't have to worry about making sure the collection holds only objects of a certain type. I can be guaranteed that the collection holds only WorldEntity class instances, because the only code that has access to this collection is the code that makes up TheWorld class, and the only line of code that adds anything to this collection is in the AddWorldEntity method, where the parameter explicitly states that the object being added has the type WorldEntity.

The Draw method fills the passed-in Graphics instance in black, then calls the Draw method on each object in the collection. Again, because of the power of encapsulation, if I choose to improve the graphics later (say I want a grassy bitmap or a star field as a background for the game), I can come right to this `Draw` method and place the code there without disturbing any other code in the game.

The `ClickedOnEntity` method compares the distance from the passed-in point to the location of each entity in the world using the `DistanceFrom` method attached to the `WorldEntity` object. If this distance is less than the hard-coded value 8, the method concludes that the entity has been clicked on. Further improvements might include taking larger and smaller entities into account and deciding how to handle the case where more than one object lies in the same place. In the current implementation, only the first object in the collection that lies close to the passed-in point gets returned.

Hopefully, this small example should outline the benefits of abstracting your code into an object-oriented framework and using encapsulation and data hiding to segregate code.

40 Merits of Inheritance

 The inheritance example can be found in the folder `prjOOPFundamentals`.

The previous section demonstrated encapsulating both code and data into a logical construct known as a *class*. The next fundamental concept of object-oriented programming stems from the requirement to have classes that share some common functionality. This usually occurs when you have abstract constructs that are similar in some ways but different in others.

Take the simple gaming example described in the previous section. We modeled an abstract `WorldEntity` class, but it might be apparent that this simple class cannot model all of the functionality that we'll require for the game. For example, you may require that an entity be able to wear some type of armor that limits the damage done on it. But not all types of entities would be able to wear armor, would they? The `WorldEntity` class in the game example is meant to model both living and non-living objects in the world. This means that while adding a `HasArmor` property to the `WorldEntity` class would work, having this property on a non-living object wouldn't make much sense. It may also be desirable to display the living and non-living objects as different color ellipses on our simple map.

It seems that splitting the `WorldEntity` class into two classes, one for living entities and one for non-living entities, is starting to make sense. But old-school procedural programmers are often averse to creating separate blocks of code that handle similar situations. (More lines of code equals more bugs, after all.) So what we really need is the ability to create these two separate classes, but have them share common functionality for the things they have in common and to encapsulate the logic that makes them separate from each other into their own class.

Obviously, I wouldn't have taken the time to set up this rather complicated example if I didn't have a solution available, and that solution is called *inheritance*. Inheritance allows you to create descendant classes off existing classes. These descendant classes share all of the functionality of the ancestor class, but they allow you to add new functionality to them. In the game example, we are going to create two new descendant classes off the WorldEntity class: an InanimateWorldEntity class and a LivingWorldEntity class. The definition of the InanimateWorldEntity class is as follows:

```
Class InanimateWorldEntity
        Inherits WorldEntity

        Public Sub New()
            MyBase.new()
            'default color of inanimate objects to gray
            Color = Color.Gray
        End Sub

        Public Overrides Function ToString() As String

            Dim cMsg As String

            cMsg &= "Class: " & Me.GetType.ToString
            If IsDead Then
                cMsg &= " (dead)"
            End If
            cMsg &= Environment.NewLine
            cMsg &= "Location: " & Me.Location.ToString & Environment.NewLine
            cMsg &= "HitPoints: " & Me.HitPoints.ToString &
                ➥Environment.NewLine
            Return cMsg

        End Function

End Class
```

Note the second line: Inherits WorldEntity. This line tells the compiler that this class descends from the WorldEntity class, and therefore shares all of the members of that class without the need to recode them. This new class, however, adds members of its own, including a new constructor (the New method), and a ToString method. The keyword Overrides on the ToString method indicates that this method also exists in one of the ancestor classes of this class. This might give you some pause, because after studying the original WorldEntity class, you would find that there is no ToString method in this ancestor class. So where is the original method? The answer lies in the fact that the WorldEntity class, although not explicitly indicated, is a descendant of the class named `Object`, and this class has a `ToString` method in it. All classes in the .NET Framework, in fact, descend from the `Object` class.

This demonstrates that inheritance can be a multi-level proposition. Class A can descend from the class `Object`, class B from A, class C from B, etc. The lowest level class in this example (class C) contains all of the members of the class `Object`, class A, and class B. This is a powerful method of code reuse, and it prevents having to duplicate code to obtain similar functionality for similar classes.

Now that you've seen the `InanimateWorldEntity` class, here's the code for the `LivingWorldEntity` class:

```
Class LivingWorldEntity
    Inherits WorldEntity

Public Sub New()
   MyBase.new()
   Color = Color.Green        'another default color
End Sub

'living objects can wear armor
Private FHasArmor As Boolean
Property HasArmor() As Boolean
   Get
       Return FHasArmor
   End Get
   Set(ByVal Value As Boolean)
       FHasArmor = Value
   End Set
End Property

'HACK: armor damage div 2 for now, add an damage reduction factor
Public Overrides Sub Damage(ByVal nAmt As Integer)
   If HasArmor Then
       HitPoints -= (nAmt \ 2)
   Else
       MyBase.Damage(nAmt)
   End If

End Sub

Public Overrides Function ToString() As String

   Dim cMsg As String
```

```
cMsg &= "Class: " & Me.GetType.ToString
If IsDead Then
    cMsg &= " (dead)"
End If

cMsg &= Environment.NewLine
cMsg &= "Location: " & Me.Location.ToString & Environment.NewLine
cMsg &= "HitPoints: " & Me.HitPoints.ToString & Environment.NewLine
cMsg &= "HasArmor: " & Me.HasArmor
Return cMsg

    End Function

    End Class
```

The `LivingWorldEntity` class also adds a constructor and an overridden `ToString` method. In addition, a new property named `HasArmor` is added, which indicates whether the living entity is wearing armor or not. This property does not exist on the `InanimateWorldEntity` class, which demonstrates how descendant classes from the same ancestor can have different features.

Another difference in the `LivingWorldEntity` class is that the `Damage` function has been changed to alter how damage is absorbed based on whether the object is wearing armor or not. Armor-wearing entities take half the intended damage.

41   The Church of Polymorphism

The polymorphism example can be found in the folder `prjOOPFundamentals`.

You've seen two of the three fundamental concepts behind the object-oriented paradigm. The third, *polymorphism*, is a bit more abstract concept. Polymorphism occurs when two or more classes have similar properties or methods and the compiler is able to automatically sort out which object is which without being explicitly told.

To see polymorphism in action, look at the code that executes in the `prjOOPFundamentals` project when an object in the world is double-clicked:

```
Private Sub pnDraw_DoubleClick(ByVal sender As _
    Object, ByVal e As _
    System.EventArgs) Handles pnDraw.DoubleClick

    Dim cMsg As String

    If oLastClickedOn Is Nothing Then Exit Sub
```

```
        oLastClickedOn.Damage(10)
        cMsg = "object damaged: " & Environment.NewLine
        cMsg &= oLastClickedOn.ToString
        Call DisplayMessage(cMsg)

    End Sub
```

This code calls the Damage method on the object instance oLastClickedOn, which is declared as type WorldEntity. This code makes no attempt to determine whether the oLastClickedOn variable is currently referring to a LivingWorldEntity or an InanimateWorldEntity; it simply calls the Damage method. At runtime, the program sorts out which method code to execute depending on which class the oLastClickedOn variable is currently pointing to.

Polymorphism is often closely linked with inheritance because of overridden methods like the Damage example in this section. However, polymorphism can act on classes that are not involved in an ancestor/descendant relationship. You could create a new class, not inherited from any current class in the project, that also has a Damage method. If you were to place instances of this object in the world and call the Damage method from the same type of code as shown in the preceding example, you would see polymorphic behavior in classes that are not directly related.

42   In Your Face Interfaces

 The interface code examples can be found in the folder prjInterfaces.

You've seen in the previous sections how object-oriented programming allows you to encapsulate members like properties, events, and methods into a class to abstract some form of functionality. Sometimes, this abstract level of functionality is common enough or important enough to be needed in multiple classes. This is when you should start thinking of using *interfaces*. An interface, like a class, is a declared set of members. Unlike classes, however, interfaces provide no implementation of these member functions. Instead, the interface provides the declaration for a set of members for the purpose of future classes fully defining these interfaces.

This might be better explained through an example. The most common example is the IList interface, which is part of the .NET Framework. The IList interface defines the members required to create a list of things (usually some form of object instances). Here is a list of the members that the IList interface declares:

Member Name	Type	Description
IsFixedSize	Boolean property	True if list has a maximum size.
IsReadOnly	Boolean property	True if items can't be added, removed.
Item	Object (indexed) property	Sets/returns object at specified position.

Member Name	Type	Description
Add	Method	Adds an item.
Clear	Method	Removes all items.
Contains	Method	True if passed-in item is in list.
IndexOf	Method	Returns index of passed-in item.
Insert	Method	Adds item to middle of list.
Remove	Method	Removes passed-in item.
RemoveAt	Method	Removes item at passed-in index.

If you wish to create a class that manages a list of items, you might consider implementing the IList interface in this class. This means that you'll have to define each of the members listed in this table and specifically denote which members implement which parts of this interface.

What benefit will you get out of implementing the IList interface? For starters, other developers using your new class learn a great deal about your new class right from the start if you tell them that the class implements a known interface. They know that all of the members in the table will be represented in your class, so they have a good expectation of how your class works.

Implementing an interface also helps during the design of your class. Once you declare that a class implements a known interface, the Visual Studio .NET debugger tells you about each member function that you have not yet implemented, which means that your program will not compile until you have correctly coded the entire interface.

Coding to an Interface

As an example, let's try and create a new class that implements the IList interface and see what the compiler does to help us out. My new list class will be classed the DoNothingList, and it will really serve no good purpose other than to demonstrate the implementation of the IList interface. The DoNothingList will hold a list of the same integer value.

The first step is to declare the new class and the fact that it will implement the IList interface:

```
Class DoNothingList
    Implements IList

End Class
```

At this point, the compiler should bark out a dozen or so errors at you, and you've barely started coding! Here's the text of one of these errors:

```
C:\Documents and Settings\mtagliaf\My Documents\vbNet2ndEdition\prjInterfaces\
➡CheesyList.vb(5): 'prjInterfaces.mCheesyList.DoNothingList' must
➡implement 'Overridable Overloads Function Add(value As Object) As
➡ Integer' for interface 'System.Collections.IList'.
```

This message is telling you that you have yet to implement the member function Add in this class, and you are required to do so in order to successfully implement the IList interface. The other error messages are identical, each telling us about a different member that you need to implement. Coding the rest of the class is a simple matter of fixing each of these errors, one by one. To fix one of the errors, you simply implement the member function in question. Make sure to instruct the compiler which member function you are implementing, as follows:

```
Function Add(ByVal Value As Object) As Integer _
    Implements IList.Add

    'no need to add any real values, just inc counter
    FCount += 1
    Return 0
End Function
```

Remember that this particular example class doesn't really store a list of objects; it simply demonstrates the implementation of the interface. This is why the Add method doesn't really do anything with the passed in the Value parameter.

Once the Add method is added to your class, one of the error messages in the Task List should disappear, and you can move on to the next error message.

One other quick word on implementing interface members. The Intellisense feature of Visual Studio really helps out. Intellisense helps you by showing you a list of the members in the given interface, as seen in the following illustration.

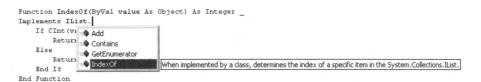

Note that the only available entries in the Intellisense drop-down list are those members that match the parameter list for the function you've defined so far. Since this function takes a single parameter of type Object, the Intellisense feature does not give us the RemoveAt method as a choice here, for example, because that method doesn't match the parameter list that you've already defined.

Creating Your Own Interfaces

Coding against a known interface is one thing, but you can also define your own interfaces to code against in Visual Studio .NET. Why might you want to do that? This is really useful in multi-developer shops, where a project manager can design an interface that defines how a class or set of classes need to be implemented, and then task his developers with actually implementing those interfaces into classes to be used by future programs.

The module CustomInterface.vb demonstrates the declaration of several interfaces and classes against those interfaces. The first declared interface is as follows:

```
Interface IBaseballPlayer
    Property Team() As String
End Interface
```

The IBaseballPlayer interface declares a single string property that represents the team that a baseball player currently plays for. The next two declared interfaces extend the first interface:

```
Interface IBaseballPositionPlayer
    Inherits IBaseballPlayer

    Property BattingAverage() As Single
End Interface

Interface IBaseballPitcher
    Inherits IBaseballPlayer

    Property ERA() As Single
End Interface
```

Note that interfaces can be inherited just like classes can. These interfaces add a batting average or an ERA property to the first interface. (Since most baseball position players don't have earned run averages, it doesn't make sense to add this property to the base interface.) This correctly models most baseball players' statistics, with one exception—pitchers in the National League also hit, so they need a batting average property as well. Let's declare a new interface to handle this:

```
Interface IBaseballNationalLeaguePitcher
    Inherits IBaseballPositionPlayer, IBaseballPitcher

End Interface
```

This example demonstrates the ability of interfaces to inherit from multiple sources. We've created a new interface that declares the members in two ancestor classes.

Finally, the sample program declares a class that implements the `IbaseballNational-LeaguePitcher` interface. Imagine that a project leader wrote the interface and then left the coding of this class definition to a developer who works for him. The developer would have to correctly code all the members of this interface before the class could be compiled and used in a program.

```
Class NationalLeaguePitchers
        Implements IBaseballNationalLeaguePitcher

        Private FTeam As String
        Private FBattingAverage As Single
        Private FERA As Single

        Property ERA() As Single Implements IBaseballNationalLeaguePitcher.ERA
            Get
                Return FERA
            End Get
            Set(ByVal Value As Single)
                FERA = Value
            End Set
        End Property

        Property AVG() As Single Implements IBaseballPositionPlayer
            ➡.BattingAverage
            Get
                Return FBattingAverage
            End Get
            Set(ByVal Value As Single)
                FBattingAverage = Value
            End Set
        End Property

        Property Team() As String Implements IBaseballPlayer.Team
            Get
                Return FTeam
            End Get
            Set(ByVal Value As String)
                FTeam = Value
            End Set
        End Property
    End Class
```

43   Calculating Elapsed Time

 The redundant function calls code can be found in the folder `prjRedundantFunctionCalls`.

During development, I often find the need to calculate the time it takes to run a given piece of code. This gives me a quantitative measure of how fast (or slow) a procedure I'm working on is running. If I decide that I can improve on the time by optimizing the code, I'll have a number in mind that I have to beat.

I whipped up a little elapsed-time calculation class for this purpose. This is a good example of a high "bang for the buck" class; it took practically no time for me to come up with this class, but I find myself using it repeatedly.

The code for the `ElapsedTime` class is so small, in fact, that I'll reproduce it here in its entirety:

```
Public Class tagElapsedTime

    Private iStartTime As Integer

    Public Sub New()
        MyBase.New()

        Call StartTimer()
    End Sub

    Public Sub StartTimer()
        iStartTime = Environment.TickCount
    End Sub

    ReadOnly Property MilliSecondsElapsed() As Double
        Get
            Return (Environment.TickCount - iStartTime)
        End Get
    End Property

    ReadOnly Property SecondsElapsed() As Double
        Get
            Return MilliSecondsElapsed / 1000
        End Get
    End Property

    ReadOnly Property MinutesElapsed() As Double
        Get
            Return SecondsElapsed / 60
        End Get
    End Property

End Class
```

Pretty simple, no? A method called `StartTimer` sets a private variable based on a .NET Framework variable named `Environment.TickCount`. This value represents the number of milliseconds that have elapsed since the system was started last. (For all of you Win32 API gurus, this is equivalent to the `GetTickCount` API call, which I could have used here with identical results.)

To calculate the number of seconds or minutes that have elapsed since `StartTimer` is called, merely call the `SecondsElapsed` or the `MinutesElapsed` method.

The sample project `prjRedundantFunctionCalls` does some time trials on converting all of the lowercase *a*'s in a block of random text to uppercase *A*'s using two different methods. (See "Redundant Function Calls" earlier in this book for more information on why these comparisons were being made.) Here is a portion of the code, showing the `tagElapsedTimer` class in action:

```
oTimer = New tagElapsedTime()

oTimer.StartTimer()
cText = SlowTextConvert(cText)
lbSlow.Text = "Time: " & oTimer.MilliSecondsElapsed & " ms."
tbExampleText.Text = cText
```

The `SlowTextConvert` function in this example is the function being timed. To get the most accurate result, I start the timer on the line immediately preceding this function call and print the milliseconds elapsed on the line immediately following the function call.

44 Reading and Writing *INI* Files

 The `INI` file code can be found in the folder `prjIniFiles`.

Microsoft has been trying to put the use of `INI` files out to pasture, but they just won't die. I find them much more convenient than writing to the Registry in many cases. For example, say I'm writing a SQL Server database application program that is to be run off a shared network drive. One of the things my program will need is the name of the database server. This server name will be the same for all users of the program, so why store it in each user's individual Registry? It is much easier to store the server name in an `INI` file in the application directory. That way, when my network manager comes and tells me she's performing a SQL Server upgrade over the weekend, and, oh by the way, she's changing the name of the server during the upgrade, I can simply change the `INI` file to point to the new server. If this information were stored in the Registry, I'd have to change it on each end user's machine.

Microsoft's desire to do away with the INI file has apparently gotten strong enough that they conveniently "forgot" to include support for them in the .NET Framework. But I'm not going to let that stop me, oh no. A bit of coding, and I have a nice, compact INI file class that performs all of the INI file support that I need.

The API Calls

The basic API declarations that I needed for my INI file class are listed here:

```
Private Declare Function GetPrivateProfileInt Lib _
    "kernel32" Alias "GetPrivateProfileIntA" (ByVal _
    lpApplicationName As String, ByVal lpKeyName As String, ByVal _
    nDefault As Integer, ByVal lpFileName As String) As Integer

Private Declare Function GetPrivateProfileString Lib _
    "kernel32" Alias "GetPrivateProfileStringA" (ByVal _
    lpApplicationName As String, ByVal lpKeyName As String, ByVal _
    lpDefault As String, ByVal lpReturnedString As String, ByVal _
    nSize As Integer, ByVal lpFileName As String) As Integer

Private Declare Function WritePrivateProfileString Lib _
    "kernel32" Alias "WritePrivateProfileStringA" (ByVal _
    lpApplicationName As String, ByVal lpKeyName As String, ByVal _
    lpString As String, ByVal lpFileName As String) As Integer

Private Declare Function FlushPrivateProfileString Lib _
    "kernel32" Alias "WritePrivateProfileStringA" (ByVal _
    lpApplicationName As Integer, ByVal _
    lpKeyName As Integer, ByVal lpString As Integer, ByVal _
    lpFileName As String) As Integer
```

There are more INI-related API calls than these, but these are the basic calls needed for reading and writing to a *private* INI file (which includes all INI files except for WIN.INI).

The last API declaration is a special-purpose declaration of WritePrivateProfileString that declares the first three parameters as type Integer instead of type String. This declaration is renamed FlushPrivateProfileString. The purpose of this function is to flush changes written to the INI file to disk, since INI file operations are cached. You probably won't need to worry about flushing INI file changes to disk in your applications, but I wanted to show the INI file contents directly after making changes to the INI file in my example program, and the program wasn't showing the changes immediately because of the caching nature of the INI file. Flushing the changes to disk before reading them from the file solved this problem for me.

Digging into the *INI* Class

The INI file class itself is small and straightforward. The constructor takes a single string as a parameter. This string is used as the INI filename in all further operations. I also made the filename available as a read-only property, as shown here:

```
Dim FFilename As String

Public Sub New(ByVal cFilename As String)
    FFilename = cFilename
End Sub

ReadOnly Property FileName() As String
    Get
        Return FFilename
    End Get
End Property
```

Because the INI filename is passed into the constructor and because the Filename property is read-only, an instance of the INIFile class can read and write to only one INI file. This can be easily rectified if your desired use of the file is to have a class that can write to more than one INI file at the same time, but I did not find this to be a necessary feature of my class.

The class contains read and write methods for strings, integers, and Booleans. Booleans are typically stored in INI files as 0 or 1, and I chose to retain that storage scheme in this class. Therefore, the GetBoolean method calls the GetPrivateProfileInt API call.

I chose to implement the writing of strings, integers, and Booleans through the single WritePrivateProfileString API call. Thus, both the WriteBoolean and WriteInteger methods end up calling the WriteString method, after converting the desired value to a string.

The prjIniFiles example application demonstrates reading and writing to an INI file. The INI file is first created with default values. The buttons to the left side of the application allow you to write information to the INI file, and the INI file is redisplayed after each change (this is where I needed the "flush" functionality in my class), as shown in the following illustration:

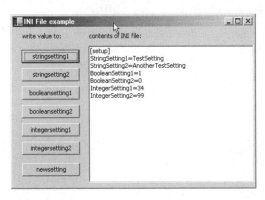

One interesting trick in this example application is the use of a single `Click` event to handle more than one button click. The following sub handles the two Boolean value buttons:

```
Protected Sub cbBS1_Click(ByVal sender As _
Object, ByVal e As System.EventArgs) _
Handles cbBS1.Click, cbBS2.Click

        Dim b As Boolean
        Dim aButton As Button

        aButton = CType(sender, Button)
        b = Ini.GetBoolean(SECTIONNAME, aButton.Text, False)
        b = Not b

        Call Ini.WriteBoolean(SECTIONNAME, aButton.Text, b)
        Call ShowINIFileContents()

    End Sub
```

Note the `Handles` clause at the end of the procedure declaration. This tells the compiler that this sub should be called as the `Click` event for buttons `cbBS1` and `cbBS2`. This type of functionality generally replaces the use of control arrays in previous versions of Visual Basic.

The next interesting part of this procedure is the line `aButton = Ctype(sender, Button)`. This line of code determines which button was clicked to call this procedure and assigns that button to a variable named `aButton`. The next line of code retrieves a value from the `INI` file, and the key name that it uses is the caption of the button that was clicked (`aButton.text`).

Finally, the Boolean value is negated (`b = Not b`), and the negated value is written back to the `INI` file.

The same `Handles` event trick is used for the two integer buttons and again for the two string buttons.

45   Adding Controls to the Toolbox

The toolbox controls code can be found in the folders `prjControlsInTheToolbox` and `prjControlsInTheToolboxUsage`.

It's always been my dream, ever since I was a little boy, to add my own components to the Visual Basic toolbox. OK, so that statement is a tad extreme. But why the heck couldn't I? Sure, I could add these things called `UserControls`, or I could write ActiveX controls and stick them in there, but that just isn't the same. Why can't I just take a regular control, add a few new properties, change a color or font or two, and drop it into the toolbox for use in all my projects?

Visual Studio .NET lets you do just that. Thanks to the magic of object-oriented programming, you can inherit new controls off of existing controls and place them in the component toolbox right where they belong.

The example code for adding controls is actually two different projects in Visual Studio. The first project, named `prjOddListBox`, is the new control that I've developed, a do-almost-nothing control that I've named the `OddListBox`. After I've explained how this control was developed, I'll describe how it can be added to the toolbox. In the second project, `prjControls-InTheToolboxUsage`, I'll demonstrate how to use the control.

Developing the Control

The `prjOddListBox` project was created as a Windows Control Library, as you can see in the following illustration:

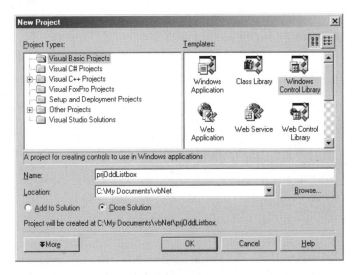

This creates a project without a main form and instead creates a single module named `Control.vb`, the contents of which is as follows:

```
Public Class UserControl1
    Inherits System.Windows.Forms.UserControl
```

```
#Region " Windows Form Designer generated code "

    Public Sub New()
        MyBase.New()

        'This call is required by the Windows Form Designer.
        InitializeComponent()

        'Add any initialization after the InitializeComponent() call

    End Sub

    'UserControl1 overrides dispose to clean up the component list.
    Protected Overloads Overrides Sub Dispose(ByVal disposing As Boolean)
        If disposing Then
            If Not (components Is Nothing) Then
                components.Dispose()
            End If
        End If
        MyBase.Dispose(disposing)
    End Sub

    'Required by the Windows Form Designer
    Private components As System.ComponentModel.Container

    'NOTE: The following procedure is required by the Windows Form Designer
    'It can be modified using the Windows Form Designer.
    'Do not modify it using the code editor.
    <System.Diagnostics.DebuggerStepThrough()> Private Sub InitializeComponent()
        components = New System.ComponentModel.Container()
    End Sub

#End Region

End Class
```

The default class that the Visual Studio .NET project creates for you is given the name Control1 and is a descendant of the class System.Windows.Forms.UserControl. Note that you don't have to inherit off this control; that's just a suggestion that VS.NET makes to you. I instead chose to inherit off a more well-defined control, the standard Listbox. To do this, I merely changed the Inherits line to read Inherits System.Windows.Forms.Listbox. I now have the makings of my own little Listbox, ready for customization.

The first thing I wanted to add to my custom Listbox was a string-based Tag property similar to that found in prior versions of Visual Basic. Now, VB .NET controls do have a Tag property (as of beta 2 of the .NET Framework, anyway), but I originally coded this object in beta 1 of Visual Studio .NET. I chose to reimplement the Tag property for two reasons:

As an exercise   The Tag property doesn't have to do a thing inside the control as long as it can store a string value for the programmer to use. Therefore, this is the easiest possible property to write and a good place to start learning about inheritance.

Backward-compatibility   In large projects, it might be easier to use a Listbox with a Tag property on it than to sort through 100,000 lines of code looking for all the places to change .Tag to .PrimaryKey, or whatever you decided to name some new property.

The code to add the Tag property is only a few lines and is shown here:

```
Private FTag As String

<Description("User-Defined Property to mimic VB6 Tag"), _
Category("UserStuff")> _
Property MyReplacementTag() As String
        Get
              Return FTag
        End Get
        Set(ByVal Value As String)
              FTag = Value
        End Set

   End Property
```

The private variable FTag is how the control will internally store the Tag data. As you see, the property definition has the simplest possible Get and Set procedures, whose functions are to simply read and write the value of the FTag variable.

NOTE   Once Visual Studio .NET beta 2 came out, my own Tag property conflicted with the one they put back on all the controls. I therefore chose to rename my own property MyReplacementTag.

The interesting part of the procedure is the stuff between the <> symbols. This information is called *metadata*. Metadata is information that helps describe your code to the Visual Studio environment. In this case, we are describing two attributes of the Tag property through the metadata. The first attribute is the Description attribute—this is a comment that will appear at the bottom of the Property Browser when the programmer is editing this property. The second attribute is called the `Category` attribute; it describes in which grouping the new property should appear in the Property Browser. You'll see how these attributes work later.

The second custom property that I created is called `AvgLength`. This is a read-only property that returns the average character length of all the elements in the `Listbox` at a given time. The code for this property is as follows:

```
<Description("Average String Length of elements"), _
Category("UserStuff")>
    ReadOnly Property AvgLength() As Integer
    Get
        Dim i As Integer
        Dim iTot As Integer = 0

        If Me.Items.Count = 0 Then
            Return 0
        Else
            For i = 0 To Me.Items.Count - 1
                iTot += CStr(Me.Items(i)).Length
            Next
            Return iTot \ Me.Items.Count
        End If

    End Get

    End Property
```

Note that there is no `Set` portion of this property because it's a read-only property. This code loops through all the items, adding up the characters and then dividing by the number of items. This property also has the same two attributes defined for it in the metadata portion.

Metadata is not only used to further describe properties; it can also be used to describe an entire class. The class definition of `OddListBox` reads as follows:

```
<ToolboxItem(True)> _
    Public Class OddListBox
    Inherits System.Windows.Forms.ListBox
```

Setting the `ToolBoxItem` attribute to `True` is necessary for controls that I intend to be placed in the Visual Studio .NET toolbox.

Adding the Control to the Toolbox

Once my new component was completed, I was ready to add it to the toolbox. After compiling, I made sure that there was an `OddListBox.dll` file in the `bin` folder of my Windows Control Library project. This is the DLL that I'll need to reference when I add my control to the toolbox.

Since this was the first toolbox control that I was adding, I decided to create a new tab in the toolbox for all of my custom controls. You add a tab by right-clicking an empty space and choosing Add Tab from the pop-up menu. I named my new tab `MattTagCustom`, referring to my custom controls. My naked, ready-to-use tab is shown here:

Finally, the time had come to add the control. With my new tab as the current tab, right-clicking and selecting Customize Toolbox brought up the following dialog box. This dialog box is used for adding different types of controls to the toolbox. I'm interested in .NET Framework Components, which is the right-most tab in the dialog box.

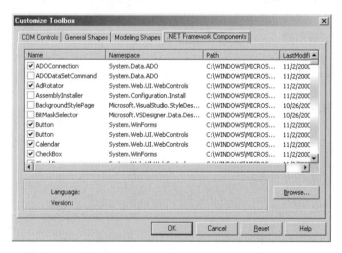

To add my new control, I clicked the Browse button and selected the `OddListBox.dll` file whose existence I had verified earlier. The final step was to make sure the `OddListBox` control had been added to the master list of Visual Studio controls and that it was checked. After closing the dialog box by clicking OK, I saw my very own custom control in the Visual Studio toolbox for the first time (insert thunderous applause here).

NOTE   The large list of components already listed in the .NET Framework Components tab of the Customize Toolbox is a good tool for familiarizing yourself with the controls and namespaces available to you.

Using the New Control

Getting your custom controls in the Visual Studio .NET toolbox is the hard part. Once you manage to get them there, using them is easy, because it's no different from using the built-in toolbox controls.

The example project `prjControlsInTheToolboxUsage` shows the `OddListBox` control that I created in the prior example dropped onto an empty form (see the following illustration). It looks just like a normal `Listbox` except for the lack of a 3D border and the somewhat odd background color. (Examining the code for this control shows that I changed these two visual elements in the constructor, mainly so I had a visual way to tell my control from a normal `Listbox`. Nothing prevents the user of my control from setting these properties back to their default values, or any other values for that matter.)

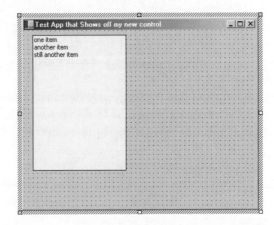

The truly cool part (to me, anyway) is examining the custom properties that I created right in the Property Browser. As shown in the next illustration, the two properties of my OddList-Box are shown at the bottom of the Property Browser. They have been placed into the category I specified (via metadata attributes) and have the correct descriptive text when they are selected (more metadata attributes).

The AvgLength property in particular is interesting to play with. If you go ahead and add some items to your OddListBox in design mode, the AvgLength property updates automatically, right in the Property Browser. Remember, this read-only property returns the average string length of the items in the OddListBox. The code that I wrote that calculates this average is running during *design mode*. To quote Keanu Reeves, "Whoa."

If you're anything like I was when I first played with this functionality, your head is probably spinning with ideas right now about all the custom components you can create for your company or your next big project and how cool they'll look all lined up side by side in the Visual Studio .NET toolbox.

46   Earning Your Inheritance

The inheriting forms code can be found in the folders prjInheritingForms and prjUsing-InheritingForms.

Inheriting existing classes to create descendant classes is an easy enough concept to understand. What about inheriting forms to create descendant forms? Could this serve a purpose?

The answer to this question is, of course, "yes." A form is a class in the .NET Framework, so every form that you make is in fact an inherited form. However, you can extend the inheritance concept more deeply by creating forms with predefined elements on them and then creating descendant classes from them. Inheriting forms gives you the same benefit that inheriting any other class does: sharing functionality, "black-boxing" code inside descendant classes, reducing code duplication, and so on. Because forms are visual elements, you can use form inheritance to give your application a consistent look, as well. If you want every form in your application to have the same status bar, for example, you can create a base form with this status bar and then subclass every form in your project from this base form. Then, if you decide to change the look of the common status bar, you need only change it in one place.

The sample projects here demonstrate how to create a base form and then use it in a new project as the descendant of a new form. The base form is located in project prjInheriting-Forms. This project starts off as a standard Windows application. The base form is very simple: a three-panel status bar at the bottom of the form and a Close button anchored to the lower-right corner. In addition, a timer control is set up and used to display the current time in one of the panels, as seen in this illustration.

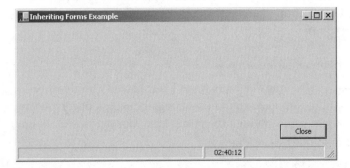

Once the base form is fully designed and finalized, the project type needs to be changed from a Windows application to a Class Library. This is done in the Property Pages dialog box, which you can access by selecting the project in the Solution Explorer, right-clicking, and selecting Properties. The following illustration shows exactly what needs to be changed:

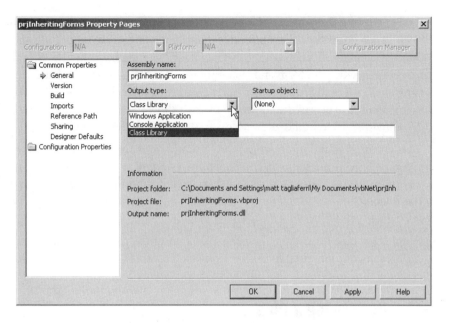

Once the project type is changed, you need to make sure to rebuild the project, which will create the necessary DLL file in which the base form class resides. The form will then be ready to be subclassed. I created a new project named `prjUsingInheritedForms` for my subclassed form example. Once this project was created, I first removed the default form that Visual Studio .NET created for me. Then, I right-clicked the project in the Solution Explorer and selected Add Inherited Form. In the Add Item dialog box, make sure Local Project Items is selected on the left and Inherited Form is selected on the right. After naming the new form file, click Open. You will be prompted to select the file containing your base form. Locate and select the DLL file built in the previous step. You will now have the base form added to your project, as seen in this illustration:

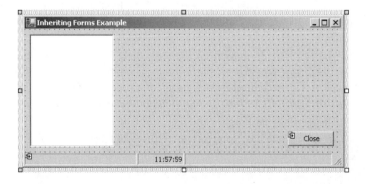

Note that the form looks a bit different in that the status bar/Close button has a little graphic in its upper-left corner. This indicates that these controls are part of the `Ancestor` class and cannot be modified. I could alter this behavior by going back into the original class library that contains the base form and changing the `Modifiers` property on the button or the status bar from `Private` to `Protected` or `Public`. A setting of `Protected` would still not allow changes to the position or size of the control but would allow access to the controls by subclassed objects. A setting of `Public` would allow access to the controls by all objects.

One thing I found interesting in my example was that my inherited form showed the accurate time in the status bar, even while in design mode. This told me my base form code was running and updating the status bar clock during the design mode of my new project. Pretty cool.

Note that if you go back and decide to make changes to your base form, make sure to rebuild that base form class library to a DLL after the changes are made, or you won't see the changes in your inherited forms.

47   Performing a Ping

 The ping code can be found in the folder `prjPinger`.

A large part of the .NET strategy is the concept of *web services*. In the world of web services, programmers write useful little black boxes of code and expose them to other programmers via the Internet. Need the shipping status of a package displayed on your e-tailer site? Just call your shipper's .NET web service. (Such a service does not exist at the time of this writing, but Microsoft is banking on the fact that it will be in the .NET future.) Want to incorporate a search engine into your own site? Just hook up to Yahoo! or AltaVista or Google's web service.

As a long-time (at least in developer years) programmer, I've been taught to look at the glass as not half full or even as half empty, but to consider the possibility that someone has stolen the glass completely, and it hasn't rained in months. Developers must consider the "worst-case scenario" when developing applications because our friend Murphy has taught them time and time again that this scenario is exactly what will face the end user of the software within the first 30 minutes of its execution.

My worst-case scenario in the web services world is building a slick, state-of-the-art VB application around a really useful web service, only to have that web service be nonfunctional half the time for myriad reasons I can't control. After all, if I'm going to use a web service in my app, then I'm at the mercy of the hardware, the developer(s), the internal network architecture, and databases upon which that web service is acting, right? In other words, if my shipper's server is down all weekend, then my app is down, too.

This gloom-and-doom scenario is not a good enough reason to abandon all hope, though. A web service from my shipper might be the only way I have to incorporate shipping information directly into my application, so if I want that functionality, I'm going to throw myself on the mercy of the resources on the shipper's side of the Internet. After all, if my shipper does offer this service, and it doesn't fulfill its intended purpose due to network outages, badly designed code, and so on, they stand to lose business.

So What to Do?

OK, so I've bitten the bullet and decided that I can't live without incorporating a certain web service in my application, but I don't want the application going boom when the code on the other side of the world isn't functioning because the server is down. I might want to code some simple diagnostic ability into my application that tells me when it can't find the server upon which the web service is running. When I need to see if a server is available, I usually perform a simple ping on the server. A ping is a command-line program that's shipped with all flavors of Windows. The results of the ping look like this:

```
C:\WINDOWS>ping espn.go.com

Pinging espn.go.com [204.202.129.230] with 32 bytes of data:

Reply from 204.202.129.230: bytes=32 time=233ms TTL=245
Reply from 204.202.129.230: bytes=32 time=165ms TTL=245
Reply from 204.202.129.230: bytes=32 time=192ms TTL=245
Reply from 204.202.129.230: bytes=32 time=192ms TTL=245

Ping statistics for 204.202.129.230:
```

```
Packets: Sent = 4, Received = 4, Lost = 0 (0% loss),
Approximate round trip times in milli-seconds:
    Minimum = 165ms, Maximum =  233ms, Average =  195ms
```

In this example, I simply typed **ping** and then a domain name (in this case, my bi-hourly-visited sports news source, espn.go.com) from a command prompt, and the ping program went out and performed a small meet-and-greet with that web server. It sent four packets of test information to the site and waited for the same information to come back. It then reported on how long the test information took to make its round-trip. I'm not usually worried about the time taken itself; as long as the information *does* return, this tells me that the web server on the other side is in good working order.

Using the *Pinger* Class

The VB .NET Pinger class does the same thing as the ping command. Given a domain name, the code will ping-test that domain and return the results of that test. This type of test might be useful in a program that relies on a web service as part of its functionality. You could easily build in a ping test to the machine upon which the web service is running to support your application. If the ping fails, then the web service probably cannot be contacted either, and the portion of your application that relies on the web service will probably not be functioning until this problem is resolved.

The Pinger class in the prjPinger application demonstrates the VB .NET equivalent of the ping command-line utility. To use it, you simply create an instance of the Pinger class and call the Ping method, passing it a web address. The object performs the ping black-box style (like all good objects should) and returns to you the results of the ping operation.

The first thing that the Pinger class needs to do is *resolve* the web address that you pass into an IP address. The human-readable form of an IP address is x.y.z.w, where x, y, z, and w are numbers from 0 to 255. The Windows-readable form of an IP address is just a large number, storable in the VB .NET integer data type.

WARNING   Keep in mind, the VB .NET Integer is equivalent to the VB6 Long data type. It might seem that Microsoft is purposely trying to drive us programmers nuts by renaming data types in this fashion. The reason they're doing this is to bring the naming convention in all of their languages (C++, C#) into a common vernacular. If you have a real problem keeping track of these, you can use the Int16 and Int32 data types, which are the strict .NET Framework–equivalent names and easier to remember. Consult the Visual Studio help section "Data Type Summary" for a complete reference on the mapping of old to new data types.

The Pinger class resolves the passed-in URL to both the human- and Windows-readable IP address in the ResolveHostName procedure. That procedure is reproduced here:

```
Private Sub ResolveHostName()

    'converts a host name to an IP address,
    'both string and int form.

    Dim IPAddress As IPAddress
    Dim IPHE As IPHostEntry

    IPHE = DNS.GetHostByName(FHostName)
    If IPHE.AddressList.Length > 0 Then

        IPAddress = IPHE.AddressList(0)
        FAddress = IPAddress.ToString
        FdwAddress = IPAddress.Address

    Else
        FdwAddress = INADDR_NONE
    End If

End Sub
```

This procedure is nice and short because there are classes in the .NET Framework that do much of the work for you. The DNS class has a method named GetHostByName, which returns an instance of the IPHostEntry class. This class contains all the information about a URL that you would ever want, including the IP address information you need for this project. The code eventually stores the human-readable IP address in the FAddress variable and the integer version of the address in the FdwAddress variable.

The Ping method itself relies on a few API calls found in the ICMP.DLL file, which is present on all 32-bit versions of Windows. This code is fairly simple to understand. The main call, to the DLL function IcmpSendEcho, fills an API structure called ICMP_ECHO_REPLY, which contains the useful information about the ping, such as the total round-trip time in milliseconds.

The remainder of the Pinger class sets up properties that can be queried by the "outside world," such as the human-readable IP address, the round-trip time, and the status of the ping (which may fail for a number of reasons, remember).

48 A Big Savings: Object Graph Serialization

 The object graph code can be found in the folder prjCollections.

If you're like me, you'll find that object-oriented programming is almost addictive on some levels. As new projects come up and you begin working on the application design, you'll most likely envision all manner of complex object structures and their interrelationships. Consider an example: an object graph that loads information about a list of employees for a human resources application. There might be a master object called `EmployeeList`, and within it a collection of `Employee` objects. Each `Employee` object might have one (or more) `Mailing-Address`, `PhoneNumber`, and `EmailAddress` objects within it. The entire `EmployeeList` might be stored in such a way so that an `OrgChart` can be easily generated from the data, either as some form of b-tree, or with a separate construct within it containing pointers to the org chart hierarchy.

In a business development environment, all of this data would probably be permanently stored in a database like Microsoft SQL Server and then loaded into your complex object graph, as just described, for manipulation. The class structure just described might be the middle tier in a three-tier architecture, for example. While this programming model works well for most business applications, one cannot always use a powerhouse back-end database like SQL Server to store data. Imagine wanting to write a little contact manager application for open source or retail shelf release. This contact manager application might need the exact same object graph as just described in the human resources application. As the developer, however, you don't want to require the presence of a back-end database to use our program.

The .NET Framework has an alternate storage solution in cases where a database might not be practical. Built into every .NET Framework class (including the ones you create yourself) is the ability to serialize, or save, object instances in a proprietary binary format to disk and then reload them later.

This opens up an entire new range of possibilities for the storage needs of your application. If you're designing your data in a well-thought-out, nested group of objects, you'll be able to add an amazingly few lines of code to your application and have the ability to save/load these objects to disk.

I haven't included very much code here, because the technique for object graph serialization is almost frighteningly easy. Here is the code to save any object graph to disk:

```
Dim f As New FileStream(BINARYFILE, FileMode.Create)
Dim b As New BinaryFormatter()

Try
  b.Serialize(f, oStack)
Catch oEX As Exception
  MsgBox(oEX.Message)
Finally
  f.Close()
End Try
```

The constant BINARYFILE in the preceding code is a string constant containing a filename. The key to serializing an object graph is the BinaryFormatter class. Once you've instantiated an object of this class, you call the Serialize method on it, passing a FileStream object and the object you want to save to disk.

To load the serialized object, you merely do the following:

```
Dim oStack As New AnotherBookEncapsulaterStack()

Dim f As New FileStream(BINARYFILE, FileMode.Open)
Dim b As New BinaryFormatter()
Try
  oStack = CType(b.Deserialize(f), _
  AnotherBookEncapsulaterStack)
Finally
  f.Close()
End Try
```

This is really just the inverse of the code to save the object. The only tricky part here is that you have to typecast the results of the DeSerialize method back to whatever class you're loading.

For quite a few years, I wrote level-editor programs for popular computer games. I wrote a level-editing program for id Software's Doom and Quake. I also wrote a level editor for a commercial game company. In all of these cases, I wish wish *wish* I'd had the ability to serialize objects to disk as described here. Such an ability would have cut dozens of hours off of each of these projects and allowed me time to concentrate on more important problems like user interface design and adding powerful features to the program, instead of writing hundreds of lines of I/O code to store my level information to disk.

49   Delegate Some Authority

 The event code can be found in the folder prjEventsAndDelegates.

As you start converting your thinking process into an object-oriented programming mode, the concept of writing properties and methods will probably come pretty easily to you. A property on your object appears just like a variable attached to your class definition, and a method is just a procedure or function. Variables, procedures, and functions are all familiar elements to programmers, so the only change in an object-oriented world is that you're now "attaching" these things to a class. Furthermore, the pseudo/almost/not-quite OOP features in Visual Basic 6 allowed you to create classes with both properties and methods.

Coding *events*, however, might be delving into some unfamiliar territory. Just when do you need an event on your class? How is it coded? We're all familiar with responding to events on existing classes, like the Click event of a button or the Changed event of a Textbox. This is called *responding* to an event, and because it's a familiar topic to any developer with Visual Basic experience, I won't cover it here. Instead, I want to talk about coding objects that *raise* events.

Why?

To think of situations in which you would want to code objects that raise events, you have to turn around your thinking a bit. Almost all of your Visual Basic coding experience to this point has been writing code that responds to events. Most VB programs start off with a blank form onto which controls are placed, followed by event-handling code written for the controls.

In the VB .NET world, you're not only using objects, but you're writing them as well. This doesn't just mean visual controls like buttons or Listbox objects, but data-driven objects like custom collections or typed datasets. When writing such classes, imagine that other coders might be using them in their own projects and that they may need to respond to something important happening to these objects. This is when you might consider adding the ability of your object to raise an event.

How?

Events in the .NET Framework are created using something called a *delegate*. A delegate is a special type of pointer to a function that handles communication between an object trying to raise an event and the event-handling code. Delegates are what allow you to dynamically attach event-handling code to events on all object instances—not only your own, but existing, well-known objects like buttons, timers, and Treeview objects.

Trying to nail down exactly what a delegate is and how it works is pretty tricky since it's such a new concept, so it might be easier (if not 100 percent dead-on accurate) to think of a delegate as a procedure of a certain type. What differentiates one type of procedure from another is the argument list passed to the procedure. As an example, the first two procedures here are of the same type, and the third is of a different type:

```
Sub SomeFuncA(p1 as integer, p2 as integer, s as string)
Sub SomeFuncB(aLeft as integer, aTop as integer, cText as string)
Sub SomeFuncC(aPoint as Point, cText as string)
```

Note that the name of the arguments in the parameter list are not important when comparing procedure types, just the number of arguments, the type of each argument, and the calling convention (by reference or by value). If the number, type, and calling convention of arguments match, then the two procedures are of the same type.

An example of declaring a delegate is shown here:

```
Delegate Sub PersonVerifier(ByVal oP As Person, ByRef bIsOk As Boolean)
```

The purpose of this statement is to declare a type of procedure having two arguments. The first argument is of type `Person` (declared elsewhere in the sample project), and the second argument is a simple Boolean, but passed by reference. Declaring this delegate means that I can now create events for my objects having this delegate signature.

The following code shows the beginning of a new class called a `PersonCollection`. The purpose of this class is to store a collection of another class, called the `Person` class. The `Person` class in the example code is trivial and is not detailed here, except to mention that it has three string properties to store a person's first name, last name, and state of residence.

```
Class PersonCollection
        Inherits System.Collections.CollectionBase

        Public Event VerifyPerson As PersonVerifier
```

Note that one of the members on the `PersonCollection` is an event named `VerifyPerson`, and the type of this event is the delegate type I defined earlier. What this means is that my custom collection now has the ability to raise an event named `VerifyPerson`, and any programmer using my `PersonCollection` will be able to write code to respond to this event.

Why did I write such an event? The purpose of the event is made much clearer when the Add method on the collection class is examined:

```
Public Function Add(ByVal oP As Person) As Boolean

    Dim bIsOk As Boolean = False

    RaiseEvent VerifyPerson(oP, bIsOk)

    If bIsOk Then
        MyBase.InnerList.Add(oP)
    End If

    Return bIsOk
End Function
```

The first line of code raises the `VerifyPerson` event. This means that if the programmer using my class has written event-handling code for my event, then that code will be called here. I pass that code two items: the `Person` object that is about to be added and a Boolean variable that has been initialized to false. The code after the `RaiseEvent` checks the Boolean, and, if found to be true, adds the `Person` object instance to the collection. This gives the programmer of my class the means to perform any type of custom validation on the `Person` object before it is added to the collection.

Handling the Event

Now that the PersonCollection is written, writing the code to use it and to handle the event is more like the coding you've done in the past. The following sample code creates an instance of the PersonCollection object and then adds not one but two event handlers to the Verify-Person event:

```
Dim oColl As New PersonCollection()

AddHandler oColl.VerifyPerson, _
AddressOf DoesLastNameEndWithVowell
AddHandler oColl.VerifyPerson, _
AddressOf IsStateOhioOrPennsylvania

Public Sub DoesLastNameEndWithVowell(ByVal oP _
As Person, ByRef bIsOk As Boolean)

    Dim cLetter As String = oP.LastName.ToLower

    bIsOk = bIsOk Or cLetter.EndsWith("a") Or _
                     cLetter.EndsWith("e") Or _
                     cLetter.EndsWith("i") Or _
                     cLetter.EndsWith("o") Or _
                     cLetter.EndsWith("u")

End Sub

Public Sub IsStateOhioOrPennsylvania(ByVal _
oP As Person, ByRef bIsOk As Boolean)
    bIsOk = bIsOk Or _
    (oP.State.Equals("OH") Or oP.State.Equals("PE"))
End Sub
```

Note that the two event-handling procedures have the same argument list as the delegate that's been used to declare the event. If this were not true, Visual Studio would report a design-time error that my event-handler signature does not match the signature of the event on the PersonCollection object.

Now that my class is instantiated and wired up to some event-handling code, I can try and create some Person objects and add them to the collection. For each Person object, both events will fire, and if both return true, the Person object will be successfully added to the collection:

```
oP = New Person("Tony", "Soprano", "NJ")
If oColl.Add(oP) Then
    console.WriteLine(oP.Fullname _
    & " from " & oP.state & " -- added")
Else
```

```
console.WriteLine(oP.Fullname _
  & " from " & oP.state & " -- NOT added")
End If
```

Tony would get added because his last name ends in a vowel. I coded my two events to return true if either the person's last name ends in a vowel, or their state of residence is Ohio or Pennsylvania. (I could have just as easily required both events to be true by ANDing the event results together instead of ORing them.)

Once you reverse your thinking to start considering how other people might use your new classes, ideas for events will start coming to you. On my simple `PersonCollection`, I could create new events that fire after a person is successfully added, after a person is rejected, and after one has been removed from the list. All of these events would allow the developer using my class to respond to these important happenings with their own code.

50   Taking Out the Trash: The Garbage Collector

 The garbage collection code can be found in the folder `prjGarbageCollector`.

Visual Studio .NET represents a complete paradigm shift for many programmers to a 100 percent object-oriented programming methodology. This affects some programmers more than others. I, for example, was used to programming a bit in C++ and even more in Inprise Delphi. (A non-Microsoft product? Shame on me!) Because of my experience in these languages, many of the object-oriented programming (OOP) concepts were already familiar to me.

But Microsoft threw a new wrench into the .NET Framework: the concept of *garbage collection*, a concept familiar to Java developers but completely foreign to C++ or Delphi programmers (and altogether alien to VB programmers). The garbage collector is like an invisible maid for your programs that cleans up all of the memory you've left behind. Consider the following code fragment:

```
Sub DoABunchOfStuff

Dim o as SomeObject
Dim i as integer

For i = 1 to 100
   o = new SomeObject(i)
   call o.SomeMethod
   call o.SomeOtherMethod
Next

End Sub
```

Reading this code fragment about six months ago would have had me breaking out in a rash. The routine declares 100 instances of the class SomeObject and does some work with each instance, but it never frees them! There they are, floating around in space like Captain Kirk in "The Tholian Web" episode, with no chance to be freed. This is what we used to affectionately call "a memory leak," and it lead to uncountable hours of debugging by coders all over the planet.

The garbage collector in the .NET Framework is a deliberate attempt by Microsoft to save you, the programmer, from spending all those untold hours hunting down memory leaks. Put in its simplest terms, the garbage collector does all the object freeing for you. This means that the previous code fragment is perfectly legal, and in fact, it is the correct way to code a loop of this nature. (Although it will still look strange to a prior-life OOP programmer, it's just something you'll have to get used to.)

The garbage collector is like a little separate process, running off on its own in the background of your application. As the programmer, you do not have 100 percent control over when and how it runs. This tends to drive some old C++ programmers loony, but overall you should eventually find the new memory scheme to your liking (perhaps after a little "getting to know you" adjustment period).

One reason this style of thinking is so different to C++ programmers is because .NET Framework classes do not have the concept of destructors in them. A *destructor* is a piece of code that executes as an object is being freed. A class destructor was a really handy place to deallocate resources used by the class instance. For example, a class that encapsulated file access could make sure that any open file handles were closed in the destructor. A class that encapsulated a GDI object like a brush could make sure the brush handle was freed in the destructor.

Deallocating Resources

So how do you deal with resource-using classes like the examples just given? Where is a good place to deallocate resources? .NET classes allow for a special method called Finalize. This is where you should put all resource-freeing code needed by your class.

The garbage collector treats a class with an overridden Finalize method much differently from one with no Finalize method. An object that requires finalization is put into a list and finalized later. That is, the garbage collector must perform its collection twice before an object with a finalization method is truly freed.

For this and other reasons, Microsoft contends that you should avoid using finalization methods whenever possible. If your class does not have any specific resources to clean up, then skip writing a finalization method. They provide much more overhead to the program and could slow down your application significantly.

Another reason that you might want to avoid writing a finalization method is that you have no control over exactly when finalization methods are called. The garbage collector is responsible for calling finalization methods. If your class allocates large memory footprint objects and doesn't get rid of them until the finalization method is called, you might have big chunks of memory hanging around long after you need them.

Since programmers don't like to be told they don't have control over parts of their program, a different programming convention has been established for memory cleanup. This new convention has you write a `Dispose` method for your classes that looks exactly like the following:

```
Public Sub Dispose()
    Call Finalize
    GC.SuppressFinalize(me)
End Sub
```

This sub calls the `Finalize` method (which is where all your resources are freed) and then tells the garbage collector not to call the `Finalize` method on this instance because you've already done it. This method provides the best of both worlds: If you want to allow the garbage collector total control, you can declare your object instances and not bother to do any cleanup, as you would with most .NET Framework classes, and the garbage collector will take care of everything. However, if you have a section of code where more control is needed, you can declare your objects and call their `Dispose` methods when you're through with them. This will free all of the resources your class requires and will prevent the now-unnecessary overhead of the garbage collector calling the `Finalize` method. Tricky, huh?

Controlling Garbage Collection

The garbage collector has a few more methods that might assist you in managing the memory of your application. You can force the garbage collector to perform a collection by calling `GC.Collect`. Most applications probably won't have to worry about telling the garbage collector when to run, but you do have that option. In addition, you can also pass an integer to the `GC.Collect` method. This integer refers to a generation of objects in the application heap. The generation of an object refers to how long it has been sitting around and how many passes of the garbage collector it has survived. A generation 0 object has never been tested by the garbage collector. A generation 1 object has survived one swing of the garbage collector's axe, and so on.

A basic assumption is made in heap management: Recently created objects have a higher probability of being destroyed sooner, and "old" objects tend to continue longer rather than be destroyed in the near future. This assumption can be used to optimize garbage collection: If recent objects are the most likely candidates for collection, then perhaps you could run through a collection test of only early-generation objects. By calling `GC.Collect(0)`, for example, you're telling the garbage collector to take a pass only through generation 0 objects, and collect them if they are no longer being used. This could be much faster than going through all the objects on your heap.

Garbage collection sounds at first like an easy topic to understand, but it quickly spirals out of control the longer you study it. The .NET programmer newsgroups rage in endless message threads about the benefits and drawbacks of the garbage-collecting scheme versus older, more manual methods of memory management. Arguing over these methods of memory management reminds me of how my father used to tell me never to argue about religion or politics: You can't win no matter what side you're on.

51   Saving Your RAM and Using It, Too

 The weak reference code can be found in the folder `prjWeakReferences`.

The space versus speed issue is a constant battle for programmers (or, at least it *should be* a constant battle), as they weigh the benefits of certain choices, such as taking up more RAM at the expense of saving computing time.

The .NET Framework has some features that let you, in some instances, have the best of both worlds (low memory *and* fast access times). There are many examples of objects that you can construct easily that take up a large amount of memory. For example, suppose you have a measuring device that takes an air pressure reading once per minute, and you put the results in some type of text file. Say you're writing a program that displays the results of those readings for the past year in many different ways (bar graphed with straight or averaged values, high/low/mean values per hour or day, greatest change in an hour interval, and so on).

For a program like this, it would be useful to take all of the air pressure readings from the past year from disk and load it into RAM at the start of the program. When the end user specifies which report she wants to see, along with her desired parameters for the report (date range, intervals, and so on), all of the detailed data is already loaded and you can easily perform the calculations for her. This is much faster than loading the data from the file for each calculation.

Of course, the downside to this approach is that you're saving speed at the expense of space (or RAM). Having all of those numbers in memory takes up a significant amount of RAM— one reading per minute for a year is 525,600 readings, times the number of bytes per reading (say four bytes for an integer), which gives you about a 2MB RAM requirement. Now, 2MB doesn't seem all that huge in today's world of 256MB+ systems, but if this air pressure functionality is just one of several different functions that our program provides, then you're taking up 2MB that might be in contention with memory that could be better used by other parts of the application.

What would be useful in a case like this is to load the measurement data up front, but to tell the .NET garbage collector that it can go ahead and collect this memory for another task if it needs to. If your program needs the data at a later time, you can always reload the information from the file.

Using Weak References

The .NET Framework accomplishes this through the use of *weak references*. A weak reference is a special type of reference to an object that tells the garbage collector, "You can collect this object if you want to," and then gives us the means to tell whether it has been collected or not.

Weak references come in handy for objects that are RAM-expensive but computationally easy to create. It allows you to guarantee that you'll have the object around when you need it, but you can mark it as expendable when you don't need it, for example, when the user is going to a different part of the application.

The example project here shows how to set up a weak reference. I invented a class that loads about one million random integers into an array—truly useless, considering the Random class built into the .NET Framework, but you can pretend that the numbers are air pressure readings for the example. Having a million integers in RAM is pretty expensive, so I decided that this object was a good candidate for a weak reference, as shown in the following code:

```
Public Class Form1
    Inherits System.Windows.Forms.Form

    Private oMyNumbers As PreLoadedRandomNumberArray
    Private oWRef As WeakReference

    Public Sub New()
        MyBase.New

        Form1 = Me

        'This call is required by the Win Form Designer.
        InitializeComponent
```

```
oMyNumbers = New PreLoadedRandomNumberArray()
oWRef = New WeakReference(oMyNumbers)
oMyNumbers = Nothing

End Sub
```

This code shows the beginning of the form definition and the constructor. There is a form-level variable for my memory-hogging class (the `PreLoadedRandomNumberArray` class), named `oMyNumbers`. There is also a variable of type `WeakReference` that will refer to variable `oMyNumbers`.

In the `New` procedure, the `PreLoadedRandomNumberArray` variable is instantiated. Then the weak reference is instantiated, passing it the object I want to be set up as weak referenced. Finally, the `PreLoadedRandomNumberArray` variable is set to `Nothing`. This step is important, as the garbage collector would never target this variable for collection if it were declared as a variable on the application's main form, because that variable would never go out of scope.

When the time comes in the program to use the `oMyNumbers` variable, the following code tests to see if it is still around or if the garbage collector has claimed it:

```
're-point the form level variable to the weak reference target property
    oMyNumbers = CType(oWRef.Target, PreLoadedRandomNumberArray)

    'if nothing, then the GC collected this puppy. Re-create it.
    If oMyNumbers Is Nothing Then
        Console.WriteLine("object was collected, re-creating...")
        oMyNumbers = New PreLoadedRandomNumberArray()
        oWRef = New WeakReference(oMyNumbers)
    Else
        Console.WriteLine("object still here, generating random numbers")
    End If
```

As you can see, I reset the form level variable to the value of `oWRef.Target`. This is the holding place for the weak reference. If the garbage collector has collected this variable, my form-level variable will have the value `Nothing`. This is my cue to recreate the object instance and to reestablish the weak reference. If the variable is not `Nothing`, then the garbage collector has not taken my memory-intensive class instance away yet, so I am free to use it. The code that actually uses the random number class in the example project simply prints the next five values in the class.

Once I am done with the random number class, it is important to reset the value back to `Nothing`, which removes the scope of the form-level variable and signals the garbage collector that it can take the variable if desired.

Controlling Garbage Collection

Writing a program to test weak references is a bit tricky, because in normal cases the programmer has no control over when and how garbage collection occurs. Garbage collection is related to things like available RAM and the general state of the PC running the program.

In my example program, I simulated a program doing different types of things in the Do Some Stuff button. When this button is clicked, the program will either load a large, empty array, or it will load a button object (which has a relatively small memory requirement). To test the program, you should hit this button repeatedly in a random fashion and then hit the Generate Numbers button, which uses the oMyNumbers variable to print the next five random numbers it has generated (after recreating it if necessary). The program reports to the console if the object had to be regenerated because the garbage collector had taken it away.

The last button explicitly performs a garbage collection, which should force the oMyNumbers variable to be recreated the next time it is tested against the weak reference.

Weak references allow you to hog chunks of RAM for objects that are nice to have around but are reasonably easy to recreate if they should happen to be collected by the garbage collector. You gain the speed benefit of having the objects in RAM and the space benefit of allowing the .NET runtime to claim that RAM if needed. Since all machines will behave differently, it might be a good idea to add some logging or debugging code around the use of the weak references in your program. At worst, the reference would have to be recreated every single time the object is needed, which would be no different from using a local variable and creating it each time. At best, the object is taken away by the garbage collector only a small percentage of the time, and you are saving valuable CPU cycles by avoid that object's recreation time and time again. Either way, the log will help determine if the weak reference is doing the job for you.

52   Get Off My Property!

 The properties code can be found in the folders prjPropertiesBad and prjPropertiesGood.

You've had it drilled into your head by now that classes consist of members named properties, events, and methods. From the outside world (the user of a class), a property can be thought of as a variable hanging off a class instance. From the inside, however, properties are often set up much differently. Here is a sample property definition named pPreviewMode, a Boolean that indicates some type of setting in a class:

```
Class SomeClass

    Private FpreviewMode as boolean
```

```
Property pPreviewMode() As Boolean
    Get
        Return FPreviewMode
    End Get
    Set(ByVal Value As Boolean)
        FPreviewMode = Value
    End Set
End Property

End Class
```

This seems like a fair number of lines of code just to set up a Boolean variable, doesn't it? Wouldn't it be simpler to set up a public variable on the class like this:

```
Class SomeClass

    Public pPreviewMode as boolean

End Class
```

The short answer, of course, is "yes," it would be easier to set up the property in this way. The user of the class could tell no difference between the two implementation methods. However, properties set up using the "harder" way, as in the first example, can save you code management problems down the road. Let's develop an example where this might be true.

Properties the "Bad Way"

The example program in this section represents a form with the pPreviewMode property on it. The intention is to have the program's user interface denote the setting of the property in two ways. First, the menu option that controls the setting of the property contains a check mark when the property is true, and second, the form's status bar displays ON or OFF depending on the setting of the property. The following two illustrations display what the application should look like with the property both on and off:

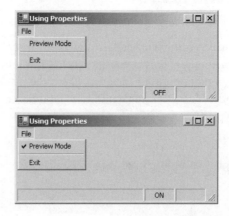

At first it appears that the pPreviewMode property changes in only one place—from the menu item that controls the property. Here then is some simple code that should set the property to the opposite of its current value, and then update the menu check mark and the status bar accordingly:

```
Public Class Form1
    Inherits System.Windows.Forms.Form

    Public pPreviewMode As Boolean

    Private Sub mPreview_Click(ByVal sender As System.Object, _
        ByVal e As System.EventArgs) Handles mPreview.Click

        pPreviewMode = Not pPreviewMode
        Call SetGuiSettings()
    End Sub

    Private Sub SetGuiSettings()
        mPreview.Checked = pPreviewMode
        sbPanel2.Text = IIf(pPreviewMode, "ON", "OFF")
    End Sub
    …
```

This looks pretty innocuous, no? The "property" is set up as a public variable on the form. When the menu item is selected (method mPreview_Click), the property is set to its opposite value, and the little procedure SetGuiSettings is called to update the menu check box and the status bar. Everything works dandy, and you move on other parts of the project.

During the testing of your application, one of your testers suggests that it would be useful if your application saved the value of the pPreviewMode property when the application exited and restored that same setting upon return. "No problem," you think to yourself as you whip up some code to save the setting to the Registry upon application close and load it back up as the application starts. Here is the code that runs as the application starts and ends to read and write the property:

```
Private Sub Form1_Load(ByVal sender As System.Object, _
    ByVal e As System.EventArgs) Handles MyBase.Load

    Dim aKey As RegistryKey

    aKey = Registry.LocalMachine

    Try
        aKey = aKey.CreateSubKey(APPSUBKEY)
        pPreviewMode = CBool(aKey.GetValue(APPSTRING, True))
    Finally
```

```
            Call aKey.Close()
        End Try

    End Sub

    Private Sub Form1_Closing(ByVal sender As Object, _
        ByVal e As System.ComponentModel.CancelEventArgs) _
        Handles MyBase.Closing

        Dim aKey As RegistryKey

        aKey = Registry.LocalMachine

        Try
            aKey = aKey.CreateSubKey(APPSUBKEY)
            Call aKey.SetValue(APPSTRING, IIf(pPreviewMode, 1, 0))
        Finally
            Call aKey.Close()
        End Try

    End Sub
```

Now, if you look very closely, I've just introduced a bug in the program. It's not a design-time error, either, so the compiler isn't going to catch it. Load up project prjPropertiesBad and start it up. You should see a screen like the following:

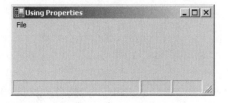

Where's the status bar text? Shouldn't there be an ON or OFF in the bar denoting the status of the property? Some quick testing shows that the menu code is still working—selecting the menu does set the status bar properly. You may not realize there's a bug until you trace through the beginning of the program. The problem is that the SetGuiSettings method is not being called after the property is set in the Form_Load event from its Registry value. You need to make sure this method is called every time you change the value of the pPreviewMode property. This is a one-line fix in this "bad" program:

```
    Private Sub Form1_Load(ByVal sender As System.Object, _
        ByVal e As System.EventArgs) Handles MyBase.Load

        Dim aKey As RegistryKey
```

```
    aKey = Registry.LocalMachine

    Try
        aKey = aKey.CreateSubKey(APPSUBKEY)
        pPreviewMode = CBool(aKey.GetValue(APPSTRING, True))
        Call SetGuiSettings
    Finally
        Call aKey.Close()
    End Try

End Sub
```

This code will work fine now that the `SetGuiSettings` method is called to update the menu and the status bar. The problem is that you had to remember that this method has to be called every time the property changes. This little sample program changes the property in only two places; consider a more complex program where properties may be set from multiple places. If you forget to "connect" the `SetGuiSettings` method call with the changing of the property, you'll introduce a bug.

Properties the "Good Way"

I don't like programs where I have to remember to include code fragment B every time I write code fragment A, as demonstrated in the preceding example. I'd much rather somehow "link" the two code fragments together so that one is executed automatically whenever the first is executed. That, my friends, is the beauty of setting up properties using the `Get` and `Set` accessor methods as shown in the very first property example. Here is the same property set up in the `prjPropertiesGood` project, as well as the menu method that changes the property to its opposite value:

```
Property pPreviewMode() As Boolean
    Get
        Return mPreview.Checked
    End Get
    Set(ByVal Value As Boolean)
        mPreview.Checked = Value
        sbPanel2.Text = IIf(Value, "ON", "OFF")
    End Set
End Property

Private Sub mPreview_Click(ByVal sender As System.Object, _
    ByVal e As System.EventArgs) Handles mPreview.Click

    pPreviewMode = Not pPreviewMode
End Sub
```

The first thing you should notice is that I didn't bother creating a private variable named FPreviewMode to hold the current value of the property. Why not? Well, I already have a Boolean property named Checked attached to my menu. Why not just use this same Boolean value to "store" the value of the property? This is why the Get accessor method of the property merely returns the Checked state of the menu.

Next, note the Set accessor method of the property. This method sets the Checked state of the menu, as well as the text on the status bar. The important thing to remember is that this code runs every time the pPreviewMode property is changed. In other words, I've "linked" the setting of the property with the updating of the interface to display the status of that property.

The best part about linking up the property to the display-updating code is that I don't have to remember to call that update code anymore. So, when it comes time to read the property from the Registry, I know that the check mark and status bar will be correct. If I add a new "extended options" dialog box later that gives the user another place to set the pPreviewMode property, I've guaranteed that once again the interface will correctly display those changes. This is what we call in the business "more elegantly written code," or as my old college roommate would joke, "more better."

One More Example

There's one other useful feature to using the Get and Set accessor methods to wire up properties. That feature allows you to get more complex in how you set up how a property stores its value. Here is a read-only property I added to project prjPropertiesGood that returns a true value if the form is close to perfectly square in size:

```
ReadOnly Property IsFormRoughlySquare() As Integer
    Get
        Dim s As Single

        s = Me.Width / Me.Height
        Return s > 0.9 And s < 1.1
    End Get
End Property
```

This property is called from the Form_Resize event, so run the program and try to resize the form into a perfect square. When you succeed, the status bar will tell you.

The interesting part of this property is that I'm not trying to calculate and store the IsFormRoughlySquare result in some type of private form-level variable. Instead, I'm calculating the value "on the fly" inside the property, thereby saving myself a variable declaration. Retrieving a property value can be as complex as you like; you can query a database or a web service, make complex calculations, and so forth, but to the user of the class, it still looks like you're accessing a variable attached to your class.

53 Got Any Cache I Can Borrow?

The global assembly cache code can be found in the folder prjGAC.

The .NET Framework helps get rid of DLL Hell in some part by encouraging developers to install private DLLs into the application folder, as opposed to dumping everything in the System32 folder as many older applications did.

There will certainly be instances, of course, where you'll write code that needs to be shared by several applications, and having multiple copies of the same DLL in multiple installation folders is neither efficient nor desired. In this case, you'll need a common place to put .NET classes that can be seen by multiple applications. That place is called the *global assembly cache*.

To be installed in the global assembly cache, the assembly has to have a *strong name*. The strong name of an assembly consists of the assembly name itself, its version number, along with a digital signature and a public key. Strong names guarantee assembly uniqueness and provide integrity checks as they are accessed.

Generating a strong name for an assembly is done using the sn.exe tool. To access this tool, select the Visual Studio .NET Command Prompt, which is in your computer's Start menu under Programs ➤ Microsoft Visual Studio .NET ➤ Visual Studio .NET Tools. The Command Prompt looks like a standard DOS box, and from within it, you run the strong name tool as follows:

```
sn -k somename.snk
```

You can use any name for the strong name key file. Once you have this file, you should copy it into the folder that your solution is kept in, and then reference that key in your project's AssemblyInfo.vb file by adding the following line:

```
<Assembly: AssemblyKeyFileAttribute("somename.snk")>
```

Once you've given your assembly a strong name, installing it into the global assembly cache is also done via a command-line tool, so you can keep open the Visual Studio .NET Command Prompt. This tool is called gacutil.exe. Adding your assembly to the global assembly cache is done by issuing this command with an -I command switch:

```
gacutil -i
```

Note how you have to fully qualify your DLL name with the path.

Using Assemblies in the Global Assembly Cache

Whether a DLL is located in the global assembly cache or not, you still need to create a reference to it in your project before you have access to its functionality. Creating a reference is done by right-clicking the project entry in the Solution Explorer and selecting Add Reference from the menu. From there, the dialog box in the following illustration appears:

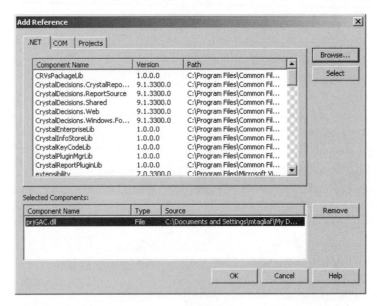

Assemblies that you have added to the global assembly cache are not in the top list of assemblies by default. You need to click the Browse button and navigate to the assembly you wish to add to your project. The preceding illustration shows the assembly already selected and ready to add.

Once added to your project, you'll see the assembly name in the References branch of the Solution Explorer, as shown here:

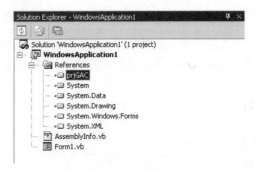

The last step is to make sure that the reference to this assembly is set to use the cache copy of the DLL, rather than a local copy. To do this, select the assembly reference in the Solution Explorer and then look at the Properties window. The property Copy Local should be set to False, as seen in the following illustration:

Viewing the Contents of the Global Assembly Cache

Visual Studio .NET installs a shell extension into Windows as you install it, meaning that you can see the contents of the global assembly cache simply by viewing the Assembly folder under your Windows folder in Explorer. The right pane of Explorer shows you the installed assemblies and their version numbers, as you can see in the next illustration:

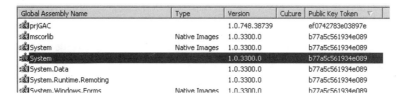

> **NOTE**   There can be multiple versions of the same assembly in the global assembly cache.

The sample project is a small DLL containing a class named CreditCardValidator, which repeats some functionality found at the beginning of Part III in "Embracing Object-Oriented Programming." That section created a Textbox with credit card validation functionality built into it. This class is a stand-alone class with a single shared method that performs the same validation routine. In the long-term interest of eliminating duplicate code, you would probably make the Textbox credit card validator use the class shown in the following code:

```
Imports System.Text

Public Class CreditCardValidator
```

```
Public Shared Function CheckCCNumber(ByVal cCCNo As String) As Boolean

    Dim I As Integer
    Dim x As String
    Dim iSum, iVal As Integer
    Dim oSB As StringBuilder

    CheckCCNumber = False

    iSum = 0
    oSB = New StringBuilder(cCCNo)
    oSB.Replace(" ", "")
    cCCNo = oSB.ToString

    If cCCNo.Length <> 16 Then Exit Function

    For I = cCCNo.Length - 1 To 0 Step -1
        x = cCCNo.Substring(I, 1)

        If IsNumeric(x) Then

            iVal = CInt(x)

            If I Mod 2 = 1 Then
                iSum += iVal
            Else
                iVal *= 2
                If iVal > 9 Then
                    iSum += ((iVal \ 10) + (iVal Mod 10))
                Else
                    iSum += iVal
                End If
            End If
        Else
            Exit Function
        End If
    Next

    CheckCCNumber = (iSum Mod 10) = 0
End Function

End Class
```

This class is compiled into a DLL named prjGAC.DLL, and then installed into the global assembly cache using the steps outlined earlier in this section. Once this is done, the Credit-CardValidator class can be added as a reference to any project and used.

PART IV

Databases

- Fast access with `DataReader`

- Unbound data access with the `DataSet`

- Binding

- Transaction programming

- Using the `SQLDataAdapter` to make database changes

- The power of stored procedures

- Formatting cells in a `DataGrid`

54   Speed Reading: Using the *DataReader*

The DataReader code can be found in the folder prjDataReader.

The workload of the database programmer can be summed up in a few simple words: *read the data*, *display the data*, *edit the data*, *and write the data*. The details under these broad tasks vary widely from project to project, of course, depending on the type of application (1-tier, 2-tier, *n*-tier), the structure of the data itself, the desired user interface, and many other factors. However, the read/edit/write cycle of the typical database application remains pretty constant.

Almost all database applications need to rip through some set of data at several points in the application. Some list-based control may need to be populated (a Listbox, Combobox, Listview, Treeview, grid, and so on), or some complex business logic may need to be applied to a set of records. The .NET Framework has a built-in construct for ripping through a group of records: the SQLDataReader. This class is optimized to perform a once-only, high-speed traversal of a set of data.

The following procedure uses a SQLDataReader to populate a Listview object with the employee records from the ever-popular Northwind database:

```
Private Sub cbDataReader_Click(ByVal sender As _
    System.Object, ByVal e As System.EventArgs) Handles _
    cbDataReader.Click

        Dim SQL As String = "Select EmployeeId, "
        SQL &= "LastName, FirstName, Title, "
        SQL &= "BirthDate from Employees"
        Dim aDate As DateTime

        Dim oConn As New SqlConnection(CONNECTIONSTRING)
        Dim oCmd As New SqlCommand(SQL, oConn)
        Dim oRD As SqlDataReader
        Dim lvItem As ListViewItem

        Call lvEmps.Items.Clear()
        Try
            oConn.Open()
            oRD = oCmd.ExecuteReader( _
            CommandBehavior.CloseConnection)

          Do While (oRD.Read())
              lvItem = New ListViewItem( _
              oRD.Item("EmployeeId").ToString)

              lvItem.SubItems.Add( _
              oRD.Item("LastName").ToString)
```

```
          lvItem.SubItems.Add( _
          oRD.Item("FirstName").ToString)

          lvItem.SubItems.Add( _
          oRD.Item("Title").ToString)

          'need to format date field
          aDate = oRD.GetDateTime( _
          oRD.GetOrdinal("BirthDate"))

          lvItem.SubItems.Add( _
          aDate.ToShortDateString)

          Call lvEmps.Items.Add(lvItem)
        Loop

    Finally
        oRD.Close()
    End Try

  End Sub
```

First, a SQLCommand object is instantiated using a simple SQL Select statement and a local connection string. (You may have to change the CONNECTIONSTRING constant in the sample app to point to an available Northwind sample database.) A SQLDataReader class is instantiated by passing it to the ExecuteReader method on the SQLCommand object. Once instantiated, the rip-through can begin.

Traversing the SQLDataReader object is done much differently than you might be used to if you have experience using ADO Recordset objects. You will not be using EOF or MoveNext methods. Instead, the Read method is called, which returns a True if the read succeeds, or a False if you are at the end of the data. The primary benefit of this new syntax is that you don't need to explicitly issue a MoveNext at the end of the loop to move on to the next record. I can't count how many times I forgot my MoveNext in the past and got myself stuck in an infinite loop. The Read method replaces the need for a separate MoveNext and the end-of-file check performed by the EOF method.

If the Read method succeeds in the previous code, a ListItem variable is populated with fields from the SQLDataReader, and this ListItem is added to the Listview. Note how the Item property is used to retrieve the string fields from the SQLDataReader. When it comes time to retrieve the date value, however, I chose a slightly different tack: I used the GetDateTime method to load the column information directly into a date variable. This allowed me to easily format the date value to my liking. The SQLDataReader has similar Get properties for all the base data types. Since the GetDateTime method required the desired column position as an ordinal (the integer position of the column in the SQLDataReader), I had to call the GetOrdinal method on the BirthDate column.

The example program has a second method that uses a SQLDataReader to return some additional data. Once the Listview is filled, if the user clicks one of the names, the address information for that user is retrieved and placed in a label control. The code to perform this is as follows:

```
Private Sub LoadAddressInfoForEmp(ByVal nID As Integer)

    Dim SQL As String = "Select * from Employees"
    SQL &= "where EmployeeID = @p"

    Dim oConn As New SqlConnection(CONNECTIONSTRING)
    Dim oCmd As New SqlCommand(SQL, oConn)
    Dim oParm As New SqlParameter("@p", SqlDbType.Int)
    Dim oRD As SqlDataReader

    oParm.Direction = Data.ParameterDirection.Input
    oParm.Value = nID
    Call oCmd.Parameters.Add(oParm)
    Try
        Call oConn.Open()
        oRD = oCmd.ExecuteReader(CommandBehavior.CloseConnection)
        If (oRD.Read()) Then

            Dim cAdd As String

            cAdd = oRD.Item("Address").ToString & _
            Environment.NewLine

            cAdd = cAdd & oRD.Item("City").ToString & _
            Environment.NewLine

            cAdd = cAdd & oRD.Item("Region").ToString & " "
            cAdd = cAdd & oRD.Item("PostalCode").ToString & " "
            cAdd = cAdd & oRD.Item("Country").ToString
            lbAddress.Text = cAdd

        End If
    Finally
        oRD.Close()
    End Try

End Sub
```

The Employee ID (the primary key on the Employee table) is passed in as the parameter to this routine. That parameter is turned into a `SQLParameter` object instance and attached to the `SQLCommand` object. Note how the SQL string for the command object contains the characters `@p`, which will be replaced with the value of the parameter when the command is executed.

Once the `SQLCommand` is executed, a `SQLDataReader` is filled with the resultant records (or, in this case, resultant single record). The `Read` method is issued, and, if successful, the employee address information is constructed in a string variable. (Note the use of the `Environment.Newline` character to add line breaks to the string.) Finally, this address string is set to be the `Text` property of the label control `lbAddress`. Once this work is complete, the `SQLDataReader`'s connection is closed inside a `Try...Finally` block to guarantee its successful closure.

NOTE   The `SQLDataReader` is part of the `System.Data.SQLClient` namespace, which contains classes specifically for connecting to Microsoft SQL Server. If you are connecting to another database, you'll want to use the classes in the `System.Data.OLEDB` namespace, which use the OLE DB layer to connect to the back-end database. The classes in this namespace are functionally equivalent, but they have different names. For example, the equivalent of the `SQLDataReader` in the `System.Data.OLEDB` namespace is `OleDB-DataReader`. You could use the `System.Data.OleDB` for SQL Server database access as well, but you will probably achieve better performance using the namespace specifically constructed for this database engine.

55   The Missing Link: The *DataSet*

 The `DataSet` code can be found in the folder `prjDataSet`.

The standard for today's database programming model is the multi-tier, or *n*-tier, application. This application is typically comprised of a database tier (like a SQL Server database with tables, views, stored procedures, and so on), a presentation tier (a VB or ASP front end that presents the information to the end user), and one or more "middle tiers," which typically contain the business rules required to act as a broker between the data and presentation tiers. For example, the application may require a grid of inventory items to be displayed on the screen, with high-selling items displayed in green and poor-selling items displayed in red (perhaps the colors are even user-configurable). This item-coloring information is a type of business rule and would often live in the middle tier.

The ADO.NET programming model has been modified extensively from prior database models to more easily allow developers to adhere to this multi-tier architectural approach. A `DataSet` class is a key component in this new architecture. The `DataSet` is best thought of as a disconnected representation of data. Like a database, it can be constructed in a relational, hierarchical fashion for easy representation of master-detail relationships between information, like customer/order information. However, the DataSet normally runs in a disconnected mode. A typical application cycle might consist of the following:

1. DataSet object instances are created and filled from a database connection. The DataSet then disconnects from the database.

2. The DataSet is used by the presentation layer to display data to the end user.

3. Changes made to the data by the end user are done on the data in the DataSet object (*not* on the database).

4. Changes are validated using business rules.

5. Once validated, all changes are written from the DataSet back to the database.

Note that the DataSet is only connected to the data tier at the beginning and at the end of this cycle; this is why it is often referred to as running in a *disconnected* state.

Because the DataSet runs most of the time in a disconnected state, it must be supplied detailed information about the structure of the data contained within it. The following code creates a DataSet containing two tables and sets up the relationship between those tables:

```
Dim aConn As New SqlConnection(CONNECTIONSTRING)

dscProducts = New _
SqlDataAdapter("Select * from Products", aConn)

dscCategories = New _
SqlDataAdapter("Select * from Categories", aConn)

aDataset = New DataSet()

dscProducts.Fill(aDataset, "Products")
dscCategories.Fill(aDataset, "Categories")

aDataset.Relations.Add("rProdCat", _
aDataset.Tables("Categories").Columns("CategoryID"), _
aDataset.Tables("Products").Columns("CategoryID"))
```

As just shown, DataSet objects can be populated using SQLDataAdapter objects. These objects allow SQL statements into your database layer to quickly load sub-objects inside your DataSet known as DataTable objects. In this example, the SQLDataAdapter that loads the result of Select * From Products is used to fill a DataTable named Products. A DataTable named `Categories` is similarly filled. The last line in the code creates a `DataRelation` between the two `DataTables`. I now have a `DataSet` that I can report out of, add and remove rows, and so forth.

Let's stop for a minute and consider what I've done. At first glance, doesn't it seem like I'm doing a great deal of extra work? My goal is to write a database application. As the sole developer on many such applications, I usually start by defining all the tables I'll need in SQL Server. Then I write some views and stored procedures to easily read and write the data, and finally, I start developing the presentation layer (a VB app or web-based Active Server Pages) to start working on the data. This is the classic 2-tier design. Now, by introducing the `DataSet` object, it seems I have to redefine all of my tables and relationships again to correctly set up the `DataSet`. What's the benefit of this?

There are a few reasons this seemingly extra setup work becomes beneficial in the long run. The first reason involves the connection between the tiers. If you're writing an application that's designed to move data over a standard dial-up Internet connection, for example, then the connection bandwidth quickly becomes an issue as the amount of data increases. Having this middle tier (depending on exactly "where" the tier lives) of `DataSet` objects can immensely ease bandwidth requirements, as adds and changes to data can happen locally as opposed to constantly reopening the database connection over the wire to read and write changes.

Another useful characteristic of the `DataSet` object is all of its communication is handled "under the hood" via XML, a text-based method of transferring data that can occur entirely over an HTTP connection. This means that you can write sophisticated data-processing applications over a standard Internet connection without doing any low-level, custom TCP/IP protocol coding. The short `DataSet` loading code in the preceding code could be run over a standard HTTP connection, where the SQL Server is on one end of the connection and the `DataSet` is on the other end, and the "loading" of the data is all done via XML.

The third reason to use the `DataSet` object is a simple division of labor: As your business grows, your applications become more complex, and your development staff grows, having a multi-tier application architecture allows you to assign developers to areas where they might be more skilled. You can hire or train "business expert" developers who can code in the middle tier (using `DataSet` objects and writing business rules), without having to learn Transact-SQL to write stored procedures. Likewise, you can hire a DBA to administer and write all the SQL Server code, without her having to know all the business logic needed to display or calculate all the data. Finally, you can have ASP or VB-interface experts that can work on the presentation layer.

OK, now that we've set up a simple `DataSet` and justified its existence, let's see how it was used in the sample project to perform a number of actions.

Filling a *Treeview*

The following code, taken and modified only slightly from the example program (to remove some bits that were extraneous to the task), loads a Treeview control with the categories and products from the DataSet I just built:

```
Sub FillTreeView()

    Dim Category As DataRow
    Dim Product As DataRow
    Dim oRoot As TreeNode
    Dim oParent As TreeNode
    Dim cCategory As String


    tvStuff.BeginUpdate()
    tvStuff.Nodes.Clear()
    Try
        For Each Category In _
        aDataset.Tables("Categories").Rows

            cCategory = Category.Item("CategoryName").ToString()
            oParent = oRoot.Nodes.Add(cCategory)
            For Each Product In aDataset.Tables("Products").Rows
                oParent.Nodes.Add( _
                Product.Item("ProductName").ToString())
            Next
        Next

        oRoot.ExpandAll()
    Finally
        tvStuff.EndUpdate()
        tvStuff.SelectedNode = oRoot
    End Try
End Sub
```

One cool feature of the DataTable objects inside a DataSet is that you can use the For Each...Next construct to iterate through all the rows in the table. Each iteration of the For Each loop returns a DataRow object, which can then be used to retrieve field values by using the Item property. Since this is a hierarchical relationship, two For Each loops are coded, one inside the other. The outer loop creates a category node named oParent, and the inner loop creates a number of product nodes off the oParent node. The Finally block makes sure that the Treeview drawing is turned back on and that the currently selected node is the topmost root node.

Adding and Removing Rows

Adding a row to a `DataTable` in a `DataSet` is a three-step process:

1. First, you call the `NewRow` method off a `DataTable` object to create a `DataRow` object.

2. Then, you fill the `Item` properties on the new `DataRow` object with the desired values.

3. Finally, you issue the `Rows.Add` method on the `DataTable`.

All three steps are shown in the following code:

```
aProdRow = aDataset.Tables("Products").NewRow
aProdRow.Item("ProductID") = PRODID
aProdRow.Item("ProductName") = "BudMeister Stout Ale"
aProdRow.Item("CategoryID") = 1
aDataset.Tables("Products").Rows.Add(aProdRow)
```

If you can find the row you want to delete and point to it using a `DataRow` object, you can simply call the `Delete` method on the object:

```
aProdRow.Delete()
```

Applying Changes to the Database

Once the user has performed all of the desired in-memory changes to the `DataSet`, the back-end database needs to be updated to reflect those changes. The `SQLDataAdapter` contains three properties to assist in sending the changes back to the database: the `InsertCommand`, `UpdateCommand`, and `DeleteCommand`. These three properties are of type `SQLCommand`. They can contain anything from simple SQL statements to complex stored procedures. The following example shows how a database insert is configured on a `SQLDataAdapter` and how an actual insert is sent to the Northwind database:

```
Protected Sub cbApply_Click(ByVal sender As Object, _
ByVal e As System.EventArgs) Handles cbApply.Click

Dim aConn As New SqlConnection(CONNECTIONSTRING)
Dim SQL As String = "Insert into Products " & _
(ProductName, "CategoryID) Values (@n, @ID)"
    Dim aParam As SqlParameter
    Dim aProdRow As DataRow

    dscProducts.InsertCommand = New SqlCommand(SQL, aConn)

    aParam = dscProducts.InsertCommand.Parameters.Add(New _
    SqlParameter("@n", SqlDbType.VarChar, 50))
    With aParam
        .SourceColumn = "ProductName"
        .SourceVersion = DataRowVersion.Current
```

```
        End With

        aParam = dscProducts.InsertCommand.Parameters.Add(New _
        SqlParameter("@ID", SqlDbType.Int))
        With aParam
            .SourceColumn = "CategoryID"
            .SourceVersion = DataRowVersion.Current
        End With

        'add a row
        aProdRow = aDataset.Tables("Products").NewRow
        aProdRow.Item("ProductName") = "BudMeister Stout Ale"
        aProdRow.Item("CategoryID") = 1
        aDataset.Tables("Products").Rows.Add(aProdRow)
         'update the database
        Try
            dscProducts.Update(aDataset, "Products")
    Catch eEx As Exception
            Call MsgBox(eEx.Message)
        End Try

        Call FillTreeView()
        sbStat.Text = "row permanently added to database"

    End Sub
```

This example maps the InsertCommand object on the SQLDataAdapter to a simple SQL Insert statement. Your database update techniques might be more complicated; for example, they might call a stored procedure to perform their inserts, updates, or deletes. If this is the case, you can specify these custom update methods using the SQLDataCommand's InsertCommand, UpdateCommand, and DeleteCommand properties to specify the stored procedure name, as in the following code:

```
With dscProducts
    .InsertCommand.CommandText = "pInsertNewProduct"
    .InsertCommand.CommandType = CommandType.StoredProcedure
    .UpdateCommand.CommandText = "pUpdateProduct"
    .UpdateCommand.CommandType = CommandType.StoredProcedure
    .DeleteCommand.CommandText = "pDeleteProduct"
    .DeleteCommand.CommandType = CommandType.StoredProcedure
End With
```

Looking at this example, you can begin to imagine now how the definition of a DataSet can vary greatly from the physical layout of your database, if you desire. You can create a SQLDataAdapter object with custom SelectCommand, InsertCommand, UpdateCommand, and DeleteCommand properties, all of which can actually be reading and writing data in many different tables. For the purposes of the presentation tier, however, this complexity can be removed and "flattened out" into a single, easier to understand, non-normalized view of the same data.

Filtering, Sorting, and Searching with the *DataView*

Once your DataSet is constructed and filled with data, you'll probably have to view the data in many different ways. For example, on one form you may need to show all the products less than a given price, in product name order. On another form, you might need to show all the products in a given category, in price order. The DataView object can help you create a custom view on a DataTable. The DataView allows you to filter and sort the data in a DataTable. Furthermore, the DataView can then be bound to a grid control for a quick listing of the desired data. The following code constructs a DataView off the DataSet object's Products DataTable, filters the products to show only those having a CategoryID of 2, and sorts the results on the ProductName field. Finally, the DataView is bound to the grid control named dgStuff:

```
aDataView = New DataView(aDataset.Tables("Products"))
aDataView.RowFilter = "CategoryID = 2"
aDataView.Sort = "ProductName"

dgStuff.DataSource = aDataview
```

The DataView can also be used to search for a record. The following code searches for a row in the DataView and reports on the results:

```
Const FINDSTRING As String = "Gula Malacca"
Dim iRow As Integer

aDataView = New DataView(aDataset.Tables("Products"))
aDataView.Sort = "ProductName"

dgStuff.DataSource = aDataview

Try
    iRow = aDataView.Find(FINDSTRING)
    If iRow = -1 Then
    sbStat.Text = FINDSTRING & " not found "
    Else
        sbStat.Text = FINDSTRING & " found at row " & iRow + 1
        dgStuff.NavigateTo(iRow, "")
    End If
Catch
    'find failed
End Try
```

The DataSet object is one of the core components of the .NET Framework database architecture. It is specifically designed to aid the developer in writing middle-tier components that pass data between the presentation and database tier, without the need for either a repeated or persistent database connection. The `DataSet` object is designed to send data to and from both layers in more of a batch update mode, taking advantage of XML to do so.

56   *SQLDataAdapter* Command Performance

 The `DataAdapter` command code can be found in the folder `prjDatasetCommands`.

The previous section dealt briefly with using the `InsertCommand`, `UpdateCommand`, and `DeleteCommand` properties on the `SQLDataAdapter` to propagate changes back to the database. This section will demonstrate this further. In order to successfully run the code in the sample section, you'll need a stored procedure in the Northwind database named `spInsertShipper`. The SQL code that creates this stored procedure can be found in a file named `StoredProcsForThisDemo.SQL`, which is in the project folder `prjDatasetCommands`. This stored procedure inserts a new shipper into the database only if the shipper name does not already exist.

The *SqlCommandBuilder*

Building the custom SQL for every `SQLDataAdapter`'s `Insert`, `Update`, and `Delete` statement can get pretty tedious, especially in simple cases where you're looking at a single table. There's a class named the `SqlCommandBuilder` that helps to automate the SQL building code for you in this simple case. To use this class, simply create an instance of it, passing the desired `SQLDataAdapter` in as the sole parameter on the constructor, as follows:

```
aSQLCB = New SqlCommandBuilder(aShip)
```

The `SqlCommandBuilder` contains the parameters `GetUpdateCommand`, `GetInsertCommand`, and `GetDeleteCommand`, which replace the `SQLCommand` properties on the `DataAdapter` when used. The sample program shows you what text is generated for a simple `Select * from Shippers` DataAdapter. The `InsertCommand` text is shown in the following illustration:

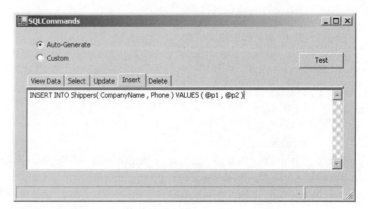

This automatically generated SQL performs a simple insert if any rows were added to the DataSet when the Update method is called on the DataAdapter, using code like the following:

```
'add a row
aRow = aDataset.Tables("Shippers").NewRow
aRow.Item("CompanyName") = "Federated Excess"
aRow.Item("Phone") = "(216) 555-1212"
aDataset.Tables("Shippers").Rows.Add(aRow)

'update the database
Try
   aShip.Update(aDataset, "Shippers")
Catch eEx As Exception

End Try
```

Any errors that occur during the Update (duplicate key, etc.) can be elegantly handled by the exception handler.

Custom Commands

The automatic command generator is useful in many situations, but there are other times when you simply need more control over how data gets sent back to the database. In this case, you can supply your own SQLCommand objects as the InsertCommand, UpdateCommand, and Delete-Command properties on the SQLDataAdapter. The following code sets up these three parameters on the example program's DataAdapter (the variable named aShip):

```
aShip.InsertCommand = New SqlCommand()
With aShip.InsertCommand
   .Connection = aConn
   .CommandType = CommandType.StoredProcedure
   .CommandText = "spInsertShipper"
   .Parameters.Add(New SqlParameter("@CompanyName", SqlDbType.VarChar))
   .Parameters("@CompanyName").SourceColumn = "CompanyName"
   .Parameters.Add(New SqlParameter("@Phone", SqlDbType.VarChar))
   .Parameters("@Phone").SourceColumn = "Phone"
End With

aShip.UpdateCommand = New SqlCommand()
With aShip.UpdateCommand
   .Connection = aConn
   .CommandType = CommandType.Text
   .CommandText = "UPDATE Shippers set CompanyName=@CompanyName," & _
                  "Phone=@Phone WHERE ShipperID=@ShipperID"
   .Parameters.Add(New SqlParameter("@ShipperID", SqlDbType.Int))
   .Parameters("@ShipperID").SourceColumn = "ShipperID"
   .Parameters.Add(New SqlParameter("@CompanyName", SqlDbType.VarChar))
   .Parameters("@CompanyName").SourceColumn = "CompanyName"
```

```
    .Parameters.Add(New SqlParameter("@Phone", SqlDbType.VarChar))
    .Parameters("@Phone").SourceColumn = "Phone"
End With

aShip.DeleteCommand = New SqlCommand()
With aShip.DeleteCommand
    .Connection = aConn
    .CommandType = CommandType.StoredProcedure
    .CommandText = "spDeleteShipper"
    .Parameters.Add(New SqlParameter("@ShipperID", SqlDbType.Int))
    .Parameters("@ShipperID").SourceColumn = "ShipperID"
End With
```

InsertCommand and DeleteCommand call stored procedures to perform their respective updates. UpdateCommand uses a standard SQL Update statement. In all three cases, parameters are set up on the commands so that the DataAdapter knows how to map its columns to the statement's columns.

Testing the Two Methods

To test the two methods of sending data back to the database, the following program adds two rows to the DataSet, then calls the Update method on the SQLDataAdapter. The wrench thrown into the works is that the two records have the exact same CompanyName value. The Northwind database has no built-in constraints to prevent this.

```
Dim aRow As DataRow

tbType.SelectedIndex = 0          'make sure datagrid visible

aRow = aDataset.Tables("Shippers").NewRow
aRow.Item("CompanyName") = "Federated Excess"
aRow.Item("Phone") = "(212) 555-1212"
aDataset.Tables("Shippers").Rows.Add(aRow)

aRow = aDataset.Tables("Shippers").NewRow
aRow.Item("CompanyName") = "Federated Excess"
aRow.Item("Phone") = "(216) 555-1212"
aDataset.Tables("Shippers").Rows.Add(aRow)

'update the database
Try
    aShip.Update(aDataset, "Shippers")
Catch eEx As Exception
    'don't do anything here, let the OnRowUpdated event figure it out
End Try
```

When the automatic method of generated SQLCommands is used, the program allows the duplicate rows, as seen in the following illustration.

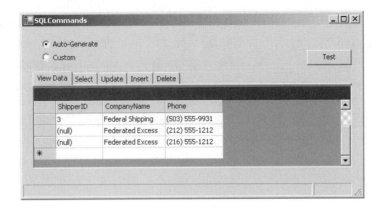

When the stored procedure is used to perform the insert, however, the second row is not added to the database because of an explicit check in the stored procedure code that prevents this. Adding a RowUpdated event handler to the SQLDataAdapter helps you keep the disconnected SQLDataAdapter in sync with the database changes that were made. When setting up the SQLDataAdapter, this line of code adds an event handler to the RowUpdated event:

```
AddHandler aShip.RowUpdated, AddressOf OnRowUpdated
```

And this is the event code:

```
Protected Sub OnRowUpdated(ByVal sender As Object, _
  ByVal e As SqlRowUpdatedEventArgs)

  Dim cMsg As String

  If e.RecordsAffected = 0 Then
      cMsg = "errors occured on row during insert "
      cMsg &= "- row removed from dataset"
      Panel1.Text = cMsg

      e.Row.Delete()
  End If
End Sub
```

Because the stored procedure does not insert the second row, the RecordsAffected property on the SqlRowUpdatedEventArgs parameter for this procedure equals 0. When this is the case, the code prints an error message on the status bar and deletes the row in the DataSet to keep the DataSet in sync with the database.

An alternate way of handling the error would have been in the exception code of the Update statement, but it would have been a bit harder to gain access to the exact row in the DataSet that caused the error, which would have made it harder to delete to keep in sync with the database.

57   Tackling Typed *DataSet* Objects

The typed `DataSet` code can be found in the folder `prjTypedDataset`.

The `DataSet` concept in .NET Framework is really powerful: It provides for a ready-made, disconnected container for hierarchical data. This is just what the doctor ordered in terms of constructing the middle tier(s) in an *n*-tier architecture.

However, the `DataSet` objects that you've used to this point are not the easiest to use. For one thing, as you've already learned, they are a bit of a pain to set up. One has to create `Sql-DataAdapter` objects, use them to fill the `DataSet`, and then add `DataRelation` objects manually. This is almost like setting up the database a second time (once in SQL Server and once again in VB code).

Secondly, the syntax required to use the `DataSet` is a bit cumbersome. Consider the following code fragment, taken from "Filling a `Treeview`," which iterates the rows in one table in a `DataSet` and adds the `ProductName` field as nodes in a `Treeview`:

```
For Each Product In aDataset.Tables("Products").Rows
    oParent.Nodes.Add(Product.Item("ProductName").ToString())
Next
```

`Product.Item("ProductName").ToString`? Cumbersome code like this kind of makes me wish for the days of ADO, when I could write something like `Product!ProductName`.

Fortunately for everyone's sanity, there is a new concept in the .NET Framework that helps to ease the burden of both these problems. This concept is the *typed* `DataSet`. A typed `DataSet` is a class that descends from a normal `DataSet`, in which all of the tables, columns, and relations are defined as properties of the class.

Why Use a Typed *DataSet*?

There are several benefits to using a typed `DataSet`. The main benefit is that it dispenses with programming in the cumbersome object model of the standard `DataSet`. Instead of writing a line of code that looks like this:

```
For Each Product In aDataset.Tables("Products").Rows
    oParent.Nodes.Add(Product.Item("ProductName").ToString())
Next
```

you instead write the much more readable

```
For Each aPRow In aCRow.ProductsByCategoriesCategories
    oParent.Node.Add(aPRow.ProductName)
Next
```

Not only is this more readable (once you get used to it), but you get the benefit of Intellisense helping you write the code. The benefit of this might be easier to demonstrate than to describe. The following illustration shows Intellisense suggesting the column name as I work with my typed `DataSet`:

The second benefit to using typed `DataSet` objects is that they are easier to set up than standard `DataSet` objects. At first, you might think the exact opposite, that setting up a descendant class with custom properties linked to all the tables, relations, rows, and columns of a `DataSet` might take a long time. However, Visual Studio provides you with an automatic means of creating typed `DataSet` objects from XSL Schema. This streamlines the entire process into a few simple steps.

Creating a Typed *DataSet*

Creating a typed `DataSet` is pretty straightforward, but the documentation doesn't give a good step-by-step example, so you might have trouble figuring out the exact sequence of steps needed to create one. Let's go through that sequence here.

1. *Create a new project.* The project type doesn't matter. The example project is a Winforms project.

2. *Create a data connection to a desired database.* From the Server Explorer on the left side of the screen, make a new data connection to the proper SQL Server or similar database, as shown here:

3. *Add a new XSD schema to the project.* From the Solution Explorer, right-click the project name, select Add from the menu, select Add New Item, and then select XSD Schema. Rename the filename as desired. This filename will become the name of the class of the typed DataSet, so choose something memorable.

4. *Create a schema.* Select the tables from the database connection in Server Explorer by dragging them onto the Schema design area. Connect the tables by creating relations. See the Visual Studio .NET help file for details on completing the schema under topic. Once your schema is complete, right-click the Schema design area and make sure the Generate Dataset menu item is checked. When all is complete, make sure to save the schema.

5. *Add a generated* .vb *file to the project.* Saving the XSD schema will create a .VB file in the project folder. This file contains the definition for the typed DataSet that corresponds to the XSD schema. This file is automatically part of the current project as long as the XSD file remains in the project.

Using the Typed *DataSet*

Once the typed DataSet is defined and part of your project, you can use it the way you use any other DataSet and get the same benefits. The first thing you need to do is populate the DataSet by bringing the data out of the database. This is done in the same way that any other DataSet is populated, by using code similar to the following:

```
Private Sub FillDataset()

    Dim dscP As New SqlDataAdapter("Select * from _
    Products", CONNECTIONSTRING)
    Dim dscC As New SqlDataAdapter("Select * _
    from Categories", CONNECTIONSTRING)

    dsPWC = New ProductsWithCat()

    dscC.Fill(dsPWC, "Categories")
    dscP.Fill(dsPWC, "Products")

End Sub
```

In this code, dsPWC is the form-level instance variable of your typed DataSet, named ProductsWithCat. (Recall that the class name of the typed DataSet is the same as the name you gave to the XSD schema you created in order to define this DataSet.) The DataSet variable is filled with SQLDataAdapter instances, just as a nontyped DataSet would be.

Once the DataSet is filled in the example program, the following code is executed to bind the Categories DataTable to a Combobox named cbCategories.

```
cbCategories.DisplayMember = "CategoryName"
cbCategories.ValueMember = "CategoryID"
cbCategories.DataSource = dsPWC.Categories

cbCategories.SelectedIndex = 0
```

The binding code defines the member (field name) of the DataTable to display and the member to use as the ValueMember, which is often used as the primary key to which the DisplayMember corresponds. Then the Combobox data source is bound to the DataTable. Because of the typed nature of your DataSet, you refer to the table by its name, instead of having to refer to it as dwPWC.Tables("Categories").

When the user changes an item in the Combobox, the following code executes to fill a Listbox with all of the products in the selected category:

```
Private Sub cbCategories_SelectedIndexChanged(ByVal _
sender As System.Object, ByVal e As System.EventArgs) _
Handles cbCategories.SelectedIndexChanged

    Dim iID As Integer
    Dim aDV As DataView

    iID = CInt(cbCategories.SelectedValue)

  'create a filtered dataview on the dataset
    aDV = New DataView(dsPWC.Products)
    aDV.RowFilter = "CategoryID = " & iID
    aDV.Sort = "ProductName"

    'bind the dataview to the listbox
    lbProducts.DisplayMember = "ProductName"
    lbProducts.ValueMember = "ProductID"
    lbProducts.DataSource = aDV
End Sub
```

To get only products within the currently selected category, a DataView is created and a RowFilter is specified. The Listbox is then bound to the DataView. Note that once again you are able to refer to a table as if it is a property in the statement dsPWC.Products.

This example only scratches the surface in demonstrating how useful the typed DataSet is. Remember that all of the table names, relations, constraints, and column names correspond to properties in the DataSet. This will aid in the coding of all of the desired I/O into your data source, including adding, editing, and deleting rows and performing data validation. And, because of the disconnected nature of the DataSet, you will be able to perform all of this validation locally and write all of the data changes back to the database in batch.

58   A Legally Binding Form

The data-binding code can be found in the folder prjBindingManager.

I don't know many VB programmers who like good old-fashioned data binding, but that might change for a number of reasons in VB .NET. One reason that binding wasn't the most popular approach was that it broke the *n*-tier model. By binding a data control to user interface (UI) elements like a Textbox and a Listbox, you're going right from the data tier to the presentation tier, bypassing any chance to use a middle tier in between.

As you've already seen, the DataSet is the .NET Framework solution for creating middle-tier business objects. As such, you'd hope that it would support decent data binding—and your hopes would be answered. The data-binding capabilities in the .NET Framework are very well defined and powerful.

Data binding on a VB .NET form is handled via a class called a BindingContext. There is an instance of this class on each form in your project. Within the BindingContext class, there will be one or more BindingManagerBase classes. There will be one Binding-ManagerBase class for every data source on the form. The following code points a local BindingManagerBase variable named aBase to a DataTable in an already-defined DataSet object:

```
Dim aTable As DataTable
aTable = aDataset.Tables("Products")

aBase = Me.BindingContext(aTable)
aBase.Position = 0

AddHandler aBase.PositionChanged, _
AddressOf aBase_PositionChanged

AddHandler aBase.CurrentChanged, _
AddressOf aBase_ItemChanged
```

Once you set up your data source and locate the corresponding BindingManagerBase class, you control the scrolling through your DataSet via the Position property on the Binding-ManagerBase. Position 0 is the first row in the data source, position Count - 1 is the last row. (Count is also a property on the BindingManagerBase.) This code attaches some code to the PositionChanged and the CurrentChanged events on the BindingManagerBase as well. The former is an event that fires every time the position is changed in the BindingManagerBase, which is good for updating a status or writing to a log, for example. The CurrentChanged event fires when data in the data source is changed. This could be a useful place to put data validation routines.

Binding Controls

Binding basic UI controls to the data source is done with the `Bindings` collection built into each control. An example for binding a `Textbox` to a column in a `DataTable` is as follows:

```
tbName.Bindings.Add("Text", aTable, "ProductName")
```

The second parameter is the data source, which was defined in the earlier sample code to be a `DataTable` off the data source variable `aDataSet`. The third parameter is the column name on the `DataSet` to which the `Textbox` is being bound. The first parameter raised my eyebrows a bit when I saw it for the first time. This parameter specifies the name of the property on the `Textbox` to which the data is bound. One would expect that most `Textbox` objects would bind their `Text` property to the desired data element. But the .NET Framework binding capabilities allow for much more. For example, you can bind the `Enabled` or the `Visible` properties to Boolean elements in the data source. How about binding color properties? The possibilities really begin to present themselves once you start thinking about them.

As an example of this binding functionality, I decided that I wanted to link some `Textbox` objects to a `DataSet`. I chose the Northwind Products table as my sample table to bind the controls. In scanning this table, I noticed an interesting column: the Discontinued column. My thought was that I could create an edit form for the common fields in this table, and I could then disable the controls for items that are discontinued by binding the `Enabled` property to this field.

The following code was my first pass at the code that binds a `DataSet` containing the Northwind Products table to five `Textbox` controls and a `Checkbox`:

```
Private Sub BindTheControls()

    Dim aTable As DataTable
    aTable = aDataset.Tables("Products")
    tbName.DataBindings.Add("Text", aTable, "ProductName")
    tbPrice.DataBindings.Add("Text", aTable, "UnitPrice")
    tbOnOrder.DataBindings.Add("Text", aTable, "UnitsOnOrder")
    tbReorder.DataBindings.Add("Text", aTable, "ReorderLevel")
    tbOnhand.DataBindings.Add("Text", aTable, "UnitsInStock")

    cbDis.DataBindings.Add("Checked", aTable, "Discontinued")
    tbName.DataBindings.Add("Enabled", aTable, "Discontinued")
    tbPrice.DataBindings.Add("Enabled", aTable, "Discontinued")
    tbOnOrder.DataBindings.Add("Enabled", aTable, _
    "Discontinued")
    tbReorder.DataBindings.Add("Enabled", aTable, _
    "Discontinued")
    tbOnhand.DataBindings.Add("Enabled", aTable, "Discontinued")
```

```
aBase = Me.BindingContext(aTable)
aBase.Position = 0

AddHandler aBase.PositionChanged, AddressOf
aBase_PositionChanged
AddHandler aBase.CurrentChanged, AddressOf aBase_ItemChanged
Call aBase_PositionChanged(aBase, Nothing)
End Sub
```

Note how I bound the same field, Discontinued, to the Checked property on a check box named cbDis, as well as the Enabled property on all five of my Textbox controls. Pure genius (or so I thought)!

One problem, though: My Enabled logic works in reverse. When I ran the project, the Textbox objects were enabled for the discontinued items and disabled for the live items. I wanted things the other way around. What I really wanted to do was somehow bind the Enabled properties of the Textbox objects to "Not Discontinued," or something similar. A few attempts at this type of logic didn't yield good results, though. Then, after sleeping on the problem for a day or so, I came up with the answer: I could just create a new, calculated column in my DataSet that represents the negative of Discontinued and bind it to the calculated column. Adding my new calculated column took about 30 seconds:

```
Dim SQL As String

SQL = "Select *,"
SQL &= "1-Discontinued as NotDiscontinued "
SQL &= "from Products "

dscProducts = New SqlDataAdapter(SQL, CONNECTIONSTRING)
aDataset = New DataSet()
dscProducts.Fill(aDataset, "Products")
```

My extra field is calculated as the opposite of Discontinued. (The 1-boolean = not Boolean is an old trick I recalled from my PDS Basic 6.1 days.) I could just as easily hide this detail in a view in the database, if I desired. What I have now is the existing Discontinued column and the new column, named NotDiscontinued. It's a trivial task to bind the Enabled property to this new column, as shown here:

```
cbDis.Bindings.Add("Checked", aTable, "Discontinued")
tbName.Bindings.Add("Enabled", aTable, "NotDiscontinued")
tbPrice.Bindings.Add("Enabled", aTable, "NotDiscontinued")
tbOnOrder.Bindings.Add("Enabled", aTable, "NotDiscontinued")
tbReOrder.Bindings.Add("Enabled", aTable, "NotDiscontinued")
tbOnhand.Bindings.Add("Enabled", aTable, "NotDiscontinued")
```

Note that the check box Checked property is still set to the original column, but the Enabled property is set to my new, calculated column.

This technique of creating new calculated data in `DataSet` objects for the purpose of data binding seems simple enough in concept, but there's a very important underlying design tactic going on here. In terms of the *n*-tier design strategy, the new binding abilities of .NET Framework allow you to move even more business logic *out* of the presentation tier (the VB program or web page used by the end user) and *into* the middle tiers (usually COM components or VB classes running either under MTS on a server or locally on the end user machine). The whole purpose of introducing the middle tiers is to abstract business logic out of the presentation and data tiers. The act of disabling controls based on data values or changing font colors to red when a number is negative are examples of business logic that could never before be designed to live in the middle tier, because VB wouldn't allow binding of `Color` or `Enabled` properties to data.

59   Still More Binding

The binding code can be found in the folder `prjBindingToACollection`.

You've seen how binding works on the database-like `DataSet`. This construct makes it easy to load information out of a database and into a `DataSet` (residing as some form of middle-tier object perhaps) and use the `DataSet` to bind to presentation tier controls. Binding is not limited to `DataSet` objects, however. You can bind your own classes and custom collections to UI controls. This is useful because not all applications are database applications, after all. You may have a custom storage solution for the data that your application is manipulating, and you simply don't need the overhead of a database to store that data. Because you can bind just about any class to a UI element, however, you don't have to give up the simplicity of data binding just because you're not using a database.

The following program contains a class named `PolygonDescriptor`, which stores a polygon name along with the number of sides:

```
Public Class PolygonDescriptor

    Private FNumSides As Integer
    Private FName As String

    Sub new(ByVal Name As String, ByVal NumSides As Integer)
        MyBase.New()
        FName = Name
        FNumSides = NumSides
    End Sub

    Property Name() As String
        Get
            Return FName
```

```
        End Get
        Set
            FName = Value
        End Set
    End Property

    Property NumSides() As Integer
        Get
            Return FNumSides
        End Get
        Set
            FNumsides = Value
        End Set
    End Property

End Class
```

To hold a group of `PolygonDescriptor` objects, I created a typed collection named (appropriately enough) the `PolygonDescriptor` collection. This special collection allows only the intended type to be added into it and removes the need for typecasting when retrieving an object from it:

```
Public Class PolygonDescriptorCollection
    Inherits CollectionBase

    Public Sub Add(ByVal P As PolygonDescriptor)
        MyBase.InnerList.Add(P)
    End Sub

    Function Remove(ByVal P As PolygonDescriptor) As Integer

        Dim iCtr As Integer = MyBase.InnerList.IndexOf(P)

        If iCtr > 0 Then
            MyBase.InnerList.Remove(P)
            Return iCtr
        End If

    End Function

    Function Item(ByVal i As Integer) As PolygonDescriptor
        Return CType(MyBase.InnerList.Item(i), _
        PolygonDescriptor)
    End Function

End Class
```

Through the magic of VB .NET binding, I can now bind this collection class to a Listbox, which will create a row in the Listbox for every element in the collection and show the desired field as the entries in the Listbox. The following code populates an instance of the Polygon-DescriptorCollection and then performs the binding:

```
Dim cPolygons As New PolygonDescriptorCollection()

cPolygons.Add(New PolygonDescriptor("Triangle", 3))
cPolygons.Add(New PolygonDescriptor("Rectangle", 4))
cPolygons.Add(New PolygonDescriptor("Square", 4))
cPolygons.Add(New PolygonDescriptor("Pentagon", 5))
cPolygons.Add(New PolygonDescriptor("Hexagon", 6))
cPolygons.Add(New PolygonDescriptor("Octagon", 8))
cPolygons.Add(New PolygonDescriptor("Dodecahedron", 12))
cPolygons.Add(New PolygonDescriptor("Icosahedron", 20))

Try
     lbShapes.DataSource = cPolygons
     lbShapes.DisplayMember = "Name"
Catch oEX As Exception
  Console.WriteLine(oEX.ToString)
End Try
```

The code that performs the binding step is two simple lines. The first line sets the Listbox DataSource property to the collection instance, and the second line tells the Listbox which property of the PolygonDescriptor to display. You can see from the following illustration that once you've set it up in this way, the Listbox is filled with the desired elements:

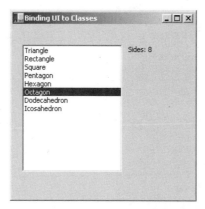

Clicking an item in the Listbox returns the PolygonDescriptor object that corresponds to this row. This makes it really easy to display further information about the selected object.

The following code resolves the selected item back into a `PolygonDescriptor` and then displays the number of sides for that polygon in a label control:

```
Private Sub lbShapes_SelectedIndexChanged(ByVal _
sender As System.Object, ByVal e As System.EventArgs) _
Handles lbShapes.SelectedIndexChanged

    Dim oPD As PolygonDescriptor

    oPD = CType(lbShapes.SelectedItem, PolygonDescriptor)
    lbSides.Text = "Sides: " & oPD.NumSides

End Sub
```

You can see that data binding to collections gives you a powerful alternative to using a database for all your data storage. Smaller apps might require a more simplistic data storage solution, but you don't have to give up binding to your controls just because you've decided against a full-blown SQL Server application.

60 Complete the (Database) Transaction

 The database transaction code can be found in the folder `prjDatabaseTransactions`.

Database transactions are not new—I'm sure many of you out there experienced in writing database applications have used transactions at one time or another. With some of the new language constructs built into Visual Basic .NET, however, you might find database transactional code a bit more "natural" to implement. Specifically, I'm talking about the vastly improved exception handling in VB .NET. Database transactions fit in perfectly with the concept of structured exception handling. Here is some pseudocode for running multiple database statements in a transaction:

```
Try
    Open Connection
    Try
        Start Transaction
        Run SQL Statement(s)
        Commit Transaction
    Catch
        Roll Back Transaction
    Finally
        Close Connection
    End Try
Catch
    Report Error
End
```

Transactions and exceptions look like they were made for each other, don't they? In the preceding pseudocode, I open a connection inside its own exception block, reporting any errors it might come across (the database is unavailable, bad login credentials, and so on). Inside a second `Try` block, I start a transaction, run a bunch of SQL statements, and then commit the transaction at the end. If any errors occur during the SQL statements (trying to insert a duplicate key, for example), the entire transaction is rolled back. The connection is closed inside a `Finally` block, which guarantees that the connection closes regardless of whether the database actions succeed or fail.

Pseudocode is good for getting a general idea; now let's look at some code that does some real work:

```
Private Sub cbEnter_Click_1(ByVal sender As _
System.Object, ByVal e As _
System.EventArgs) Handles cbEnter.Click

    Dim SQL As String
    Dim aConn As SqlConnection = New _
    SqlConnection(CONNECTIONSTRING)

    Dim aCmd As SqlCommand = New SqlCommand(SQL, aConn)
    Dim aTrans As SqlTransaction
    Dim o As Object
    Dim nID As Integer

    tbError.Text = ""
    lbResults.Items.Clear()

    Try

        Call LogEntry("open connection")
        aConn.Open()

        Try

            Call LogEntry("start a transaction")
            aTrans = _
            aConn.BeginTransaction(IsolationLevel.ReadCommitted)
            Call LogLastEntrySuccess(True)

            Call LogEntry("run the order header insert")
            SQL = "Insert into Orders "
            SQL &= "(CustomerID,EmployeeId,"
            SQL &= "OrderDate,RequiredDate,"
            SQL &= "ShipVia,Freight,ShipName,"
            SQL &= "ShipAddress,ShipCity,ShipPostalCode,"
```

```
SQL &= "ShipCountry "
SQL &= ") VALUES ("
SQL &= Quoted("SUPRD") & ","
SQL &= "4,"
SQL &= "getdate(),"
SQL &= Quoted("10/1/2002") & ","
SQL &= "1,"
SQL &= "7.00,"
SQL &= Quoted("Mr. Big") & ","
SQL &= Quoted("123 Anytown Lane") & ","
SQL &= Quoted("Cleveburg") & ","
SQL &= Quoted("55112") & ","
SQL &= Quoted("USA") & ");"
SQL &= "select @@identity"

aCmd.Transaction = aTrans
aCmd.CommandText = SQL
nID = CInt(aCmd.ExecuteScalar())
Call LogLastEntrySuccess(True)

Call LogEntry("enter an line item on the order")

SQL = "Insert into [Order Details] "
SQL &= "(OrderID, ProductID, UnitPrice,"
SQL &= "Quantity, Discount"
SQL &= ") VALUES ("
SQL &= nID & ","
SQL &= "77,"
SQL &= "10.40,"
SQL &= "1,"
SQL &= "0)"
aCmd.CommandText = SQL
aCmd.ExecuteNonQuery()
Call LogLastEntrySuccess(True)

If cbRollback.Checked Then
   Call LogEntry("enter a bogus line item")
   SQL = "Insert into [Order Details] "
   SQL &= "(OrderID, ProductID, UnitPrice,"
   SQL &= "Quantity, Discount"
   SQL &= ") VALUES ("
   SQL &= nID & ","
   'invalid product number
   SQL &= "399,"
   SQL &= "99.95,"
   SQL &= "1,"
   SQL &= "0)"
```

```
            aCmd.CommandText = SQL
            aCmd.ExecuteNonQuery()
            Call LogLastEntrySuccess(True)
        End If

        Call LogEntry("committing transaction")
        aTrans.Commit()
        Call LogLastEntrySuccess(True)
        Call LogEntry("Order " & nID & " written to database")

    Catch eEx As Exception
        Call LogLastEntrySuccess(False)
        aTrans.Rollback()
        tbError.Text = eEx.ToString()
    Finally
        aConn.Close()
    End Try

Catch eEx As Exception
    Call LogLastEntrySuccess(False)
    tbError.Text = eEx.ToString()
End Try


End Sub
```

The structure of this procedure is identical to the pseudocode shown earlier. The database code is attempting to enter an order into the Northwind database. A record is entered into the Orders table, and two items are entered into the Order Details table. The second item has a bad product ID, which causes a constraint error against the Products table. Because I have structured all of this code inside a database transaction, all of the database inserts are rolled back once this error is encountered. The project reports the error as seen in the following illustration:

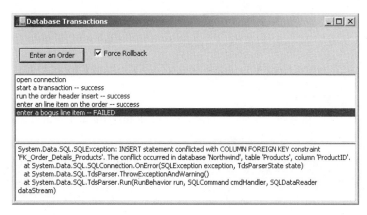

A note about coding style. I do a great deal of database programming and find myself writing a ton of SQL statements inside my VB code. (Probably way more than I should, actually—shouldn't I be using stored procedures or something?) I find it difficult to build SQL statements in VB strings because they are often very long, and one is often embedding quote characters inside the double quotes required to set up the VB strings. And these SQL-building statements are often next to impossible to read by other programmers. To aid in this task, I've developed a few conventions to make the SQL-building statements as easy to read as possible. Some of the conventions in the following list are shown in the previous statements:

Use a consistent naming convention.   I always build my SQL statements in a variable named SQL. It's easy to read, easy to understand, and consistent from project to project. I've often been tempted to declare SQL as a project global variable, but to this point I've refrained and declared it locally everywhere it's needed.

Don't use the line continuation character.   Some of my SQL statements have gotten so long that I need to break them into multiple statements. (You can only have so many line continuation statements before the VB IDE barks at you.) Rather than doing this, however, I build my SQL with lots of single-line statements, starting all but the first with SQL &= <new stuff>.

Don't embed single quotes.   I find it really hard to read a statement like this:

```
SQL = "Insert into Tbl VALUES ('" & _
cVal1 & "','" & cVal2 & "')"
```

Huh? I call this delimiter hell. The single and double quotes alongside the string concatenating ampersands and parentheses make my head spin. I can't even be sure I built a valid SQL string there without actually running it. I find it much more readable to use a function named Quoted whenever I need to embed a quoted variable inside my SQL statements. The previous statement would then be converted to something like this:

```
SQL = "Insert into Tbl VALUES ("
SQL &= Quoted(cVal1) & ","
SQL &= Quoted(cVal2) & ")"
```

The function Quoted is simply this:

```
Private Function Quoted(ByVal s As String) As String
    Return "'" & s & "'"
End Function
```

You can build similar helper functions for double quotes, brackets, braces, and so on.

I realize this is all a matter of personal style, but getting your database-building statements correct is critical, and it takes a good deal of debugging time. Having easy-to-read code in these parts of the application can save you (and your developer peers) headaches in the future.

61   Legal (Stored) Procedures

The stored-procedure code can be found in the folder prjStoredProcedures.

Most database programmers learn the power and usefulness of the stored procedure as they become familiar with client-server programming. Stored procedures are chunks of code that are written in Transact-SQL that run on the database server machine, as opposed to the client machine. When your database server is a $20,000 multiprocessor box and your client is a $1,200 box, which one should you choose to perform most of the database processing? If you're interested in speed and performance, the answer is, of course, the server. The stored procedure is the place to make much of that database processing happen.

NOTE   We'll be dealing with Microsoft SQL Server stored procedures here. Results will vary by database vendor.

Like procedures in most languages, database stored procedures accept and return parameters with which they do their work. There are three types of parameters on a stored procedure:

Input   Anything you need to send to a stored procedure goes into an input parameter.

Output   Most data that you want the stored procedure to return to your application is done so via an output parameter.

Return values   Return values are a special type of output parameter. They are limited to integers, and only one return value can be returned per procedure. Return values are most often used to return whether the procedure succeeded or failed in its intended task.

My goal was to demonstrate using all three types of parameters in a stored procedure in the Northwind database. Unfortunately, none of the built-in stored procedures had all three types of parameter types, so I wrote my own:

```
CREATE PROCEDURE CustOrderTotals
    @CustomerID varchar(5),
    @AmtSpent money OUTPUT
AS

DECLARE @NumOrd INT

SELECT @NumOrd = COUNT(*) FROM Orders
WHERE CustomerID = @CustomerID

IF (@NumOrd = 0)
    RETURN 1
ELSE BEGIN
```

```
SELECT @AmtSpent =SUM(ExtendedPrice)
    FROM [Order Details Extended] OD
    INNER JOIN Orders O ON O.OrderID = OD.OrderID
    WHERE O.CustomerID = @CustomerID

RETURN 0
END
```

This stored procedure takes a customer ID as its input parameter and returns the total amount spent by that customer. If the customer has never ordered (or is an invalid ID), the return value parameter is set to 1.

With this stored procedure in place, here's how it is called in a VB .NET application:

```
Private Sub cbGet_Click(ByVal sender As _
System.Object, ByVal e As _
System.EventArgs) Handles cbGet.Click

    Dim SQL As String = "Select CustomerID, "
    SQL &= "CompanyName from Customers"

    Dim ocConn As New SqlConnection(CONNECTIONSTRING)
    Dim opConn As New SqlConnection(CONNECTIONSTRING)

    Dim oCmd As New SqlCommand(SQL, ocConn)
    Dim oParm As SqlParameter
    Dim oRD As SqlDataReader
    Dim cCustId As String
    Dim cTot As String
    Dim lvItem As ListViewItem

    Dim oProc As New SqlCommand("CustOrderTotals", opConn)
    oProc.CommandType = CommandType.StoredProcedure

    oParm = New SqlParameter("rVal", SqlDbType.Int)
    oParm.Direction = ParameterDirection.ReturnValue
    oProc.Parameters.Add(oParm)

    oParm = New SqlParameter("@CustomerID", _
    SqlDbType.VarChar, 5)
    oParm.Direction = ParameterDirection.Input
    oProc.Parameters.Add(oParm)

    oParm = New SqlParameter("@AmtSpent", SqlDbType.Money)
    oParm.Direction = ParameterDirection.Output
    oProc.Parameters.Add(oParm)

    ocConn.Open()
```

```
opConn.Open()
Call lvCust.Items.Clear()
Try
    oRD = oCmd.ExecuteReader(CommandBehavior.CloseConnection)
    Do While (oRD.Read())
        cCustId = oRD.Item("CustomerID").ToString

        lvItem = New ListViewItem(cCustId)
        lvItem.SubItems.Add(oRD.Item("CompanyName").ToString)

        oProc.Parameters("@CustomerID").Value = cCustId
        Try
            oProc.ExecuteNonQuery()
        Catch oEX As Exception
            MsgBox(oEX.Message)
        End Try

        If CInt(oProc.Parameters("rVal").Value) = 1 Then
            cTot = "<never ordered>"
        Else
            cTot = Format(oProc.Parameters( _
            "@AmtSpent").Value, "####.00")
        End If

        lvItem.SubItems.Add(cTot)
        Call lvCust.Items.Add(lvItem)
    Loop

Finally
    opConn.Close()
End Try
End Sub
```

This code loops through all the customers in the Northwind database and calls the stored procedure for each customer. The customer ID, customer name, and the total amount ordered are placed into the columns of a Listview. If the return value of the stored procedure comes back as 1, then the total amount spent is replaced with the string <never ordered>.

Setting up the stored procedure is done using a SQLCommand object. Parameters are added using SQLParameter instances, as shown here:

```
Dim oProc As New SqlCommand("CustOrderTotals", opConn)
oProc.CommandType = CommandType.StoredProcedure

oParm = New SqlParameter("@AmtSpent", SqlDbType.Money)
oParm.Direction = ParameterDirection.Output
oProc.Parameters.Add(oParm)
```

This code sets up the output parameter. Note that the `AmtSpent` parameter matches the name as defined in the procedure itself. Once the stored procedure is executed, you access its value as follows:

```
cTot = Format(oProc.Parameters("@AmtSpent").Value, "####.00")
```

This line takes the `AmtSpent` output parameter and formats it to use two decimals. The final results of my `Listbox` loader are shown in the following illustration:

CustomerID	CustomerName	Total Spent
ALFKI	Alfreds Futterkiste	4273.00
ANATR	Ana Trujillo Emparedados y helados	1402.95
ANTON	Antonio Moreno Taquería	7023.98
AROUT	Around the Horn	13390.65
BERGS	Berglunds snabbköp	24927.58
BLAUS	Blauer See Delikatessen	3239.80
BLONP	Blondesddsl père et fils	18534.08
BOLID	Bólido Comidas preparadas	4232.85
BONAP	Bon app'	21963.24
BOTTM	Bottom-Dollar Markets	20801.61
BSBEV	B's Beverages	6089.90
CACTU	Cactus Comidas para llevar	1814.80
CENTC	Centro comercial Moctezuma	100.80
CHOPS	Chop-suey Chinese	12348.88
COMMI	Comércio Mineiro	3810.75
CONSH	Consolidated Holdings	1719.10
WANDK	Die Wandernde Kuh	9588.42
DRACD	Drachenblut Delikatessen	3763.21
DUMON	Du monde entier	1615.90
EASTC	Eastern Connection	14761.04

Working with Stored Procedures — Get Order Totals

62   Kiss My Grids!

The `DataGrid` code can be found in the folder `prjDataGrid`.

I'll admit it—I thought this was going to be a pretty short, relatively easy chapter when I started researching it. I wanted to do an example on conditional formatting in the cells of a `DataGrid`. After some brief research into the Visual Studio .NET help file, I came across the `ItemCreated` event, which appears to pass in each piece of the `DataGrid` just before it is being rendered and gives you the chance to change the colors and font of that item. Piece of cake!

A bit more research, however, and I found that the `ItemCreated` event is applicable only to the *Web*Forms `DataGrid` control, and isn't present in the *Win*Forms `DataGrid`. Drat! This gave me two choices—either change my example to be web-based (which would certainly still be a useful demonstration), or find a different way to create custom formatting in the Windows Forms `DataGrid` control. I decided to choose the latter, mainly because the Web-Forms example is extremely simple, given the presence of the `ItemCreated` event. The

WinForms example had a bit more meat to it, which is why I finally decided that it made a more interesting example.

Data to Display

The data I chose to put in my DataGrid is the total amount spent by customer in the Northwind database for a given year. The SQL statement that returns such a list is as follows:

```
select o.customerid,
    sum(od.quantity * od.unitprice) as AmtSpent,
    max(orderdate) as LastOrdered,
    case when datepart(mm,max(orderdate)) = 12 then 1 else 0 end as
        ➡ChristmasOrder
from orders o inner join [order details] od on o.orderid = od.orderid
where datepart(yy,orderdate) = 1998
group by o.customerid
order by 1 asc
```

This query sums up the dollar amount spent (quantity sold times unit price) and also returns the maximum order date for each customer. The final column, named ChristmasOrder, is set to a value of 1 if the last date ordered for each customer is December; otherwise the column is set to a value of 0.

Getting this query into a DataGrid is done by feeding this query to an SQLDataAdapter class, populating a DataSet with the contents of this SQLDataAdapter, then binding the DataSet to the DataGrid. These steps are all shown in the following procedure:

```
Private Sub LoadDataset()

    Dim SQL As String
    Dim aConn As SqlConnection
    Dim aDA As SqlDataAdapter

    aConn = New SqlConnection(CONNECTIONSTRING)

    SQL = "select o.customerid, sum(od.quantity * od.unitprice) as AmtSpent,"
    SQL &= " max(orderdate) as LastOrdered, "
    SQL &= " case when datepart(mm,max(orderdate)) = 12 then 1 else 0 end as
        ➡ChristmasOrder "
    SQL &= " from orders o inner join [order details] od on"
    SQL &= " o.orderid = od.orderid"
    SQL &= " where datepart(yy,orderdate) = " & _
        cbYear.Items(cbYear.SelectedIndex)
    SQL &= " group by o.customerid "
    SQL &= " order by 1 asc"

    aDA = New SqlDataAdapter(New SqlCommand(SQL, aConn))
```

```
aDataset.Clear()
aDA.Fill(aDataset, "CustTot")
aDG.DataSource = aDataset
aDG.NavigateTo(0, "CustTot")

End Sub
```

Note that the current year is retrieved from a Combobox control named cbYear.

Custom Formatting

All of the preceding setup code gets you a DataGrid with the desired rows, but it does not give you any way to conditionally format the grid's cells. To accomplish this, you need to look to the DataGridTextBoxColumn class. This class represents a column of data in your grid that will be edited via a Textbox control when the user chooses to edit the data. This class also contains a Paint method, meaning you should be able to override the Paint method and do some nifty custom painting.

As soon as you talk about overriding methods, you need to start thinking about creating a descendant class. Here's the start of a descendant to the DataGridTextBoxColumn class:

```
Class CustomTextBoxColumn
    Inherits DataGridTextBoxColumn

    Private FBackColor As Color = Color.Red
    Property BackColor() As Color
        Get
            Return FBackColor
        End Get
        Set(ByVal Value As Color)
            FBackColor = Value
        End Set
    End Property

    Private FForeColor As Color = Color.White
    Property ForeColor() As Color
        Get
            Return FForeColor
        End Get
        Set(ByVal Value As Color)
            FForeColor = Value
        End Set
    End Property

End Class
```

This class adds a `ForeColor` and `BackColor` property to the original `DataGridTextBoxColumn` class. The next step is to override the `Paint` method. In this class, there are three overloaded `Paint` methods, so you have to override all three:

```
Protected Overloads Overrides Sub Paint( _
    ByVal g As Graphics, ByVal r As Rectangle, _
    ByVal cm As CurrencyManager, ByVal rownum As Integer)

    Dim b As Color = BackColor
    Dim f As Color = ForeColor
    RaiseEvent GetColors(rownum, b, f)

    Call MyBase.Paint(g, r, cm, rownum, New SolidBrush(b), New SolidBrush(f), _
        ➥False)
End Sub

Protected Overloads Overrides Sub Paint( _
    ByVal g As Graphics, ByVal r As Rectangle, _
    ByVal cm As CurrencyManager, ByVal rownum As Integer, _
    ByVal bAlignRight As Boolean)

    Dim b As Color = BackColor
    Dim f As Color = ForeColor
    RaiseEvent GetColors(rownum, b, f)

    Call MyBase.Paint(g, r, cm, rownum, New SolidBrush(b), New SolidBrush(f), _
        ➥bAlignRight)
End Sub

Protected Overloads Overrides Sub Paint( _
    ByVal g As Graphics, ByVal r As Rectangle, _
    ByVal cm As CurrencyManager, ByVal rownum As Integer, _
    ByVal bBack As Brush, ByVal bFore As Brush, ByVal bAlignRight As Boolean)

    Dim b As Color = BackColor
    Dim f As Color = ForeColor
    RaiseEvent GetColors(rownum, b, f)

    Call MyBase.Paint(g, r, cm, rownum, New SolidBrush(b), _
    New SolidBrush(f), bAlignRight)
End Sub
```

These three methods are all very similar—they end up calling one of the `Paint` methods in the base class (referred to as `MyBase` in a descendant class). They pass in brush objects having the color of the new `ForeColor` and `BackColor` properties you've set up. The only thing left to explain is the `RaiseEvent GetColors` line in each method.

The CustomTextBoxColumn descendant class has a new event on it named GetColors. The purpose of this event is to provide a callback to the user of your CustomTextBoxColumn class to allow that user to change the colors of the cell on the fly based on some external condition that he chooses. If that event is not handled, then the BackColor and ForeColor properties will act as the column's default colors. If the new GetColors event is handled and the colors are changed, then those changed colors will be used on the cell. Here is the declaration of the GetColors event in the descendant class:

```
Public Event GetColors(ByVal rownun As Integer, _
    ByRef bBack As Color, ByRef bFore As Color)
```

Using the New Class

Having a new DataGridTextBoxColumn class is all well and good, but now you have to make a DataGrid control use this class instead of the base class. Here is the code that sets up the DataGrid at the start of the example program:

```
'clear the existing columns
aDG.TableStyles(0).GridColumnStyles.Clear()

oCTBC = New CustomTextBoxColumn()
With oCTBC
    .HeaderText = "CustID"
    .MappingName = "CustomerID"
    .Alignment = HorizontalAlignment.Left
    .ForeColor = aDG.ForeColor
    .BackColor = aDG.BackColor
End With
aDG.TableStyles(0).GridColumnStyles.Add(oCTBC)

oCTBC = New CustomTextBoxColumn()
With oCTBC
    .HeaderText = "Spent"
    .MappingName = "AmtSpent"
    .Alignment = HorizontalAlignment.Right
    .ForeColor = aDG.ForeColor
    .BackColor = aDG.BackColor
    .Format = "c"
End With
AddHandler oCTBC.GetColors, AddressOf GridAmtColorOverride
aDG.TableStyles(0).GridColumnStyles.Add(oCTBC)

oCTBC = New CustomTextBoxColumn()
With oCTBC
    .HeaderText = "Last Ord"
    .MappingName = "LastOrdered"
```

```
      .Alignment = HorizontalAlignment.Center
      .ForeColor = aDG.ForeColor
      .BackColor = aDG.BackColor
   End With
   AddHandler oCTBC.GetColors, AddressOf GridDateColorOverride
   aDG.TableStyles(0).GridColumnStyles.Add(oCTBC)

   oCTBC = New CustomTextBoxColumn()
   With oCTBC
      .HeaderText = "Dec. Ord"
      .MappingName = "ChristmasOrder"
      .Alignment = HorizontalAlignment.Center
      .ForeColor = aDG.ForeColor
      .BackColor = aDG.BackColor
   End With
   AddHandler oCTBC.GetColors, AddressOf GridDateColorOverride
   aDG.TableStyles(0).GridColumnStyles.Add(oCTBC)
```

There are four blocks of nearly identical code here, but the slight differences between the blocks are very important. Each block creates a new instance of the `CustomTextBoxColumn` class, binds it to a column name, and adds it to the `DataGrid`. Each block also sets up the `ForeColor` and `BackColor` properties to be the same values as the `ForeColor` and `BackColor` of the `DataGrid` itself.

The second of the four blocks sets up an event handler for the `GetColors` event:

```
AddHandler oCTBC.GetColors, AddressOf GridAmtColorOverride
```

This provides the "callback;" whenever a cell in the second column is to be rendered, the `GridAmtColorOverride` method will be called. Here is the listing for that method:

```
Private Sub GridAmtColorOverride(ByVal rownun As Integer,_
   ByRef bBack As Color, ByRef bFore As Color)

   Try
      Dim aRow As DataRow = aDataset.Tables(0).Rows(rownun)
      If CSng(aRow.Item(1)) > 12000.0 Then
         bFore = Color.Red
      End If

      Catch oEX As Exception
         Debug.WriteLine(oEX.Message)
   End Try
End Sub
```

In this method, the value of the current row, column 1 (the amount spent by a customer in a year), is retrieved, and if that value is greater than 12,000, then the passed-in foreground color is set to red.

The color parameters on the `GetColors` delegate of the new `CustomTextBoxColumn` class are set to be passed by reference (`ByRef`), meaning that changes you make to these color variables in this method will go back to the method's caller.

A second method named `GridDateColorOverride` is set up to conditionally format the third and fourth columns of the grid. In this case, if the value of the final column is set to 1 (meaning the final order for the customer that year took place in December), then the background color is set to light gray. Here's the code for the `GridDateColorOverride` method:

```
Private Sub GridDateColorOverride(ByVal rownun As Integer, _
    ByRef bBack As Color, ByRef bFore As Color)

    Try
        Dim aRow As DataRow = aDataset.Tables(0).Rows(rownun)
        If CInt(aRow.Item(3)) = 1 Then
            bBack = Color.LightGray
        End If

        Catch oEX As Exception
            Debug.WriteLine(oEX.Message)
    End Try

End Sub
```

Note that this event handler is attached to both the third and fourth columns of the Data-Grid, meaning that the background colors of each row should match for these columns—they will either both remain white or both be changed to light gray.

The following illustration shows the final product. Obviously, it would be pretty easy to extend this custom painting to include icons, font changes, and many different other custom formatting possibilities.

CustID	Spent	Last Ord	Dec. Ord
GODOS	$3,524.05	8/12/1997	0
GOURL	$8,205.23	12/22/1997	1
GREAL	$9,148.55	9/25/1997	0
GROSR	$387.50	12/18/1997	1
HANAR	$6,605.30	12/18/1997	1
HILAA	$14,026.18	12/25/1997	1
HUNGC	$2,283.20	9/8/1997	0
HUNGO	$23,959.05	11/11/1997	0
ISLAT	$2,560.50	12/26/1997	1
KOENE	$9,879.40	12/26/1997	1
LAMAI	$7,465.80	12/19/1997	1
LAUGB	$335.50	8/5/1997	0
LAZYK	$357.00	5/22/1997	0
LEHMS	$14,433.17	12/10/1997	1
LETSS	$2,039.42	11/10/1997	0
LILAS	$5,953.60	12/16/1997	1
LINOD	$7,803.95	11/4/1997	0

PART V

More Framework Topics

- Creating owner-drawn menus

- Creating classes at runtime

- Version control

- Code access security

- Talking to Microsoft Office applications

63   Creating Owner-Drawn Menus

The owner-drawing menu code can be found in the folder `prjNetNotePad`.

"Modern" Microsoft applications, such as Word 2000 and Excel 2000, have menus with bitmaps embedded in them, as shown in the following graphic:

Microsoft has never made it very easy to duplicate this functionality in Visual Basic. VB .NET makes it easier than ever before, although I'll admit that I think Microsoft could make it simpler still. (Can't we just have an `Image` property right on the `MenuItem` class? But that's another story for another version of VB.)

If you want pictures on your menus, you'll have to code them yourselves. What you need to create are *owner-drawn* menus. Owner-drawn means that Windows is relying on you, the programmer, to draw the menu-item text, instead of drawing it for you.

Creating Your Menu

The first step is to create a menu for your application. My `prjNetNotePad` application has a small, simple menu, one that allows the user to create a new file, save it, or open an existing file. Once the menu is created, you should set the `OwnerDraw` property of each `MenuItem` object to `True`, as shown in the following illustration:

Now VB is expecting you to handle all the drawing of the menu items. To accomplish this, two events need to be coded for each `MenuItem`. The first is called the `MeasureItem` event. This event is called to specify the height and width that you want the menu item to be and to pass that information back to Windows. The `MeasureItem` event in `prjNetNotePad` is shown in the following code:

```
Public Sub mNew_MeasureItem(ByVal sender As Object, _
ByVal e As _
System.Windows.Forms.MeasureItemEventArgs) _
    Handles mNew.MeasureItem, mOpen.MeasureItem, _
    mSave.MeasureItem, mExit.MeasureItem

    Dim mi As MenuItem = CType(sender, MenuItem)
    Dim textSize As Size
    Dim textFormat As New StringFormat()

    If (ShowKeyboardCues) Then
        textFormat.HotkeyPrefix = _
        Drawing.Text.HotkeyPrefix.Show
    Else
        textFormat.HotkeyPrefix = _
        Drawing.Text.HotkeyPrefix.Hide
    End If

    textSize = _
    e.Graphics.MeasureString(mi.Text, aFont).ToSize()

    maxMenuTextWidth = Math.Max(maxMenuTextWidth, _
    textSize.Width + 20)

    textSize = e.Graphics.MeasureString(mi.Text, _
    aFont, New PointF(0, 0), textFormat).ToSize()

    e.ItemHeight = Math.Max(textSize.Height + 2, _
    SystemInformation.SmallIconSize.Height + 2)
    e.ItemWidth = maxMenuTextWidth
End Sub
```

Note the `Handles` clause on the `mNew.MeasureItem` event. This `Handles` clause specifies that this event should serve as the `MeasureItem` event for four different `MenuItem` controls. This is a big time saver, because you no longer need to call the same function in multiple event procedures for multiple objects, nor do you have to create control arrays. (In fact, this functionality replaces the need for control arrays entirely, and they are not available at all in VB .NET.)

The `MeasureItem` event needs to fill the `ItemHeight` and `ItemWidth` properties of the `System.Windows.Forms.MeasureItemEventArgs` parameter, which is passed into it. It does this by calling the `MeasureString` method against the text of each menu item. The string is compared against a form-level variable named `maxMenuTextWidth`. This variable will end up containing the widest line of text of all of your owner-drawn menus, plus 20 pixels to take the width of the bitmap into account. (The bitmap is 16×16, and 4 pixels for buffer equal 20.)

Placing Your Menu

The second event that needs to be created is the one that actually draws the menu into the proper area. It is called the `DrawItem` event:

```
Public Sub mNew_DrawItem(ByVal sender As Object, _
ByVal e As System.Windows.Forms.DrawItemEventArgs) _
Handles mNew.DrawItem, mOpen.DrawItem, mSave.DrawItem, _
mExit.DrawItem

    Dim mi As MenuItem = CType(sender, MenuItem)
    Dim iImage As Integer

    Dim textColor As Color = SystemColors.MenuText

    Dim textBounds As New _
    RectangleF(e.Bounds.Left + 20, _
    e.Bounds.Top + 2, e.Bounds.Right, _
    e.Bounds.Bottom - 2)

    Dim textFormat As New StringFormat()
    Dim tabStops() As Single = {0}

    textFormat.SetTabStops(maxMenuTextWidth, tabStops)

    If (ShowKeyboardCues) Then
        textFormat.HotkeyPrefix = _
        Drawing.Text.HotkeyPrefix.Show
    Else
        textFormat.HotkeyPrefix = _
        Drawing.Text.HotkeyPrefix.Hide
    End If

    Dim selected As Boolean = False

    selected = ((e.State And DrawItemState.Selected) = _
    DrawItemState.Selected)

    If selected Then
        e.DrawBackground()
        textColor = SystemColors.HighlightText
```

```
Else
    e.Graphics.FillRectangle(SystemBrushes.Menu, _
    e.Bounds)
End If

Select Case mi.Text
    Case "&New"
        iImage = 0
    Case "&Open"
        iImage = 1
    Case "&Save"
        iImage = 2
    Case Else
        iImage = -1
End Select

If iImage > -1 Then
    e.Graphics.DrawImageUnscaled( _
    oImageList.Images(iImage), e.Bounds.Left + 1, _
    e.Bounds.Top + 1)
End If

e.Graphics.DrawString(mi.Text, aFont, _
New SolidBrush(textColor), textBounds, textFormat)

End Sub
```

The DrawItem event has a Handles clause as well, which allows this routine to be called for all four of my owner-drawn menus. This function first determines if the menu to be drawn is currently selected by the user, since a selected menu is visually different from a normal menu. If it is a selected menu, it is filled in with the default background drawing method, named FillRectangle, which is a method of the passed-in System.Windows.Forms.DrawItemEvent-Args object. If the menu is not currently selected, then a FillRectangle method is called to draw the menu a basic gray (or whatever the SystemBrushes.Menu color is defined as on this system).

The Case statement maps the current menu being drawn to an image in the ImageList control. The New, Open, and Save menu options all have bitmaps to go with them, and the Exit menu has no bitmap. If it is determined that a bitmap is to be drawn on this menu, it is drawn with the DrawImageUnscaled method. You can see the images in the menus in the first illustration in this section (which shows menus with bitmaps embedded in them).

Finally, the text itself is drawn into place. Note that the Tahoma font is used in this example. (The form-level variable aFont is initialized to an 8-point Tahoma font.) This also makes the menu look more like Microsoft Office application menus.

There is no Font property on the MenuItem class, so you'll have to create owner-drawn menus even if all you want to do is change their font. The good news is that once you take the leap into using owner-drawn menus, you have *total* control over that menu's appearance. You can draw background bitmap patterns, use any font color or size, make menu items bold or italic, or get fancy with graphics instead of normal menu text.

64   Creating UI Elements at Runtime

 The UI code can be found in the folder prjRuntimeUIElements.

I have a big confession to make: Visual Basic hasn't been my language of choice for every programming project that I've done in the past. I experimented with different languages through the years, checking out the features of each, comparing and contrasting. (But I didn't compile. Ba-dum-BAH!)

But seriously…

One of the *other* languages that I did grow fond of was Delphi. This object-oriented version of Pascal by Inprise (formerly Borland) was a great combination of the power of a "true" compiled language with a great visual programming development and form designer like Visual Basic. I did quite a few projects in Delphi, in both my professional "day jobs" and my nighttime hobby programming.

Because of my prior experience with Delphi, my interest was piqued when I learned that one of Delphi's original designers, Anders Hejlsberg, had moved over to the Microsoft team to help work on Visual Studio .NET. The buzz was that some of Delphi's functionality would be migrating over into Visual Basic. The feature I describe here is one of those Delphi-like tricks.

Creating Buttons on the Fly

In certain cases, you might find the need to create user interface (UI) elements at runtime as opposed to doing so at design time. For example, you may want to load a set of choices out of a database and display them on a form as a group of radio buttons. Because you have no idea how many choices there are going to be, you can't use the form designer to put the radio buttons on the form at design time. What you need is the ability to programmatically create new user interface controls. This allows for a much more flexible and maintainable application that can respond to different business logic in a data-driven way.

Now, if you're a VB6 (or earlier) guru, you might be thinking, "Hey, wait a minute, you can create controls on a form in VB6, so why is this so different?" The answer to that question is that in order to programmatically create user interface elements in VB6, you had to utilize control arrays. VB .NET doesn't support control arrays. Instead, a much more flexible method for programmatically creating controls has been introduced.

The way to create new controls on forms is easy to understand once you remember that controls are implemented as classes in the .NET Framework. So, to create a new control on a form, you merely instantiate an instance of the appropriate class:

```
Dim b As Button

b = New Button()
b.Size = new Size(48, 16)
b.Text = "A New Button"
b.Location = new Point(10,10)
Me.Controls.Add(b)
```

The preceding code creates a new object of class `Button`, sets the size and location properties of the button (how big will it be and where on the form will it be positioned), sets the `Text` (formerly `Caption`) property of the button, and then calls the all-important `Me.Controls.Add(b)`. This last line is what *attaches* (for lack of a more precise word) the button to the current form.

This code creates a button that you can see, but the button won't do anything. Why not? Well, you haven't told the button what code to run when the user clicks it. To connect an event to a button, you use the `AddHandler` statement:

```
AddHandler b.Click, AddressOf cbCreate_Click
```

The `AddHandler` statement takes two parameters. The first parameter is an event on an object. In the example, you are adding a handler to the `Click` event on `Button` control b. The second parameter of the `AddHandler` statement is what's known as a *delegate*. The best way to think of a delegate is as a *type-safe* function pointer. By type-safe, I mean that the parameter list of the function must match the parameter list that the event requires.

NOTE   Code completion becomes a handy learning tool for learning the Microsoft .NET Framework in places like this. If you have code completion turned on, you will get a list of valid events on object b as soon as you type **b.** in the AddHandler code line. Take a minute to browse through the list and see if you see any events you might not recognize, and make a note to learn about those events later. (To enable code completion, go to the Tools ≻ Options menu, then navigate the left-side `Treeview` to Text Editor, General. The Auto List Members check box can be found under Statement Completion.)

In the example code, the `Click` event of a button requires two parameters. The first parameter must be of type `object`, and the second parameter must be of type `System.EventArgs`. (The name of each parameter is not important, only the type.) Any sub in your application with this matching parameter list can be assigned as an event handler for a button.

The previous `AddHandler` line links the `cbCreate_Click` event to the new button control. This procedure is, of course, the procedure that creates yet another button. This means that any time any button on the form is clicked, an additional button is created, whose action is the same: to create a new button when clicked. (This might be easier to see in action than to explain in text—try out the `prjRuntimeUIElements` program and see it for yourself.)

To further demonstrate the type-safe nature of delegates, try performing an `AddHandler` statement on a function pointer whose signature does not match that of the event you are trying to define. The sample application has a commented line of code that attempts to make a procedure named `BadCreate_Click` the `Click` event of a button:

```
AddHandler b.Click, AddressOf BadCreate_Click

Protected Sub BadCreate_Click(ByVal sender As Object)
    Call Msgbox("this sub cannot be attached to a button")
End Sub
```

This code yields the following design-time error:

```
Could not find method 'Protected Sub BadCreate_Click(sender As Object)' with
    the same signature as the delegate 'Delegate Sub EventHandler(sender
    As Object, e As System.EventArgs)'.
```

This error message is telling you that the `BadCreate_Click` procedure does not have the correct parameter list to be used as a button's `Click` event.

Creating Menus Dynamically

The sample application in this section has two other examples of dynamic control creation. The first example is displayed when you select Add Menu Item from the File menu. The following code runs when the menu item is selected:

```
Private Sub mAddMenu_Click(ByVal sender As Object, _
ByVal e As System.EventArgs) handles mAddMenu.Click

    Dim m As MenuItem

    'create a new menuitem
    m = New MenuItem()

    'set the caption (er, Text) property
    '(change it for every menu)
    m.Text = "Menu " & iMenuCtr

    'add this menu to File menu
    mFile.MenuItems.Add(1, m)
```

```
    'make this new menu add another menu when selected
    AddHandler m.Click, AddressOf Me.mAddMenu_Click

    'increment the counter
    iMenuCtr += 1
End Sub
```

This example is similar to the button example. A new menu item is created, its Text property is assigned, and its Click event is assigned to this same sub. To show a second example, here is a new menu item and its event handler being created in a single line of code:

```
mAddSubMenu.MenuItems.Add(New _
MenuItem("SubMenu " & iSubMenuCtr, New _
EventHandler(AddressOf mAddSubmenu_Click)))
```

This code smashes most of the same concepts into a single line of code. A new MenuItem is added to the control mAddSubMenu. The MenuItem uses an alternate constructor, one that requires the menu's Text property, and another that's the delegate for the Click event. Note that the structure of this delegate is a bit different. Instead of simply writing AddressOf mAdd-Submenu_Click, this example uses New EventHandler(AddressOf mAddSubmenu_Click). Although this seems confusing, in actuality, the first syntax is simply a form of shorthand for this syntax.

An EventHandler is actually a type of object, and when you call AddHandler, you are really creating an instance of an EventHandler object. VB .NET lets you omit this, however, and simply pass in the delegate function address; the compiler understands all of this. To better understand what's going on with delegates, you may want to use the "long" syntax at first—it helps to explain exactly how you're linking up events to the code underneath.

65   Dynamic Object Creation Using RTTI

 The dynamic object code can be found in the folder prjRTTI.

Earlier, you learned about creating user interface controls such as buttons and menu items at runtime. The code for creating a button at runtime looks something like the following:

```
Dim b As Button

b = New Button()
b.Size = new Size(48, 16)
b.Text = "A New Button"
b.Location = new Point(10,10)
Me.Controls.Add(b)
```

Now I'd like to take dynamic object creation a few steps further. The preceding code works fine as long as you know at design time that you want to create a button, because that's what you declare in the Dim statement. What if you know you want to create an object, but don't know which class that object needs to be until runtime? This is where *runtime type information* (often abbreviated RTTI) comes in. RTTI provides the necessary constructs to determine an object's type at execution time and to dynamically create different types of objects based on values determined at execution type.

Consider a simple example. Suppose I write a class that handles the verification of a user-entered state. (Ohio and OH are valid; Californika and CX are invalid.) I also write a class that verifies countries. (U.S.A. and United Kingdom are valid; XXX is invalid.) I have a simple form for the user to enter address information, which is arranged in such a way that the user enters either a state (if he lives in the U.S.) or a country, and then I need to validate the input using my object. The pseudocode for such logic might look something like the following:

```
If (user entered a state)
    Dim oSV as New StateValidator
    oSV.Validate(cState)
else
    Dim oCV as New CountryValidator
    oCV.Validate(cCountry)
end if
```

This pseudocode would work just fine. A more abstract way to look at the same logic might be as follows, however:

```
If (user entered a state)
    cClassName = "StateValidator"
else
    cClassName = "CountryValidator"
end if

dim o as object
o = NewObjectofType(cClassName)
```

The last line is the odd one: I'm telling VB to instantiate an object whose type name is stored in a string variable. This is the art of using RTTI. The actual VB syntax is not exactly as shown here; you'll see a true example a bit later.

Using RTTI in the Real World

The previous example might seem a bit strange—why use RTTI when you can use a much more standard method to accomplish the same thing? However, if you give it some thought, you might be able to conceive of some interesting uses for RTTI. Consider a database of information that contains not only the data, but also the VB class information used to edit that data. For example, you might have a series of custom data types that represent your business objects (customers, orders, and so on). Given some well-thought-out design, you could create classes for these business objects and specify which class to load for which object, all in database tables. The VB client application would end up being very thin—it would just handle the dynamic loading and display of the business objects specified in the database.

The example project (shown next) creates a simple class named GenericButtonMaker and two more specific classes that descend from it, RedButtonMaker and GreenButtonMaker. The GenericButtonMaker and RedButtonMaker classes are shown here:

```
MustInherit Class GenericButtonMaker

    Protected FB As Button

    Public Sub New()
        MyBase.new()
    End Sub

    Property TheButton() As Button
        Get
            Return Fb
        End Get
        Set
            Fb = value
        End Set
    End Property

    Public MustOverride Sub ChangeButtonCaption()
    Public MustOverride Sub ChangeButtonColor()

End Class

Class RedButtonMaker
    Inherits GenericButtonMaker

    Public Sub New(ByRef aButton As Button)
        MyBase.new()
        FB = aButton
    End Sub

    Public Overrides Sub ChangeButtonCaption()
        Try
            FB.Text = "I am RedButtonMaker"
        Catch
            Call msgbox("button not initialized")
        End Try
    End Sub
```

```
    Public Overrides Sub ChangeButtonColor()
        Try
            FB.BackColor = color.Red
        Catch
            Call msgbox("button not initialized")
        End Try
    End Sub
End Class
```

The `RedButtonMaker` class contains two methods: `ChangeButtonColor` and `ChangeButton-Caption`. Each method relies on the fact that a button has been assigned to the `TheButton` property on the generic class, which is done as part of the constructor. The descendant classes override the two methods, changing the button's caption or color. (Have I won the award yet for most useless, do-nothing class definition? I hope so.)

Based on the value of a radio button in the main project (see the following illustration), the program dynamically loads one of the specific descendant classes and has it perform some work on the button control. The work done is to change either the button caption or the button color, depending on which class is called.

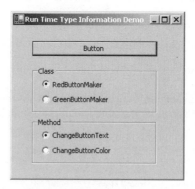

The following code loads the class and calls the desired method:

```
Private Sub Button1_Click(ByVal sender As System.Object, _
ByVal e As System.EventArgs) Handles Button1.Click

        Dim t As Type
        Dim o As Object
        Dim cClassName As String
        Dim cMethodName As String

        'reset the button back to the default look
        Button1.BackColor = Form1.BackColor
```

```
Button1.Text = "Button"

If rbRed.Checked Then
    cClassName = "prjRTTI." & rbRed.Text
Else
    cClassName = "prjRTTI." & rbGreen.Text
End If

If rbText.Checked Then
    cMethodName = "ChangeButtonCaption"
Else
    cMethodName = "ChangeButtonColor"
End If

t = Type.GetType(cClassName)
o = Activator.CreateInstance(t, New Object() {Button1})
t.GetMethod(cMethodName).Invoke(o, Nothing)

End Sub
```

This is the routine that handles the RTTI work. Based on the setting of the top radio button, a string is assigned to one of the two descendant class names. (Note that the namespace prjRTTI must be added to the class name or the program won't be able to find the class.) The desired method to call is also stored in a string, based on the setting of the bottom radio button.

The line t = Type.GetType(cClassName) is where an object of class Type is instantiated from the class name. The Type class contains all of the necessary information about a class. The next line instantiates the object o off the type t. Note the second parameter of the Create-Instance method. This parameter is an array of objects, constructed on the fly, that contains a single object; that object is Button1. When you create an instance of any object using Activator.CreateInstance, the second parameter of the CreateInstance function must be an object array containing all the parameters required by the constructor. My RedButtonMaker and GreenButtonMaker classes require a button to be passed in as the lone parameter on the constructor, and the previous syntax places that button into an array of objects.

The last line of the preceding code calls a method on the new object. The name of the method to call is stored in variable cMethodName. This variable is populated by one of the radio buttons on the lower half of the form. The second parameter on the Type.Invoke call would be an array of objects that represent any parameters that the method you're trying to call expects. The two methods on my ButtonMaker classes don't expect any parameters, so I've left the second parameter as Nothing.

Debugging RTTI

I'd like to give one final word about coding using runtime type information. Although it can be extremely powerful, it also adds a layer of complexity that can make debugging an application much more difficult. This is because many errors that are normally design-time errors become runtime errors in the RTTI world. Consider the following simple line of code:

```
Dim B as new SomeButtonOutThere()
```

This line of code declares a variable of type SomeButtonOutThere. This type must be locatable by Visual Studio in your current defined list of Imports clauses, or Visual Studio gives you an error and disallows you from compiling the program. Now, consider the same declaration using an RTTI style:

```
Dim o as Object
Dim t As Type

t = Type.GetType("SomeButtonOutThere")
o = Activator.CreateInstance(t, Nothing)
```

This code compiles fine under Visual Studio. However, if the SomeButtonOutThere class is unknown, you will get a runtime error when this snippet is executed, telling you that the class can't be located. Obviously, runtime errors are much harder to debug than compile-time errors, because they rely heavily on the state of the program, the current values of all the variables, the procedure call stack, and so on. Make sure to have some good exception handling around your RTTI code to appropriately handle errors that might occur.

66   Versioning and the End of DLL Hell

 The versioning code can be found in the folder prjVersioning.

The original purpose of the dynamic link library (DLL) was to provide a means for many applications to share the same code. Without DLLs, every application would have to have the Win32 API libraries statically linked into the EXE. This is impractical, especially in a multi-tasking environment. Pretty much every Windows program has to call the CreateWindow API call, as an example. If there were no DLLs, every program would have the code for this function loaded in their own little part of RAM. If the user is running 10 different programs, then this function is sitting in RAM in 10 different places. And this is only the first of the hundreds of shared functions that make up the Win32 API.

So the DLL provides an important function. Now, only one copy of the CreateWindow code is taking up RAM, leaving more available RAM for your own program code.

DLL Hell refers to a situation where a commonly used DLL gets replaced and is not backward compatible. This seems to have become a frequent problem in newer releases of Internet Explorer, for example. A new installation of Internet Explorer replaces a shared DLL, and suddenly the accounting package doesn't work on the PC. Careful diagnosis reveals the problem to be a bad version of SHAREME.DLL, but one cannot go back to the old version because the new version of Internet Explorer requires the latest DLL. This forces the end user (or the company's IS department) to make a choice between two programs.

The .NET Framework allows for alternatives to DLL Hell through the use of *assembly versioning*. You can now instruct certain applications to use certain versions of a shared DLL if you deem that conflicts might exist. As developers, you know that an application will use DLLs only if they are the exact same version of the DLL that you built and tested the application against. However, if you choose, you can override this action and instruct your application that it's OK to use a newer version. This should give you the best of both worlds and the end of DLL Hell.

What's a Version?

Versions are assigned at the assembly level. An assembly is a block of code that provides for deployment, security, reuse, and version control. Single-file assemblies are usually DLL or EXE files, but you can create multifile assemblies as well.

Each assembly is given a version number. The complete version number has four components and is written as follows:

```
1.0.0.0
1.2.2034.1
```

The four components of the version number are known as the major number, the minor number, the build number, and the revision number. In the second example just shown, the assembly in question is major version 1, minor version 2, build number 2034, and revision number 1.

These numbers can mean anything you want them to mean, and it's up to you as the developer to version all of your assemblies in an intelligent manner to allow the assemblies in your application to play nicely together. Forgetting to change the version number between releases of your assemblies can cause disastrous results. For example, suppose you release an application that uses a shared component library, and both assemblies start off at version 1.0.0.0. Then, you decide to make some changes to the component library. Depending on the changes you make, you may or may not be able to simply upgrade the component library without releasing a new version of the executable. If this is true, but you fail to change the version number on your library, then the executable will load the new library without problems (since it was tested against version 1.0.0.0) and possibly fail to recognize the changes you have made.

Setting the Version

When you create a new project in Visual Studio, a file named `AssemblyInfo.vb` is created as part of the project. Here are the contents of this file in one of my projects (with comments removed):

```
Imports System.Reflection
Imports System.Runtime.InteropServices

<Assembly: AssemblyTitle("myProgressBar")>
<Assembly: AssemblyDescription("Progress Bar version 1.0")>
<Assembly: AssemblyCompany("")>
<Assembly: AssemblyProduct("")>
<Assembly: AssemblyCopyright("")>
<Assembly: AssemblyTrademark("")>
<Assembly: CLSCompliant(True)>

<Assembly: Guid("3359E44B-034D-4C14-8204-C4EB12CB9539")>
<Assembly: AssemblyVersion("1.0.0.0")>
```

Several attributes have been assigned to this assembly, including the version number. Changing the assembly version is as simple as typing a new version number into the `AssemblyVersion` attribute and recompiling your application.

A Version Example

To demonstrate .NET Framework versioning, I decided to create a component that acts like the `ProgressBar` component that comes as a built-in .NET class. No, I didn't fail to realize that such a component already exists, but I wanted to see if I could create a slightly different visual look to my progress bar. Here's what I came up with:

```
Imports System.ComponentModel

<ToolboxItem(True)> _
Public Class myProgressBar
    Inherits Panel

    Sub New()
        MyBase.New()
        Me.BorderStyle = BorderStyle.Fixed3D
    End Sub

    'properties for Minimum, Maximum, and Value
    Private FMin As Integer = 0
```

```
Property Min() As Integer
    Get
        Return FMin
    End Get
    Set(ByVal Value As Integer)
        FMin = Value
        Invalidate()
    End Set
End Property

Private FMax As Integer = 100
Property Max() As Integer
    Get
        Return FMax
    End Get
    Set(ByVal Value As Integer)
        FMax = Value
        Invalidate()
    End Set
End Property

Private FValue As Integer = 0
Property Value() As Integer
    Get
        Return FValue
    End Get
    Set(ByVal iValue As Integer)
        If iValue <= FMax Then
            FValue = iValue
        Else
            FValue = FMax
Throw New OverflowException(_
"Cannot set myProgressBar Value" & _
"to greater than Max.")
        End If
        Invalidate()
    End Set
End Property

'override Onpaint and paint the progress rectangle
Protected Overrides Sub Onpaint(ByVal e As _
System.Windows.Forms.PaintEventArgs)
    Call MyBase.OnPaint(e)

    Dim iRight As Integer
    Dim b As Brush = Brushes.Navy
    Try
```

```
            iRight = FValue * Me.Width / FMax
            e.Graphics.FillRectangle(b, _
            New Rectangle(0, 0, iRight, Me.Height))
        Catch oEx As Exception
            'nevermind
        End Try
    End Sub
End Class
```

This component inherits from a standard `Panel` control and adds the `Min`, `Max`, and `Value` integer properties to mimic the functionality of the standard progress bar. The `Onpaint` method is overridden to draw a filled navy rectangle in proportion to the percentage that the progress bar is to display. Any type of exception (such as divide by zero) is ignored.

After coding my progress bar, I dutifully set the version number to 1.0.0.0, compiled it into a DLL, and then created a new Windows Forms project to test it out. After adding my new component to the toolbar, I created a simple app that incremented the new progress bar off of a timer. The end result looks something like this:

Finally, to test out the "XCOPY Install" ability of .NET projects, I copied the EXE from my test program and the DLL that contains the progress bar into a folder named `C:\TEMP` and reran the program from there. Copying the EXE and DLL to their own folder simulates an installation version of my application.

Version 2 (Actually, 1.1.0.0)

My progress bar was pretty good, but after a while, two ideas for enhancements came to mind:

- The ability to change the color of the progress meter
- Displaying the percentage as text in the center of the bar

Because I was being mindful of my versions, I created a new folder for my progress bar project and left the old one. (Yes, I could/should be using SourceSafe, but I'm not, so there.) After changing the version number to 1.1.0.0, I made the following changes (duplicate code from previous example omitted):

```
Private FProgressColor As Color = Color.Maroon
Property ProgressColor() As Color
    Get
```

```
            Return FProgressColor
        End Get
        Set(ByVal Value As Color)
            FProgressColor = Value
        End Set
    End Property

'override Onpaint and paint the progress rectangle
 Protected Overrides Sub Onpaint(ByVal e As _
 System.Windows.Forms.PaintEventArgs)
     Call MyBase.OnPaint(e)

     Dim iRight As Integer
     Dim b As New SolidBrush(FProgressColor)

     Try
         iRight = FValue * Me.Width / FMax
         e.Graphics.FillRectangle(b, _
         New Rectangle(0, 0, iRight, Me.Height))
     Catch oEx As Exception
         'nevermind
     End Try

     Dim iPct As Integer

     Try
         iPct = FValue / FMax * 100
         If iPct < 48 Then
             b = Brushes.Black
         Else
             b = Brushes.White
         End If
         e.Graphics.DrawString(iPct & "%", _
         Me.Font, b, (Me.Width / 2) - 10, 4)
     Catch oEx As Exception
         'nevermind
     End Try
```

As you can see, I added the property ProgressColor, which I defaulted to maroon (to make it really easy to tell which version of the control was being used), and I changed the Onpaint procedure to use this color when painting. I also drew the text that represents the percentage in roughly the center of the progress bar and used either black or white for this text depending on the position of the bar.

The next thing I had to decide was if my original project would require a recompile due to changes in this component. For example, if I had changed the Value property to something like `Position` or `CurrentValue`, then any reference to the old property name would fail. However, I hadn't made any changes of this nature. My two changes involved adding a property, which can't cause errors in the old application since it never knew about the property to begin with, and changing what was drawn on the control, which again shouldn't require any coding changes in the application.

Now, to prove that assembly versioning is working, I took my compiled version 1.1.0.0 DLL, copied it to the `C:\TEMP` folder (thereby overwriting the 1.0.0.0 version of the same DLL), and reran my test application. As expected, I received an error which read `"An exception System.IO.FileLoadException has occurred in prjVersioning.exe"`, and the application halted.

Version Control

To allow version 1.1.0.0 of my component to work with a program compiled against version 1.0.0.0 of that assembly, I need to place some instructions in an application configuration file. This file is an XML-format file that can contain several different commands concerning assemblies.

Before I can set up the application configuration file, however, I must do one more thing to my component; I need to set up a *strong name* for the assembly in which the component resides. A strong name incorporates the assembly's simple name and version number, along with a public/private key crypto-pair, which guarantees uniqueness for your assembly name as you install it on other machines.

Generating a strong name for an assembly is done using the `sn.exe` tool. To access this tool, select the Visual Studio .NET Command Prompt, which you can find in your computer's Start menu under Programs ➤ Microsoft Visual Studio .NET ➤ Visual Studio .NET Tools. The Command Prompt looks like a standard DOS box, and from within it, you run the strong name tool as follows:

```
sn -k myProgressBarKeyFile.snk
```

You can use any name for the strong name key file. Once you have this file, you should copy it into the folder that your solution is kept in, and then reference that key in your project's `AssemblyInfo.vb` file by adding the following line:

```
<Assembly: AssemblyKeyFileAttribute("myProgressBarKeyFile.snk")>
```

Next, you need to find out what the public key for your assembly is. To do this, compile your project to a DLL, go back to the .NET Command Prompt, and run the following:

```
sn -Tp myProgressBar.dll
```

You'll either have to copy the DLL into the current folder or specify the path to that DLL on the command line. The results of that program look something like the following.

```
Microsoft (R) .NET Framework Strong Name Utility  Version
    1.0.2914.16
Copyright (C) Microsoft Corp. 1998-2001. All rights reserved.

Public key is
0024000004800000940000000602000000240000525341310004000001 0
00100fdb965f524e287575eb66aed705a7ca5242f2b7c9690b61ecf1168
2c9edd3527baf3bcbaa5c4bd67fe495061231a6177b512ccbff4248d22f
0248bd0d8977237a3556847a38919dc3f1750564d9474ffd868c2d042f7
bb70ce35491cf22794f479536279e23ff4b88f97abdcb213475854fcc98
d5bffa1c1d5b962ca7198b2b2

Public key token is 5274ff09512bfcf5
```

The value that you're interested in is the public key token value. I saved this value in a convenient spot and then created a file named prjVersioning.exe.config that had the following contents:

```
<?xml version="1.0"?>
<configuration>
  <runtime>
    <assemblyBinding xmlns="urn:schemas-microsoft-com:asm.v1">
      <dependentAssembly>
        <assemblyIdentity name="myProgressBar" publicKeyToken="5274ff09512bfcf5"
          ➥/>
        <bindingRedirect oldVersion="1.0.0.0" newVersion="1.1.0.0" />
      </dependentAssembly>
    </assemblyBinding>
  </runtime>
</configuration>
```

The values I needed to customize were the name and publicKeyToken values (under assemblyIdentity). The name is the name of my component assembly, and the publicKeyToken is the value that was the result of me running the sn utility. The other values that require changing are the oldVersion and newVersion values, which, as you can see, instruct the .NET Framework to allow the 1.1.0.0 version of this assembly to replace the 1.0.0.0.

This application configuration file is placed into the C:\TEMP folder along with the EXE and the component DLL. Once this is all in place, my program runs with the new DLL, as you can see in the following illustration:

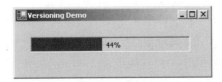

67   The New Security Model

The security model code can be found in the folders `prjCodeAccessSecurity` and `prj-CodeAccessSecurity2`.

It's a brave new world in code development, or rather, it will be if the Microsoft .NET strategy is adopted and widely used. (Are you going to be against Microsoft? Nah, me neither.)

The .NET strategy relies heavily on modular code, either built into units called assemblies that exist as DLLs on the end user's system, or as web services that send data across HTTP. No matter the source, the evil Microsoft scheme is to have developers writing modular code and sharing these modules in order to save work. Why write a binary tree class for the 50th time in your career (not including a dozen times in college) when someone's already written one that you can snap into your program?

A common concern in this brave new world is security. If I'm going to rely on someone else's code module, can I really be sure of everything that module does? Could a module actually appear to perform its published task and at the same time gather up my Microsoft Money backup file for upload to some strange FTP site?

The .NET Framework attempts to deal with these issues through a new concept called *code access security*. Code access security allows you as the developer to publish the permissions that your program will require and to establish trust relationships between your code and the modules that your program will use, even if those modules are from unknown or unreliable sources.

Permissions

The first example program denies the program access to the `C:\WINNT` folder, a pretty common security permission that you might want to deny. (I'm sure most of you have trashed your PC by nuking something in the Windows folder at one time or another.) The following code sets up a `PermissionSet` object instance that includes all access permissions to the `C:\WINNT` folder:

```
Private Sub SetupApplicationPermissionSet()

    Dim ofp As New _
    FileIOPermission(FileIOPermissionAccess.AllAccess, _
    "c:\winnt")

    oPS = New PermissionSet(PermissionState.None)
    oPS.AddPermission(ofp)
End Sub
```

Note that a specific object instance of the `FileIOPermission` class is created, and this object is added to the `PermissionSet` object through the use of the `AddPermission` method. This syntax allows you to add several different types of permissions to a single permission set (which is exactly what the final version of the sample program does).

Once this permission set is created, you can do several things with it. You can call the `Demand` method against it, for example, to request all of the enclosed permissions. Based on the security policy established on the end user's PC, the `Demand` method will succeed or fail with an exception. (Most users in a networked environment don't have local write access to the Windows folders, for example, so the `Demand` method would fail.) You can also call the `Deny` method on the `PermissionSet`, which would prevent your code any access to the resources described.

The sample program calls the `Deny` method and then goes right ahead and attempts to copy a text file into the `C:\WINNT` folder. This copy operation fails with a `SecurityException`.

Now, why would you ever set up a security permission and then deny it? If your intention is to never write to the `C:\WINNT` folder on a computer, why go through all the trouble of setting up a permission to deny it?

The answer becomes clear when you go back to the fact that your application may rely on code that isn't yours, and you're not exactly sure what it does. If you're going to use third-party modules, you can set up and deny various security permissions before you call that module. If that module attempts to do anything against your `PermissionSet`, it too will be denied.

There are other permission types besides the `FileIOPermission`. The sample program in this section adds four different types of permissions to the `PermissionSet`, as seen here:

```
Private Sub SetupApplicationPermissionSet()

    Dim ofp As New FileIOPermission _
    (FileIOPermissionAccess.AllAccess, "c:\winnt")

    Dim ors As New RegistryPermission _
    (RegistryPermissionAccess.AllAccess, _
    "HKEY_LOCAL_MACHINE\SOFTWARE")

    Dim orf As New ReflectionPermission _
    (PermissionState.Unrestricted)

    Dim oev As New EnvironmentPermission _
    (PermissionState.Unrestricted)
```

```
      oPS = New PermissionSet(PermissionState.None)
      oPS.AddPermission(ofp)
      oPS.AddPermission(ors)
      oPS.AddPermission(orf)
      oPS.AddPermission(oev)
   End Sub
```

Each additional permission can be described as follows:

RegistryPermission   This permission describes access to a Registry key. Permission can be given (or removed) to create keys or to read or write Registry values. The preceding code sets up a permission for full access to the HKEY_LOCAL_MACHINE\SOFTWARE Registry key.

ReflectionPermission   This permission sets up access to perform reflection on a .NET Framework assembly. Without specific permission, only public members are available for reflection. The sample program shows that only 107 classes are counted via reflection if the permission is denied, while 158 classes are counted if the permission is granted.

EnvironmentPermission   This permission allows access to read or write system environment variables.

Declarative Security

The type of permission checking in the sample program is called *imperative security*—it is performed at runtime. A second type of code access security can be employed called *declarative security*. This type of security is defined by using security attributes (metadata) at the assembly level.

Declarative security offers different types of benefits. For one, a program could be written that scans an assembly and lists exactly what types of permissions that assembly is defined as having. This might have the effect of making the assembly more trusted to other users because the permissions you've granted to your own code are verifiable.

The next sample program, prjCodeAccessSecurity2, gives a solid example of declarative security using the StrongNameIdentityPermission attribute. This permission, when used with the LinkDemand security action as in this example, denies access to this class by any assembly except the one with the strong name key described by the long hex string shown. (See "Versioning and the End of DLL Hell" for information on the strong name.)

```
Imports System
Imports System.Security.Permissions
Imports System.Reflection

<assembly: AssemblyKeyFileAttribute("friend.keys")>
```

```
< StrongNameIdentityPermission( SecurityAction.LinkDemand, _

    PublicKey:="00240000048000009400000060200000024000052534131000400000100010
        ➡041fa118e7994d91ba823ee72d911ca7612fc87515633f83b168d2413ebd3b27710d8
        ➡61314c5de0cfe6f9240e1764b8597bb57692d104f375fcb177dd346ee51e8c1016ee6
        ➡b327944e98010638d6b77f24eafbafc72de04c965f3a91f5ef3dc950f2148dc95531d
        ➡9326ede5f1ba90b6fd8fb4b7d856034b2f70ac3a7f44797fe1" ) > _
public class Utility
    public shared sub Work()
        Console.WriteLine("Utility.Work")
    end sub
end class
```

This has the effect of locking down a class so that only one assembly can call it. A situation like this would allow a developer to put up a web service on the Internet to take advantage of that technology but to have the appropriate security so that unauthorized users can't access the potentially sensitive code or the data it exposes.

NOTE   Mike Woodring, who maintains a coding web site at http://staff.develop.com/ woodring, graciously donated the project in folder prjCodeAccessSecurity2. This project was not created using the Visual Studio IDE, because I found out that the beta 2 version of Visual Studio could not successfully parse Visual Basic modules using declarative security attributes. Mike helped me diagnose this problem by converting this example from the original C# example he had written. The end result was a great little example of using a declarative attribute, which prompted me to request its addition to the book. I later found this bug to be already known by Microsoft and reported fixed for the final version.

68   Excel-lent—Talking to Excel

 The talking-to-Excel code can be found in the folder prjOffice.

I'm sure many of you have written VB applications that send data to Microsoft Office applications for formatted reporting, label generation, automated mail merges, etc. Visual Basic .NET allows you to communicate with Office applications using a COM interface as well. This section shows you how to create an Excel spreadsheet from a .NET console application.

Once you've created an empty .NET console application, you need to locate the Excel COM library and add a reference to it in the current project. This is done from the Add Reference entry in Project menu of Visual Studio. The dialog box shown in the following illustration shows the Add Reference dialog box, as well as the COM library name required for talking to

Excel 2000. (The name of the COM library may be different on your development machine depending on what version of Office you have installed.)

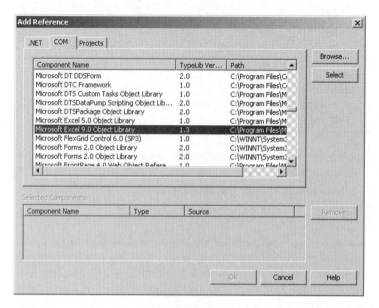

If you're not familiar with the Excel COM library, you might want to take a stroll through the Object Browser to see what the basic objects are. You'll more than likely use an `Excel.Workbook` object, one or more `Excel.Worksheet` objects, and a few `Excel.Range` objects.

The example program in this section creates a table of dates and values and then a chart based on that table. Here are some of the highlights from the example program code:

```
Dim e As New Excel.Application()
Dim r As Excel.Range
Dim ws As Excel.Worksheet

e.Workbooks.Add(XlWBATemplate.xlWBATWorksheet)
'NOTE: array is 1-based, not 0-based
ws = e.Workbooks(1).Worksheets(1)
ws.Name = "Test"
ws.Cells(2, 1) = "Excel Output Demonstration"
ws.Cells(3, 1) = Now
ws.Cells(5, 1) = "Date"
ws.Cells(5, 2) = "Sales"
```

```
r = ws.Range("A2", "B5")
r.Font.Bold = True
```

The preceding block of code creates a new workbook with a single worksheet named Test. It then fills in a few cells of header information and the two-header column cells for the upcoming table. It ends by making all of this header text bold.

The second part of the code is a loop that fills up the table. The first column is a date from Dec 1–Dec 15, and the second value is a random number between 50 and 100. (You would most likely be pulling real sales numbers out of a database as opposed to creating a spreadsheet of random values.)

```
Dim iRow As Integer = 7
Dim dDate As Date = #12/1/2001#
Dim oRand As New Random()

Do While dDate < #12/15/2001#
    ws.Cells(iRow, 1) = dDate.ToShortDateString
    ws.Cells(iRow, 2) = oRand.Next(50, 100)
    iRow += 1
    dDate = DateAdd(DateInterval.Day, 1, dDate)
Loop
iRow += 1
r = ws.Range("B" & iRow, "B" & iRow)
r.Formula = "=sum(B7:B" & iRow - 2 & ")"
r.Font.Bold = True
```

The third and last section of the code creates a formula at the bottom of the second column to add up all the values above it and makes the formula cell bold:

```
r = ws.Range("B" & 7, "B" & iRow - 2)
c = ws.Parent.Charts.Add
With c
    .ChartWizard(r, Excel.XlChartType.xl3DColumn, , _
        Excel.XlRowCol.xlColumns, , , False)
    .Name = "SalesChart"
    .SeriesCollection(1).Name = "Sales"
    .Location(Excel.XlChartLocation.xlLocationAsObject, ws.Name)
End With

' Move the chart over
With ws.Shapes.Item("Chart 1")
    .Top = ws.Rows(7).Top
    .Left = ws.Columns(4).Left
End With
```

This last section creates the chart. It uses the `ChartWizard` object built into the Excel automation library. The final result can been seen in the following illustration:

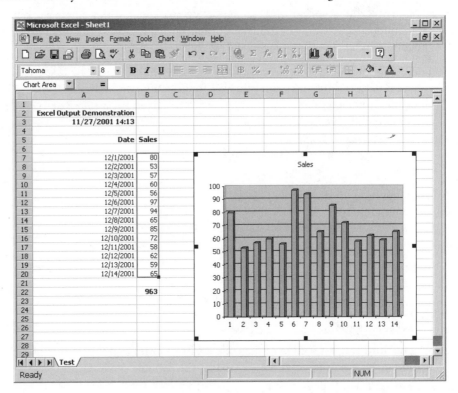

69   Word Up—Talking to Word

 The talking-to-Word code can be found in the folder `prjOffice`.

Excel isn't the only Microsoft Office application that you can rip open from VB .NET and force to do your bidding—all of the Office apps can be exposed through good old-fashioned COM libraries. The demo in this section expands on a demo found in the Microsoft Knowledge Base. It creates mailing labels from scratch, using the names in the Customers table of the Northwind database as the source of the names.

To set up your project to talk to Word, you first have to select Add Reference from the Project menu, and find the Microsoft Office COM library, as seen in the following illustration.

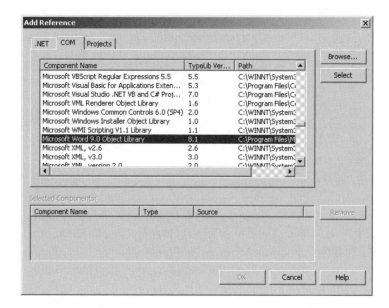

The exact name of the library might be different depending on the version of Office you have installed on your PC.

The first part of the mailing label demo has nothing to do with Word at all—it opens up the Northwind database and exports all of the names and addresses in the Customers table into a comma-delimited text file:

```
Private Sub NorthWindCustomersToTextFile(ByVal cFileName As String)

    Const CONNECTIONSTRING As String = "DATABASE=Northwind;SERVER=localhost;
      ➥UID=sa;PWD=;"

    Dim SQL As String = "Select * from Customers"
    Dim tOut As StreamWriter
    Dim cLine As String

    Dim oConn As New SqlConnection(CONNECTIONSTRING)
    Dim oCmd As New SqlCommand(SQL, oConn)
    Dim oRD As SqlDataReader

    tOut = New StreamWriter(cFileName)
    Try
        cLine = """Name"",""Address"",""City"",""PostalCode"",""Country"""
        Call tOut.WriteLine(cLine)
        Try
```

```
            oConn.Open()
            oRD = oCmd.ExecuteReader(CommandBehavior.CloseConnection)
            Do While (oRD.Read())
                cLine = DblQuoted(oRD.Item("ContactName").ToString) & ","
                cLine &= DblQuoted(oRD.Item("Address").ToString) & ","
                cLine &= DblQuoted(oRD.Item("City").ToString) & ","
                cLine &= DblQuoted(oRD.Item("PostalCode").ToString) & ","
                cLine &= DblQuoted(oRD.Item("Country").ToString)
                Call tOut.WriteLine(cLine)
            Loop

        Finally
            oRD.Close()
        End Try
    Finally
        tOut.Close()
    End Try

End Sub
```

Once the text file is created, the Word mail merge export is created. The more interesting parts of this routine are in this code, followed by some explanation:

```
With oDoc.MailMerge

With .Fields
    .Add(oApp.Selection.Range, "Name")
    oApp.Selection.TypeParagraph()
    .Add(oApp.Selection.Range, "Address")
    oApp.Selection.TypeParagraph()
    .Add(oApp.Selection.Range, "City")
    oApp.Selection.TypeText(", ")
    .Add(oApp.Selection.Range, "PostalCode")
    oApp.Selection.TypeText(", ")
    .Add(oApp.Selection.Range, "Country")
End With
Dim oAutoText As Word.AutoTextEntry
oAutoText = oApp.NormalTemplate.AutoTextEntries.Add("MyLabelLayout",
    ➡oDoc.Content)
oDoc.Content.Delete()
```

This first part of the mail merge routine creates the mail merge fields as an AutoText entry named MyLabelLayout. This is done because of a feature in the Word automation library that lets you create mailing labels with the contents of an AutoText entry as the source. This part of the routine creates the data source from the passed-in file `cFilename`, and then performs the mail merge.

```
.MainDocumentType = Word.WdMailMergeMainDocType.wdMailingLabels
.OpenDataSource(Name:=cFileName)

oApp.MailingLabel.CreateNewDocument(Name:="5160", Address:="", _
    AutoText:="MyLabelLayout",
  LaserTray:=Word.WdPaperTray.wdPrinterManualFeed)

.Destination = WdMailMergeDestination.wdSendToNewDocument
.Execute()
```

The result is a slick set of mailing labels automatically generated from a SQL Server table, as shown in the following illustration:

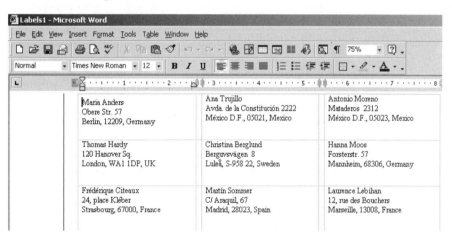

NOTE   Putting together a .NET console application like this `prjOffice` demo and the ability to output Excel and Word documents should get the wheels spinning on all types of automated export/reporting tools you might be able to write.

PART VI

Visual Studio

- Visual Studio .NET macro development

- Visual Studio .NET add-in development

- The Visual Studio .NET Task List

70 The Visual Studio "HoneyDo" List

 The Task List code can be found in the folder `prjDataset`.

At my home, as in many homes I'm sure, we have what we call a "HoneyDo" list—a list of outstanding jobs around the house for me to do. These jobs range in size from small projects like sweeping out the garage or putting up some shelves to larger tasks like removing wallpaper or staining the deck. Sometimes, I'll be working on one chore that reveals the need for a second chore—like when I pull up old carpet in the basement only to reveal some rust-stained concrete underneath. Or when I discover a hole created by chipmunks while cleaning out the garage. It never ends.

When things like this happen, I often don't have time to get to the second job in the same day (the ballgame awaits, after all...). Instead, I add it to the HoneyDo list, complete the first job, and get back to the second job another day. Visual Studio .NET has a feature much like the HoneyDo list (except that it doesn't call me "honey"—good thing): the Task List. The Task List is similar to that found in Microsoft Outlook, or even in previous versions of Visual Studio, with one important distinction: You can auto-fill Task List entries with specially constructed comments. Let's look at how this works.

Task List categories are set up under the Tools ➤ Options dialog. The Task List settings are under the Environment category, as shown in the following illustration:

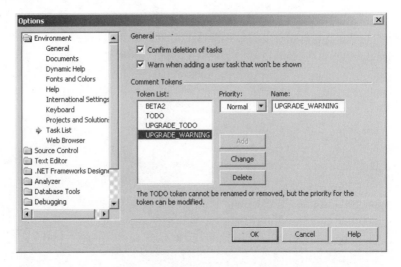

NOTE   As you can see in the illustration, I created a BETA2 token that I used throughout the development of this book. Whenever something wasn't working in VS .NET beta 1 and I suspected that the problem might be because the language was an early beta, I left myself a note to recheck the problem once I received VS .NET beta 2.

You can modify the entries under Token List. A *token* is a special phrase with which you can begin a comment. If you do begin a comment with one of the predefined tokens, an entry is automatically added to the Task List. The text of the task is the text of the comment. This code snippet shows a comment entered into the sample project:

```
' TODO - replace connection object later
Dim aConn As New SQLConnection(CONNECTIONSTRING)
```

Because the comment begins with the TODO token, a task is automatically placed into the Task List, as shown here:

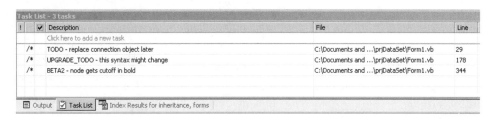

Once the comment is set up in this way, you can double-click the item in the Task List and it will zoom your code directly to the corresponding comment. Deleting the comment deletes the task in the Task List. This functionality acts as the HoneyDo list for your project. You can set up open tasks as comments, and they'll show up in the Task List. Using different tokens allows you to group tasks under different categories and priorities.

71   Macro-Economics

 The macro example can be found in the folder prjMacros.

Any time you find yourself performing repetitive keyboard commands in Visual Studio, you might want to think about combining these keystrokes into a macro. Macros work similarly to the way they work in Microsoft Office. First, you set the macro recorder on, then you perform the keystrokes you wish to turn into a macro, and then you stop the recording. You can then name the macro, or even open it up on the code level to edit it.

One macro that I like to have around is something I call the EqualsSwitch macro. This macro takes a line of code with an equal (=) sign in it and swaps the right-hand and left-hand sides. Thus, it takes this line

```
f.cbCheckSpellingAsYouType.Checked = fCheckSpellingAsYouType
```

and turns it into this line

```
fCheckSpellingAsYouType = f.cbCheckSpellingAsYouType.Checked
```

I find this type of macro useful when programming "properties" or "settings" dialog boxes. The example program shows this well. I've created a sample "settings" dialog box with some check boxes that I ripped out of Word, as seen in the following illustration:

I store the value of each of the properties in form-level Boolean variables, like so:

```
Private fCheckSpellingAsYouType As Boolean = True
Private fHideSpellingErrors As Boolean = False
Private fAlwaysSuggest As Boolean = True
Private fSuggestMainOnly As Boolean = False
Private fIgnoreUpperCase As Boolean = True
Private fIgnoreNumbers As Boolean = True
Private fIgnoreInternetAndFile As Boolean = True
```

When it comes time to display the dialog box, the following code is executed to populate the values of the check boxes with the current values of the Boolean variables:

```
Dim f As New FSettings()
f.cbCheckSpellingAsYouType.Checked = fCheckSpellingAsYouType
f.cbHideSpellingErrors.Checked = fHideSpellingErrors
f.cbAlwaysSuggest().Checked = fAlwaysSuggest
f.cbSuggestMainOnly().Checked = fSuggestMainOnly
f.cbIgnoreUpperCase().Checked = fIgnoreUpperCase
f.cbIgnoreNumbers().Checked = fIgnoreNumbers
f.cbIgnoreInternetAndFile().Checked = fIgnoreInternetAndFile

f.ShowDialog()
```

Now if the user clicks the OK button on the dialog box, I need to save the values of the check boxes back into the Boolean variables:

```
If f.DialogResult = DialogResult.OK Then
    fCheckSpellingAsYouType = f.cbCheckSpellingAsYouType.Checked
    fHideSpellingErrors = f.cbHideSpellingErrors.Checked
    fAlwaysSuggest = f.cbAlwaysSuggest().Checked
```

```
    fSuggestMainOnly = f.cbSuggestMainOnly().Checked
    fIgnoreUpperCase = f.cbIgnoreUpperCase().Checked
    fIgnoreNumbers = f.cbIgnoreNumbers().Checked
    fIgnoreInternetAndFile = f.cbIgnoreInternetAndFile().Checked
End If
```

Note that the assignment statements inside the IF block are the same as the ones before the ShowDialog statement, except that their equal statements are flipped. This is where my EqualsSwitch macro comes in handy; I can copy the original block of code down into the new place and run the EqualsSwitch macro on each line, getting the statement I want.

Recording a Macro

Recording a macro is done from the Tools ➤ Macros ➤ Record TemporaryMacro menu option. (Ctrl+Shift+R is the default shortcut key.) Once you select this menu option, macro recording begins immediately, so make sure the cursor is exactly where you want to start the macro keystroke recording before choosing this menu option.

The EqualsSwitch macro consists of the following sequence of actions:

- Press the Home key (go to the beginning of the current line).

- Perform an Exact Word search on the equal sign.

- Press the Delete key (delete equal sign).

- Press and hold the Shift key (start text selection mode).

- Press the Home key (select all text backward from the equal sign to the beginning of line, or everything to the left of the equal sign).

- Cut selected text.

- Press the End key (move to end of line).

- Type an equal sign.

- Paste the text in the clipboard.

Once the macro keystrokes are recorded, select the Tools ➤ Macros ➤ Save Temporary-Macro menu option.

Editing a Macro

The macro you've created through the recording process has a hard-coded name of Temporary-Macro. This is fine if your macro is a part-time thing that you don't wish to save, but if you want to keep the macro for future projects, you'll probably want to edit it at least to change the name.

To see the code for all your macros, select the Tools ➤ Macros ➤ Macro Explorer menu option. The Macro Explorer window looks like any other project window, as seen in the following illustration. You can open the `TemporaryMacro` that you've just created for editing by right-clicking it and selecting Edit.

You'll probably make the mistake of double-clicking the macro to edit it, since this is how the Solution Explorer works. In actuality, double-clicking a macro in the Macro Explorer *runs* the macro, so make sure you undo any unintended editing if you accidentally double-click when you meant to edit.

The Visual Basic code for the `EqualsSwitch` macro is as follows:

```
Option Strict Off
Option Explicit Off
Imports EnvDTE
Imports System.Diagnostics

Public Module RecordingModule


    Sub TemporaryMacro()

    DTE.ActiveDocument.Selection.StartOfLine(VsStartOfLineOptions
        ➡.VsStartOfLineOptionsFirstColumn)
        DTE.ExecuteCommand("Edit.Find")
        DTE.Find.FindWhat = "="
        DTE.Find.Target = vsFindTarget.vsFindTargetCurrentDocumentFunction
        DTE.Find.MatchCase = False
        DTE.Find.MatchWholeWord = True
        DTE.Find.Backwards = False
        DTE.Find.MatchInHiddenText = False
        DTE.Find.PatternSyntax = vsFindPatternSyntax.vsFindPatternSyntaxLiteral
        DTE.Find.Action = vsFindAction.vsFindActionFind
        DTE.Find.Execute()
        DTE.Windows.Item(Constants.vsWindowKindFindReplace).Close()
        DTE.ActiveDocument.Selection.Delete()

    DTE.ActiveDocument.Selection.StartOfLine(VsStartOfLineOptions
        ➡.VsStartOfLineOptionsFirstText, True)
        DTE.ActiveDocument.Selection.Cut()
        DTE.ActiveDocument.Selection.EndOfLine()
```

```
        DTE.ActiveDocument.Selection.Text = "="
        DTE.ActiveDocument.Selection.Paste()
    End Sub
End Module
```

You'll want to change the name of the module from `RecordingModule` to something else, as well as the name of the sub from `TemporaryMacro` to something else. Take this time to study the code and see how the Development Tools Extensibility (DTE) object works to interface with the Visual Studio .NET environment.

Adding a Macro to the Toolbar

To add your new macro to the Visual Studio toolbar, select Tools ➤ Customize from the menu. In the dialog box in the following illustration, on the Commands tab, select the Macros menu on the left side of the Categories list box. You should see the macro you've created on the right side of the dialog box. To add this macro to the toolbar, drag the right-side macro name off this dialog box and directly onto the toolbar in Visual Studio .NET. With the Customize dialog box still in place, right-click the new button for options such as setting the tool button bitmap and whether text should appear on the button.

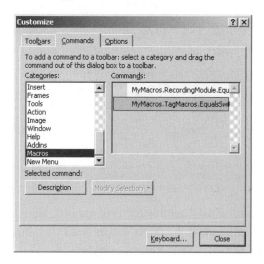

72 Adding in Add-ins

 The add-ins example can be found in the folder `prjSimpleAddin`.

Add-ins are a second method of using the Visual Studio .NET automation model to extend and customize the VS .NET IDE. While the code and object model for add-ins and macros is the same, writing an add-in gives you more functionality within the IDE, such as the ability to programmatically disable the menu option associated with your add-in (depending on the current state of the IDE), or the ability to create new types of windows in the IDE that display the output of your add-in.

Add-ins are created using the Add-in Wizard. To start the wizard, you want to create a new Visual Studio project. Under the project type, select Extensibility Projects under Other Projects, then select Visual Studio .NET Add-in. The dialog box for choosing this new project type is as follows:

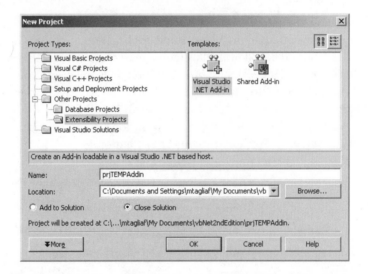

This starts the Add-in Wizard. The first page of the wizard is an introductory page. Once you click Next to get past the first page, you will be asked the following questions:

- Page 1: Choose a language. Your choices are Visual C#, Visual Basic (meaning VB .NET), or Visual C++/ATL.

- Page 2: Choose application host(s). You can write an Add-in for Visual Studio .NET, and/or the VSMacros IDE (the IDE that comes up when you choose to edit a macro). Future IDEs may find their way into this step, as well, if they are installed on your computer. Choose at least one of the application hosts.

- Page 3: Select a unique name and give descriptive remarks to your add-in.

- Page 4: Choose add-in options. There are four check box options to select (shown in the following illustration). These options are reasonably self-explanatory. I recommend that you make sure that the first box is selected for your first add-in, so that a menu option is created to start your add-in.

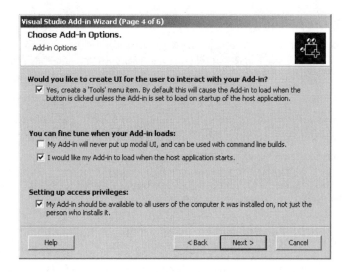

- Page 5: Display About Box text. You can create custom text that displays on the Visual Studio .NET About Box.

For my first add-in, I chose something relatively simple coding-wise, yet still pretty useful. I'm having trouble remembering the syntax to the new classes in ADO.NET. As a database developer, I'll be using `DataSets` and `DataReaders` quite frequently in my day-to-day life. For my first add-in, I decided to spit out a template `DataReader` loop. Here is the template code fragment I want my code to spit out:

```
Const CONNECTIONSTRING As String = "DATABASE=Northwind;SERVER=localhost;UID=sa;
    ➥PWD=;"
Dim SQL As String = "Select * from Customers"
Dim oConn As New SqlConnection(CONNECTIONSTRING)
Dim oCmd As New SqlCommand(SQL, oConn)
Dim oRD As SqlDataReader

Try
    oConn.Open()
    oRD = oCmd.ExecuteReader(CommandBehavior.CloseConnection)
    Do While (oRD.Read())
        'stuff here
        'syntax for field: oRD.Item("ContactName").ToString
    Loop

Finally
    oRD.Close()
End Try
```

Note that the comments inside the read loop are part of what I want to be inserted into the current IDE window when the add-in is executed.

Coding the Add-in

Once you've completed the Add-in Wizard, you'll get a nice amount of setup code generated for you in the form of a class called Connect. Inside the Connect class, you'll see a variable named applicationObject of type EnvDTE.DTE. This is the same DTE type you used in the previous macro section. This object is your interface into all of the current open windows of the IDE.

The only important procedure you'll need to code to get a bare-bones functionality add-in working is the Exec method. This function is started for you here:

```
Public Sub Exec(ByVal cmdName As String, _
    ByVal executeOption As vsCommandExecOption, _
    ByRef varIn As Object, ByRef varOut As Object, ByRef handled As Boolean) _
    Implements IDTCommandTarget.Exec

    handled = False
    If (executeOption = _
      vsCommandExecOption.vsCommandExecOptionDoDefault) Then
        If cmdName = "prjSimpleAddin.Connect.prjSimpleAddin" Then
            handled = True
        End If
    End If
End Sub
```

You need to complete the routine by putting code right above the handled = true line. My DataReader template spitter-out code looks like this:

```
Dim objTD As TextDocument
Dim objEP As EditPoint
Dim cCode As String
Dim NL = Environment.NewLine

Try
    objTD = applicationObject.ActiveDocument.Object("TextDocument")
    objEP = applicationObject.ActiveDocument.Selection.TopPoint.CreateEditPoint()

    cCode = "Const CONNECTIONSTRING As String = "
    cCode &= """"DATABASE=Northwind;SERVER=localhost;UID=sa;PWD=;""" & NL
    cCode &= "Dim SQL As String = ""Select * from Customers""" & NL
    cCode &= "Dim oConn As New SqlConnection(CONNECTIONSTRING)" & NL
    cCode &= "Dim oCmd As New SqlCommand(SQL, oConn)" & NL
    cCode &= "Dim oRD As SqlDataReader" & NL & NL
    cCode &= "Try" & NL
    cCode &= "oConn.Open()" & NL
    cCode &= "oRD = oCmd.ExecuteReader(CommandBehavior.CloseConnection)" & NL
    cCode &= "Do While (oRD.Read())" & NL
    cCode &= "'stuff here" & NL
    cCode &= "'syntax for field: oRD.Item(""ContactName"").ToString" & NL
    cCode &= "Loop" & NL & NL
```

```
        cCode &= "Finally" & NL
        cCode &= "oRD.Close()" & NL
        cCode &= "End Try" & NL
        objEP.Insert(cCode)

    Catch oEx As Exception
        MsgBox(oEx.Message)
    Finally
        handled = True
    End Try
```

What you're really doing here is finding the current position of the cursor in the current editing window, building a big string that contains that text you want to put in, and then inserting it. Note that I also moved the `handled = true` line into a `Finally` clause, just to make sure it always executes.

Testing the Add-in

To begin testing your add-in program, you compile and run it from Visual Studio .NET, just as you would any other program. What might throw you off at first, however, is that a second instance of Visual Studio is created where you can see the `prjSimpleAddin` menu option, as shown in the following illustration. Selecting the `prjSimpleAddin` from the menu will run it. (In the case of this add-in, start a dummy project in Visual Studio and open up a code window or the add-in will error out, since it won't have anywhere to insert its code.)

73   Add-ins and Event Hooks

 The advanced add-in example can be found in the folder `prjMoreAddins`.

The add-in in the preceding section was activated by a menu option from the Visual Studio .NET IDE, but there are many other ways to interface your add-in code. In particular, the DTE object has a full-featured set of events that can be hooked from your programs to allow new add-in IDE features to be executed in dozens of different parts of the application-development process.

The sample project in this section demonstrates a way of automating the code documentation process by adding event hooks into two places—whenever a solution is opened in the IDE and whenever a solution is built.

Event Hook on Solution Open

The object that allows solution-specific event hooking is called `SolutionEvents`. To hook any of the events within this object within your add-in, you first need to declare a variable of this type in your add-in class, as follows:

```
Dim WithEvents oevSolution As SolutionEvents
```

Once this variable is declared, you point it to the available DTE object's `SolutionEvents` property. The most logical place to do this is in the `OnConnection` event of your add-in class:

```
Public Sub OnConnection(ByVal application As Object, _
        ByVal connectMode As Extensibility.ext_ConnectMode, _
        ByVal addInInst As Object, ByRef custom As System.Array) _
        Implements Extensibility.IDTExtensibility2.OnConnection

        oApp = CType(application, EnvDTE.DTE)
        oevSolution = oApp.Events.SolutionEvents
```

You now have the ability to write event code for any of the events defined in the `Solution-Events` object. These events include the following:

- `AfterClosing`
- `BeforeClosing`
- `Opened`
- `ProjectAdded`
- `ProjectRemoved`
- `ProjectRenamed`
- `QueryCloseSolution`
- `Renamed`

I chose to write event code for the `Opened` event. This code creates an XML file that contains the name of the user and the time that the solution was opened. That code is as follows:

```
Public Sub SolutionOpened() Handles oevSolution.Opened
        Call ExportLastOpenedDataToXML()
End Sub

Private Sub ExportLastOpenedDataToXML()
    Dim cFilename As String
```

```
        Dim f As New FileInfo(oApp.DTE.Solution.FullName)
        Dim oPrj As Project
        Dim oItem As ProjectItem

        cFilename = f.DirectoryName & "\ProjOpened.xml"
        Dim oW As New XmlTextWriter(cFilename, Nothing)
        Try
            oW.Formatting = Formatting.Indented
            oW.WriteStartDocument()
            oW.WriteComment("XML Visual Studio.NET Solution Last Opened record")
            oW.WriteComment("generated " & Now)
            oW.WriteStartElement("solutionopened")
            oW.WriteAttributeString("name", f.Name)
            oW.WriteAttributeString("when", Now)
            oW.WriteAttributeString("who", Environment.UserName)
            oW.WriteEndElement()
            oW.Flush()
        Finally
            oW.Close()
            Console.WriteLine("XML Last Opened spec published")
        End Try

    End Sub
```

The XML-formatted output of this file is as follows:

```
<?xml version="1.0" ?>
<!—XML Visual Studio.NET Solution Last Opened record—>
<!— generated 11/29/2001 12:50:08 PM —>
<solutionopened name="prjMacros.sln" when="11/29/2001 12:50:08 PM" who=
    ➡"mtagliaf" />
```

This XML file could be published to a web server and serve as the source for a development manager report showing the last time each VB .NET project in his department was opened, and by whom.

Event Hook on Solution Build

Hooking code into a solution build is done in almost the same way, except that a different class is required. This class is called the BuildEvents class. Once again, you need to declare a variable of this type within your add-in class:

```
Dim WithEvents oevBuild As BuildEvents
```

Next, you point this variable to the property of the same type on the DTE object. Again, do this within the OnConnection event of your add-in:

```
Public Sub OnConnection(ByVal application As Object, _
        ByVal connectMode As Extensibility.ext_ConnectMode, _
```

```
              ByVal addInInst As Object, ByRef custom As System.Array) _
              Implements Extensibility.IDTExtensibility2.OnConnection

       oApp = CType(application, EnvDTE.DTE)
       oevBuild = oApp.Events.BuildEvents
```

You can now write event code based on the following events in the `BuildEvents` class:

- `OnBuildBegin`

- `OnBuildDone`

- `OnBuildProjConfigBegin`

- `OnBuildProjConfigDone`

The example program exports a different type of XML document whenever a solution is built. This XML document creates project summary data, including the files contained in the current solution, and a list of all the tasks in the Task List for this solution. Here's the method that produces the XML document:

```
Public Sub BuildDone(ByVal bs As _
        vsBuildScope, ByVal ba As vsBuildAction) _
        Handles oevBuild.OnBuildDone

        Call ExportProjectToXML()
End Sub

Private Sub ExportProjectToXML()
        Dim cFilename As String

        Dim f As New FileInfo(oApp.DTE.Solution.FullName)
        Dim oPrj As Project
        Dim oItem As ProjectItem

        cFilename = f.DirectoryName & "\ProjData.xml"
        Dim oW As New XmlTextWriter(cFilename, Nothing)
        Try
            oW.Formatting = Formatting.Indented
            oW.WriteStartDocument()
            oW.WriteComment("XML Visual Studio.NET Solution summary")
            oW.WriteComment("generated " & Now)
            oW.WriteStartElement("solution")
            oW.WriteAttributeString("name", f.Name)
            For Each oPrj In oApp.DTE.Solution.Projects
                oW.WriteStartElement("project")
                oW.WriteAttributeString("name", oPrj.Name)
                For Each oItem In oPrj.ProjectItems
                    oW.WriteStartElement("file")
```

```
                oW.WriteAttributeString("name", oItem.Name)
                oW.WriteEndElement()
            Next
            oW.WriteEndElement()
        Next


        oW.WriteComment("Summary of Task List")
        oW.WriteStartElement("TaskList")
        Dim oWin As Window =
oApp.DTE.Windows.Item(Constants.➡vsWindowKindTaskList)
        Dim oTL As TaskList = oWin.Object
        Dim oTask As TaskItem
        For Each oTask In oTL.TaskItems
            oW.WriteStartElement("task")
            oW.WriteAttributeString("category", oTask.Category)
            oW.WriteAttributeString("checked", oTask.Checked.ToString)
            oW.WriteAttributeString("file", oTask.FileName)
            oW.WriteAttributeString("line", oTask.Line)
            oW.WriteAttributeString("priority", oTask.Priority)
            oW.WriteEndElement()
        Next
        oW.WriteEndElement()      'tasklist
        oW.WriteEndElement()      'solution
        oW.Flush()
    Finally
        oW.Close()
        Console.WriteLine("XML Project spec published")
    End Try

End Sub
```

The XML output from this code is as follows:

```
<?xml version="1.0"?>
<!-XML Visual Studio.NET Solution summary->
<!-generated 11/29/2001 1:54:51 PM->
<solution name="prjOOPFundamentals.sln">
  <project name="prjOOPFundamentals">
    <file name="AssemblyInfo.vb" />
    <file name="Form1.vb" />
    <file name="WorldObjects.vb" />
  </project>
  <!-Summary of Task List->
  <TaskList>
    <task category="Comment" checked="False" file="WorldObjects.vb" line="146"
      ➡priority="2" task="TODO: collision detection?" />
```

```
    <task category="Comment" checked="False" file="WorldObjects.vb" line="110"
    ➥priority="2" task="HACK: armor damage div 2 for now, add an damage
    ➥reduction factor" />
    <task category="Comment" checked="False" file="WorldObjects.vb" line="55"
    ➥priority="2" task="TODO: ellipse just placeholder for now, will switch
    ➥to actual graphics later" />
    <task category="Comment" checked="False" file="WorldObjects.vb" line="50"
    ➥priority="2" task="todo: create event for dying" />
    <task category="Comment" checked="False" file="WorldObjects.vb" line="39"
    ➥priority="2" task="TODO: check the math here" />
    <task category="Comment" checked="False" file="WorldObjects.vb" line="27"
    ➥priority="2" task="TODO : decide if negative HitPoints allowed, remove
    ➥0 check if yes" />
  </TaskList>
</solution>
```

PART VII

Beyond Visual Basic

- Console application programming

- Mixing C# and VB .NET

- ASP.NET custom control development

74   Expanding Your Horizons: Mixing Languages

 The mixed language code can be found in the folders `clHoverButton` and `prjMixingLanguages`.

I've already read (and even participated in) some online debate on which language is "better," Visual Basic .NET or C#. The arguments range from interesting to inane to inaccurate. The VB vs. C++, or VB vs. Delphi, or VB vs. anything wars have been raging on and on since the release of our favorite language.

I have the feeling, though, that this latest incarnation of the VB wars won't last long. After all, both VB and C# are built on top of the same framework, and there really isn't any important thing you can do in one language that you can't do in the other. This means that the answer to the VB vs. C# question really boils down to personal preference. What's the point in arguing about that?

In all truthfulness, I'm thinking it might be a good idea to become proficient in both VB .NET and C#. Being able to call myself a .NET guru in either language will probably look good on the resumé. But I'm pretty sure that my own personal preference will always be the Basic syntax over the C syntax.

The point is, you really don't have to choose one or the other, even within the same project. The language you choose must be the same across each assembly, but you can have a project with multiple assemblies, like an EXE calling a DLL, for example. And these two assemblies can be in different .NET languages.

Trying It Out

To test out the language-mixing abilities of the .NET Framework, I decided to create a component in C# and then use it in a VB project. My C# component is called a `HoverButton`—it's simply a button that highlights its caption when the mouse moves over the button. Here's the code for `HoverButton`:

```
namespace clHoverButton
{
    using System;
    using System.Windows.Forms;
    using System.Drawing;

    public class HoverButton: Button
    {

      Color FChangedForeColor = Color.Red;
      Color FSaveForeColor;
      public Color ChangedForeColor
      {
            get { return FChangedForeColor; }
            set { FChangedForeColor = value; }
      }
    }
```

```
protected override void OnMouseEnter(System.EventArgs e)
{
        base.OnMouseEnter(e);
        FSaveForeColor = ForeColor;
        ForeColor = FChangedForeColor;
}

protected override void OnMouseLeave(System.EventArgs e)
{
        base.OnMouseLeave(e);
        ForeColor = FSaveForeColor;
}


}
}
```

Looks pretty alien, no? You should have seen me trying to write it. All those curly braces and such, yuck! (Just kidding.) Anyway, this button descendant has a new property named ChangedForeColor that represents the color that the caption turns to when the button is hovered over. The hover code is accomplished in the OnMouseEnter and OnMouseLeave methods. These methods save the original color, set the ForeColor to the value of the new property, and then set the original color back when the mouse leaves the control.

Mixing It Up

After compiling my new HoverButton control, I started up a new Visual Basic project and wrote some code to put a ton of hover buttons on my form. This double loop creates 64 hover buttons in an 8×8 grid and reports which button is clicked:

```
Dim i As Integer
Dim j As Integer
Dim aB As HoverButton
For i = 0 To 7
    For j = 0 To 7
        aB = New HoverButton()
        aB.Text = "Button " & ((i * 8) + j)
        aB.Size = New Size(64, 32)
        aB.Location = New Point(4 + (i * 68), 4 + (j * 36))
        aB.Visible = True
        AddHandler aB.Click, AddressOf ClickMe
        controls.Add(aB)
    Next
  Next
```

Not being completely satisfied with this, however, I stumbled across a new idea: I wanted my new control's caption to change to still another color when clicked. To summarize, it would be one ForeColor when the control was idle, a second ForeColor when the mouse was hovering over, and a third `ForeColor` when the button was in the down state. Now, I had two different ways of adding this new functionality: I could either modify the original control or I could create a new descendant control that inherits off of the original `HoverButton` and adds this new functionality. To further show off the abilities of mixing languages, I chose the latter solution, and created the new descendant `HoverButton` in my "native" Visual Basic:

```
Class NewHoverButton
    Inherits HoverButton

    Private FSaveColor As Color
    Private FDownColor As Color = Color.Navy
    Property DownColor() As Color
        Get
            Return FDownColor
        End Get
        Set(ByVal Value As Color)
            FDownColor = Value
        End Set
    End Property

    Protected Overrides Sub OnMouseDown(ByVal e As _
    system.Windows.Forms.MouseEventArgs)
        MyBase.OnMouseDown(e)
        FSaveColor = Me.ForeColor
        Me.ForeColor = FDownColor
    End Sub

    Protected Overrides Sub OnMouseUp(ByVal e As _
    system.Windows.Forms.MouseEventArgs)
        MyBase.OnMouseUp(e)
        Me.ForeColor = FSaveColor
    End Sub

End Class
```

Pretty cool, no? I created a control in C# and inherited off it in Visual Basic. This type of power might come in handy in larger development shops (by larger, I mean larger than one programmer), where a new hire might be more fluent in one .NET language over the other and wouldn't be forced to switch right away before she became productive.

NOTE   When you load up the `prjMixingLanguages` sample project in Visual Studio, you may encounter several errors about not being able to find the `clHoverButton` assembly. This is because the `clHoverButton` assembly resides in a different folder from this project, and Visual Studio is having trouble finding this folder depending on where you installed the sample projects on your hard drive. To correct the error, go to the Solution Explorer, right-click References, select Add Reference, and then navigate to and select `clHover-Button.dll`. Adding this reference should remove all of the errors in the project.

75   The Joy of Console Applications

 The console applications code can be found in the folder prjConsoleApp.

I write a great deal of utility programs in my current job. These programs usually run unattended at some ghastly hour and perform one or more tasks, like taking all the data over *here*, summing it up, and putting the results over *there*. For these types of applications, the user interface isn't important, obviously—there's usually nobody around to watch the program when it's running anyway.

VB .NET allows you to write a new kind of application known as a *console application*. Actually, calling it a new kind of application is not really correct—console applications are really "old school" apps from back in the pre-Windows days of DOS. (Ask your grandfather or that 38-year-old senior developer in your company about those days.) All of the input and output in a console app happens in a simple console command line, similar to a DOS prompt.

Creating a Console App

Creating a console application is a simple task. When you create a new project in Visual Studio .NET, Console Application is one of the project options, as shown in the following illustration:

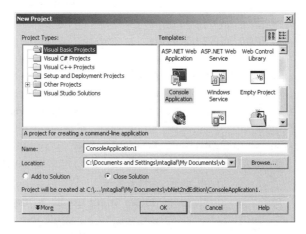

The empty project contains a blank Sub Main inside of a Module1, as seen here:

```
Module Module1
    Sub Main()
    End Sub
End Module
```

Sub Main is the procedure that executes first when your application runs. This is where you start your coding.

Producing Input/Output in a Console App

The Console class handles most of the features of your console app. You don't have to create an instance of the Console class, either; an instance is created automatically as part of the application.

To produce a line of output in your console application, use the WriteLine method of the Console class:

```
Console.WriteLine("Here is some Output")
```

The WriteLine method will output whatever you specify, and follow that up with a carriage return and linefeed so that the next output will start on a new line. If you want to output only part of a line and have subsequent output on the same line, use the Write method:

```
Console.Write("Here is some Output...")
Console.Write("and some more output")
```

If your application needs to query the user for some information, use the ReadLine method. The following snippet of code asks the user for his age and stores the result into a string variable named sResult:

```
Console.Write("Enter your Age: ")
sResult = Console.ReadLine()
```

OK, you might have noticed something a bit odd. I mentioned that console apps are often used for creating unattended jobs. If that's the case, why is there a need for writing output to the screen or asking a user for input—there's supposedly no user around to read the output or answer the prompts.

Ah, good point, Number One. As usual, Microsoft anticipated this exact question and designed the Console class in a somewhat unique way to handle input from sources other than user input. The Console class has a property named IN that represents the current *stream* of input to the program. By default, the input stream is the console input itself (where you can type entries). Say, for example, that you want to write a program that processed the contents of a text file. One way to handle this is to change the Console.In property to be an instance of the text stream that contains the desired program input.

Output is handled in a similar way. There might not be anybody around to read the output of your program, but you can write the results to a text file log, which can be examined in the morning. There is a Console.Out property that holds a StreamWriter object that serves as the destination to all console application output.

The Console.In and Console.Out properties are read-only and therefore cannot be changed directly. There are methods named Console.SetIn and Console.SetOut that accomplish this, however.

The ConsoleApp project included on the CD that accompanies this book is a silly little program that can run two different types of programs. The first function of the program demonstrates simple user interaction by playing a number-guessing game with the user. You are prompted to guess a number between 1 and 100 and told whether your number is too high or too low, until you get the number correct.

The second part of the program takes a command line that represents the name of a valid text file. (The text file must be in the same folder as the ConsoleApp executable.) This part of the program redirects console input to that text file and redirects console output to a second, new text file, and then writes the contents of the source file into the destination file, converting all the text to uppercase along the way. The reading and writing of the two text files is done using the Console.ReadLine and Console.WriteLine methods. The procedure that accomplishes this function is as follows:

```
Private Sub MakeFileContentsUpperCase(ByVal cInputFile _
As String)

    Dim tIn As StreamReader
    Dim tOut As StreamWriter
    Dim bDone As Boolean = False
    Dim cLine As String
    Dim cOutputFile As String

    Dim oSaveIn As TextReader
    Dim oSaveOut As TextWriter

    If Not File.Exists(cInputFile) Then
        Console.WriteLine(cInputFile & " does not exist")
        Exit Sub
    End If

    cOutputFile = Application.StartupPath & _
    "\TextOutput.txt"

    Console.WriteLine("processing file " & cInputFile)
    Console.WriteLine("output filename is " & cOutputFile)
    tIn = New StreamReader(cInputFile)
    tOut = New StreamWriter(cOutputFile)

    oSaveIn = Console.In
    oSaveOut = Console.Out
    Call Console.SetIn(tIn)
    Call Console.SetOut(tOut)
```

```
Try
    While Not bDone
        cLine = Console.ReadLine()
        If cLine Is Nothing Then
            bDone = True
        Else
            Call Console.WriteLine(UCase(cLine))
        End If
    End While
Finally
    Call tIn.Close()
    Call tOut.Close()

    Call Console.SetIn(oSaveIn)
    Call Console.SetOut(oSaveOut)
End Try

    End Sub
```

Note that the `TextReader` and `TextWriter` objects are instantiated and set to console input and output using the `SetIn` and `SetOut` methods. Note also that the original input and output streams are saved to variables so they can be restored later. This step isn't necessary except that I wanted to write a message to the console that the program was complete, and I couldn't write to the console once I had redirected output to the text file.

The loop itself is not extraordinary. `Console.ReadLine` is called in a loop, which retrieves one line of the input text file at a time. The uppercase version of that string is written to the console (again, redirected to an output text file) using `Console.WriteLine`. This continues until the end of the input file is reached. When that happens, the input and output streams are closed, and the console streams are restored to their original state. The loop is enclosed in a `Try…Finally` block to make sure that the streams are closed and the console streams are restored, no matter what errors you might encounter during the loop.

76   Getting Entangled in Some Web Development

 The web development code can be found in the folder `prjWebApp`.

Developing browser-based apps instead of "fat" Visual Basic clients has both advantages and disadvantages to the user community and to the developer. The browser app can be deployed over the Internet, meaning your users can sit at their home PCs and use your application without having to install anything. In addition, new types of wireless handheld devices are being invented seemingly every day (things like WAP phones, PDAs, portable instant messengers, and so on), and browser-based applications are a good choice for designing applications to run on these devices. The downsides to browser-based applications include the requirement for an Internet connection (no running your app on a laptop while flying in a plane, for example) and the lack of the rich client interface you can provide your user base in a VB front end. On the developer side, I find web development much more difficult than Visual Basic coding, mainly because the development tool set is much more primitive.

Still, both types of applications fill a need given the application requirements, and to be a well-rounded developer, it's probably a good idea to be able to throw at least a little web development experience on your resumé. Fortunately, in the .NET world, web development and VB development have gotten much closer to each other in both coding style and development tool usage.

An ASP.NET Primer

Browser-based development is done using ASP+, or ASP.NET. (They keep renaming it, but I think ASP.NET is the name that's sticking now.) ASP, for the uninitiated, stands for Active Server Pages, and it contains code built to interact with web pages. This code runs on the web server (as opposed to VBScript or JavaScript code that runs on the client machine). The purpose of most ASP code is to render HTML pages for the user to view. If the end user selects View Source in his browser, the ASP code isn't there—it runs on the web server, creates the final web page, and sends that to the browser.

In Visual Studio .NET, an ASP.NET application uses something called *Web Forms*, which are collectively the set of user interface controls that you can use to design your web pages. This is much closer to designing a Visual Basic application than previous web development environments. Controls are dragged onto Web Forms and positioned along a grid. When a control is double-clicked in the design environment, a code window appears for you to edit the event code behind that control. After designing a simple web page with a text box, a button, and a label, the resulting HTML code looks as follows:

```
<%@ Page Language="vb"
 AutoEventWireup="false" Codebehind="CustLookup.aspx.vb"
   Inherits="prjWebApp2.WebForm1"%>
<!DOCTYPE HTML PUBLIC "-//W3C//DTD HTML 4.0 Transitional//EN">
<HTML>
   <HEAD>
      <title>customer lookup</title>
      <link rel="stylesheet" href="Styles.css">
      <meta name="GENERATOR"
```

```
         content="Microsoft Visual Studio.NET 7.0">
       <meta name="CODE_LANGUAGE" content="Visual Basic 7.0">
       <meta name="vs_defaultClientScript" content="JavaScript">
       <meta name="vs_targetSchema"
        content="http://schemas.microsoft.com/intellisense/ie5">
   </HEAD>
   <body MS_POSITIONING="GridLayout">
      <form id="aForm"
            method="post"
            runat="server"
            action="CustList.aspx">
            <p>
            Enter the Last Name of the Customer to Look up (partial name ok)
            </p>
            <asp:TextBox id="tbName"
            style="Z-INDEX: 100;
            LEFT: 8px; POSITION: absolute;
            TOP: 38px"
            runat="server"
            Width="208px"
            Height="24px"></asp:TextBox>
            <asp:Label id="lbMessage"
            style="Z-INDEX: 102;
            LEFT: 13px; POSITION: absolute;
            TOP: 83px"
            runat="server"
            Width="207px"
            Height="17px"></asp:Label>
            <asp:Button id="cbSearch"
            style="Z-INDEX: 103;
            LEFT: 232px;
            POSITION: absolute;
            TOP: 40px" runat="server"
            Text="Search"></asp:Button>
      </form>
   </body>
</HTML>
```

This looks like pretty standard HTML, with a few new elements. There are several <asp:something> tags, which represent the Web Forms controls I added to the page. The top line refers to a "code-behind" file, which points to a standard Visual Basic .NET (or C#) file that contains the event code for the controls on the web page. The following is the code-behind file for this page.

```
Imports System.Data.SqlClient

Public Class WebForm1
    Inherits System.Web.UI.Page
    Protected WithEvents tbName _
    As System.Web.UI.WebControls.TextBox
    Protected WithEvents cbSearch _
    As System.Web.UI.WebControls.Button
    Protected WithEvents lbMessage _
    As System.Web.UI.WebControls.Label

    Private Sub cbSearch_Click(ByVal sender As _
    System.Object, ByVal e As _
    System.EventArgs) Handles cbSearch.Click

        Dim cName As String

        cName = tbName.Text
        cName = cName.Trim

        If cName.Length > 0 Then
            Response.Redirect("custlist.aspx?Name=" & cName)
        End If
    End Sub
End Class
```

The preceding chunk of code shouldn't intimidate anyone who has some VB .NET experience. It's the exact same VB .NET code you'd put in a non-web project. The only thing that might be new to you is the Response.Redirect command. This command tells the browser to load up a new page and that you're adding something called a *query string* to the end of the web page. (A query string is like passing a parameter as part of the URL.)

Creating Page 2

The second page in the web application contains an empty data grid and a label control. The code-behind file is as follows:

```
Imports System.Data.SqlClient

Public Class CustList
    Inherits System.Web.UI.Page
    Protected WithEvents lbMessage _
    As System.Web.UI.WebControls.Label
    Protected WithEvents aDataGrid _
```

```
As System.Web.UI.WebControls.DataGrid

Private Sub Page_Load(ByVal sender As _
System.Object, ByVal e As _
System.EventArgs) Handles MyBase.Load

Const CONNECTIONSTRING As String = _
 "DATABASE=Northwind;SERVER=localhost;UID=sa;PWD=;"

    Dim aDR As SqlDataReader
    Dim aConn As SqlConnection
    Dim aCmd As SqlCommand
    Dim SQL As String
    Dim cName As String

    cName = Request.QueryString("Name") & ""
    cName = cName.Trim

    lbMessage.Text = "names matching '" & cName & "'"
    SQL = "Select CustomerID, CompanyName, "
    SQL = SQL & " ContactName from Customers "
    SQL = SQL & " where ContactName like '%" & cName & "%'"

    aConn = New SqlConnection(CONNECTIONSTRING)
    aCmd = New SqlCommand(SQL, aConn)

    aConn.Open()
    Try
        aDR = aCmd.ExecuteReader
        aDataGrid.DataSource = aDR
        aDataGrid.DataBind()
    Catch oEX As Exception        'no records
        aDataGrid.Visible = False
        lbMessage.Text &= " (none)"
    Finally
        aConn.Close()
    End Try

End Sub

End Class
```

Again, this code is syntactically just like any other VB .NET code you've worked on to this point. Note that one of the first lines in the Page_Load event pulls the parameter off the current

URL by using `Request.QueryString`. This allows you to retrieve whatever the user typed into the text box on the previous page. Then, a `DataReader` is opened and filled with all of the customers in the Northwind database that contain the typed-in string. Finally, the `DataGrid` is bound to that `DataReader`. The end result is the web page shown in the following illustration:

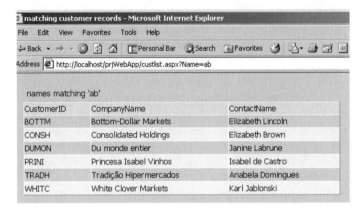

ASP.NET programming can (and will) be the subject of many books by itself, so I can't do it full justice here. The point to understand is that once you become a .NET Framework and VB .NET syntax expert, your path to also becoming a web developer is much shorter than it used to be because you'll be able to use most of the techniques and code from your VB .NET projects. In fact, you'll most likely be able to use many of your actual classes (at least the nonvisual classes) in both VB and ASP projects.

A quick note on web projects: Setting up a web project requires a machine running Microsoft Internet Information Server (IIS) components. This can be a local Windows NT or 2000 workstation, or a "real" web server. From IIS, you can set up "web applications" and configure their default start pages, security, and other functions. To run the web programs in this book, you'll need to create web applications in IIS and give them the same name as the VS .NET project file.

77   ASP.NET Reusability

The reusability code can be found in the folder `prjWebUserControl`.

One of the things that made "old school" ASP programming difficult was the difficulty in reusing code. I always found myself either copying files from one application folder to another (programmer's bad habit #214) or having to add all sorts of strange include file directives with relative-pathed filenames to my pages.

ASP.NET solves that problem by making web development much closer to "standard" application development. One of the ways that this was done was in the implementation of *User Controls*. User Controls are reusable controls that you create using Web Forms user interface (UI) elements. The main difference between a Web Form and User Controls is that User Controls are not usable by themselves—they must be placed on another page.

NOTE   Although the class name is identical, don't confuse the ASP.NET `UserControl` class (found in namespace `System.Web.UI`) with the Windows Forms `UserControl` class (found in namespace `System.Windows.Forms`). The two classes share a common name and the same basic purpose, but have little in the way of common members.

A User Control Example

A useful User Control might be something that connects to the Northwind database and displays a list of product categories from which the end user can select. A control of this type might be useful on many different types of pages within the Northwind application, such as the page where new items are created and edited, or in selected sales report parameters (show me all sales in category *x*). The end result should look like the following illustration:

Select a Category

Select	Category	Description
○	Beverages	Soft drinks, coffees, teas, beers, and ales
○	Condiments	Sweet and savory sauces, relishes, spreads, and seasonings
○	Confections	Desserts, candies, and sweet breads
○	Dairy Products	Cheeses
○	Grains/Cereals	Breads, crackers, pasta, and cereal
○	Meat/Poultry	Prepared meats
○	Produce	Dried fruit and bean curd
○	Seafood	Seaweed and fish

Thank you for your Selection

Note that in the preceding illustration, the labels above and below the table are not part of the User Control; they are part of the web page upon which the User Control is placed.

Creating a new User Control is done from the Solution Explorer. With the project high-lighted, right-click and select Add ➤ Add Web User Control from the context menu, as seen here:

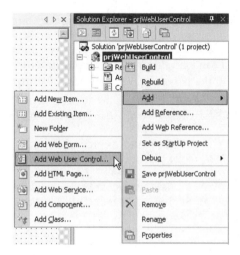

A design view appears that's identical to the view used when creating Web Forms. You can place any Web Form UI element on the User Control surface. I chose the main element in my User Control to be a Repeater—a slick little data-bound list that allows you to create custom HTML for the start of the items in the list, the end, each individual item, and between items. I chose to bind my Repeater to an ArrayList that contains instances of a trivial two-property class shown in the following code:

```
Protected Class CategoryData

    Private FCat As String
    Private FDesc As String

    Public Sub New(ByVal cCat As String, ByVal cDesc As String)
        FCat = cCat
        FDesc = cDesc
    End Sub

    Public ReadOnly Property pCategory() As String
        Get
            Return FCat
        End Get
    End Property
```

```
Public ReadOnly Property pDescription() As String
    Get
        Return FDesc
    End Get
End Property

End Class
```

Once declared, I can load the `ArrayList` up from Northwind and then bind it to the Repeater control in the `InitMe` event of the User Control:

```
Private Sub InitMe(ByVal sender As System.Object, _
    ByVal e As System.EventArgs) Handles MyBase.Init

        Const CONNECTIONSTRING As String = _
            "DATABASE=Northwind;SERVER=localhost;UID=sa;PWD=;"

        Dim oArray As New ArrayList()
        Dim SQL As String = "Select CategoryName, Description from Categories"
        Dim cCat As String

        Dim oConn As New SqlConnection(CONNECTIONSTRING)
        Dim oCmd As New SqlCommand(SQL, oConn)
        Call oConn.Open()
        Dim oRD As SqlDataReader = oCmd.ExecuteReader(CommandBehavior
            ➥.CloseConnection)

        Try
            Do While (oRD.Read())
                cCat = oRD.Item("CategoryName").ToString.Trim
                oArray.Add(New CategoryData(cCat, _
                    oRD.Item("Description").ToString.Trim))
            Loop

        Finally
            oRD.Close()
            Repeater1.DataSource = oArray
            Repeater1.DataBind()
        End Try
    End Sub
```

The code that sets up the Repeater templates is found on the HTML page of the design view of the User Control:

```
<asp:Repeater id="Repeater1" runat="server">
    <HeaderTemplate>
        <table border="1" style="FONT-SIZE: 8pt; FONT-FAMILY: Tahoma">
            <tr>
                <td><strong>Select</strong></td>
                <td><strong>Category</strong></td>
```

```
                <td><strong>Description</strong></td>
            </tr>
    </HeaderTemplate>
    <ItemTemplate>
        <tr>
            <td align="right">
                <% dim cLine as string
                cLine = "<INPUT type='radio' name='selectme'>"
                response.write(cLine) %>
            </td>
            <td><%# DataBinder.Eval(Container.DataItem, "pCategory") %></td>
            <td><%# DataBinder.Eval(Container.DataItem, "pDescription") %></td>
        </tr>
    </ItemTemplate>
    <FooterTemplate>
        </table>
    </FooterTemplate>
 </asp:Repeater>
```

Note the special template sections defined as part of the Repeater. The HeaderTemplate declares the HTML table and column header row. The FooterTemplate merely ends the table definition. Most of the fun happens in the ItemTemplate section. There, each item in the data-bound list is defined as a row in the table that's being defined. An HTML radio button control (INPUT type='radio') is placed in the first column of each table row. The second and third cells are populated by evaluating the property of the object instance associated in the list that's bound to the repeater. In this example, that object is of the trivial two-property CategoryData class created in the preceding code.

Using the User Control

Once the User Control is set up, using it on another web page is as easy as can be. All you have to do is drag the User Control out of the Solution Explorer and plop it down on your web page in the desired location. You should see a placeholder icon for your control as shown here:

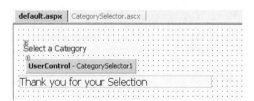

Once placed on a web page, you should be able to test the control and see it in action. You've just created a reusable piece of ASP code. Hurrah! After all the hassle I've gone through in the pre-.NET days, that's definitely worth a hurrah.

Part VIII

Internet and Distributed Development

- Reading and writing XML

- Using XML from SQL Server

- Message queue programming

- Remoting

- XML Web Service development

- Accessing other XML Web Services

- Writing COM+ transactions

- Talking to Microsoft TerraServer

- Writing applications for mobile devices

78 XML Speed Reading

 The XML-reading code can be found in the folder prjSlashdDotReader.

XML has been a major topic of conversation lately, commanding attention from books and articles and websites and the like. The .NET strategy uses XML as a critical part of its communication, though in many cases this is an "under-the-hood" technology, so you as the developer need never know it. However, many websites and third-party sources are starting to make their data available via the web as XML, and it's probably a good idea to learn how to directly parse XML. The prjSlashDotReader project introduced earlier in this book takes advantage of the fact that the SlashDot news site makes their current news pages an XML document. Let's see how I retrieved this document and parsed it out so that the current news became menu items in my project.

The Class to Know

The XMLDocument class in the .NET Framework gives you everything you need for parsing valid XML data for your own purpose. This class contains members for creating and reading all of the different types of XML data. (And, since the XML spec seems to grow and morph on a weekly basis, I'm sure we'll be seeing some changes to this class as well.)

If you have a valid XML document URL, you can load that XML file into an XMLDocument object instance using the following code:

```
Dim doc As New XmlDocument()
Dim wr As WebRequest
Dim ws As WebResponse
Dim sr As StreamReader
Try
    wr = _
    WebRequest.Create("http://www.slashdot.org/slashdot.xml")
    ws = wr.GetResponse()
    sr = New StreamReader(ws.GetResponseStream(), _
    Encoding.ASCII)

    'Read entire document
    cLine = sr.ReadToEnd()

    'Load the text into the xml document
    doc.LoadXml(cLine)
Catch oEX As Exception
    MsgBox(oEX.ToString)
Finally
    sr.close()
    ws.Close()
End Try
```

The location for the SlashDot news XML document is `http://www.slashdot.org/ slashdot.xml`. This document is retrieved by first opening a `WebRequest` class, retrieving the response off that `WebRequest`, and then converting that response into a stream. Finally, the complete contents of the stream are loaded into a single string variable named `cLine`.

Once the document content has been loaded into a local string, the `XMLDocument` instance can import it using the `LoadXml` method. Now the document is loaded into the object and you're ready to parse. A small portion of this XML code has been reproduced here so that you may refer to it as I describe how the code parses it:

```
<?xml version="1.0" encoding="ISO-8859-1" ?>
- <backslash xmlns:backslash=
"http://slashdot.org/backslash.dtd">
- <story>
  <title>Slashback: Mono, Names, Locking Up</title>
  <url>http://slashdot.org/article.pl?sid=01/07/09/136208</url>
  <time>2001-07-09 23:59:34</time>
  <author>timothy</author>
  <department>goin'-south-again</department>
  <topic>slashback</topic>
  <comments>118</comments>
  <section>articles</section>
  <image>topicslashback.gif</image>
  </story>
- <story>
  <title>Canada Post Kills Free
Internet-For-Life Program</title>
  <url>http://slashdot.org/article.pl?
sid=01/07/09/2223227</url>
  <time>2001-07-09 22:44:48</time>
  <author>timothy</author>
  <department>only-kidding</department>
  <topic>internet</topic>
  <comments>124</comments>
  <section>articles</section>
  <image>topicinternet.gif</image>
  </story>
```

Scanning the XML Document

The highest level in the XML just shown appears to be a collection of `<story>` elements. Within these elements are several different nodes, the most important of which are the `<title>` and `<url>` nodes. You're going to use the `<title>` nodes as the menu text, and you also want to save the URLs that correspond to each title.

If you'll recall from "System Trays in Their Full, Upright Position," I created a descendant class from a standard `MenuItem` that contained an extra string property named `URL` for the purpose of storing the URL for each story right in the menu item that the user will select when he wants to read that story. That class, the `MenuItemWithURL`, is used in the parsing code:

```
Dim nlStories As XmlNodeList = _
doc.GetElementsByTagName("story")
Dim oNode As XmlNode
Dim oChild As XmlNode

For Each oNode In nlStories
    cTitle = ""
    cURL = ""
    For Each oChild In oNode.ChildNodes
        If oChild.Name = "title" Then
                cTitle = oChild.InnerXml
        ElseIf oChild.Name = "url" Then
                cURL = oChild.InnerXml
        End If
    Next

    If cTitle.Length > 0 And cURL.Length > 0 Then
        aUMenuItem = New MenuItemWithURL(cTitle, cURL)
        AddHandler aUMenuItem.Click, AddressOf MenuClick
        aMenu.MenuItems.Add(aUMenuItem)
    End If
  Next
```

What this code does is load all of the `<story>` nodes into a collection known as an `XMLNodeList` in order to iterate through them. Each item in an `XMLNodeList` is of type `XMLNode`. `XMLNode` objects themselves can have an `XMLNodeList` collection under them. (Remember, an XML document is a fully recursive structure.)

For each XML node that represents a story, you loop through all the child nodes. You're looking for the `<title>` tag and the `<url>` tag, and, if you find each, you store their values into a string variable. If you end up finding both tags, then a `MenuItemWithURL` object instance is created, and it is added to your menu.

Writing code to rip through an XML document is really easy in theory. In practice, however, you usually have to have some idea of exactly what you're looking for as you rip through it. In this case, you want to load up the `<title>` and `<url>` tags for each `<story>` node in your document. Of course, XML documents can get infinitely complex, and your parsing logic will have to grow more complex as you try and extract data out of such documents.

79   Producing XML

The XML-writing code can be found in the folders prjDataSet and prjManualXML.

I'm sure that sooner or later, some outside party will ask you to make the data from your application available in an XML format so that they might import it into their own applications. There are several ways to do this.

Database XML

If your application uses database data and you've already implemented the I/O using the DataSet, then creating XML is about as trivial as you can get. Once your DataSet is defined and populated, you can use the GetXml method to return the XML representation of that DataSet as a string variable:

```
tbXML.Text = aDataset.GetXml
```

A sample of the XML produced by the sample project and the GetXml method is as follows:

```
<NewDataSet>
  <Products>
    <ProductID>1</ProductID>
    <ProductName>Chai</ProductName>
    <SupplierID>1</SupplierID>
    <CategoryID>1</CategoryID>
    <QuantityPerUnit>10 boxes x 20 bags</QuantityPerUnit>
    <UnitPrice>18</UnitPrice>
    <UnitsInStock>39</UnitsInStock>
    <UnitsOnOrder>0</UnitsOnOrder>
    <ReorderLevel>10</ReorderLevel>
    <Discontinued>false</Discontinued>
  </Products>
  <Products>
    <ProductID>2</ProductID>
    <ProductName>Chang</ProductName>
    <SupplierID>1</SupplierID>
    <CategoryID>1</CategoryID>
    <QuantityPerUnit>24 - 12 oz bottles</QuantityPerUnit>
    <UnitPrice>19</UnitPrice>
    <UnitsInStock>17</UnitsInStock>
    <UnitsOnOrder>40</UnitsOnOrder>
    <ReorderLevel>25</ReorderLevel>
    <Discontinued>false</Discontinued>
  </Products>
```

If you're interested in writing a DataSet's XML to a file, you can use the WriteXml method in one of its many incarnations:

```
Call aDataset.WriteXML("c:\fred.xml")
```

DataSets can export their schema as XML as well. The schema of an XML document is a list of the nodes and their relationships, just as the schema of a database is a listing of the tables, columns, and relationships between them. The tricky part is that an XML schema is itself an XML document. The schema document describes the structure of the data document, if you will.

The GetXmlSchema method on the DataSet class is used to create the schema. The following code is an example of the DataSet schema from the sample project prjDataSet:

```xml
<xsd:schema id="NewDataSet" targetNamespace=""
    xmlns="" xmlns:xsd="http://www.w3.org/2001/XMLSchema"
    xmlns:msdata="urn:schemas-microsoft-com:xml-msdata">
  <xsd:element name="NewDataSet" msdata:IsDataSet="true">
    <xsd:complexType>
      <xsd:choice maxOccurs="unbounded">
        <xsd:element name="Products">
          <xsd:complexType>
            <xsd:sequence>
              <xsd:element name="ProductID"
                  type="xsd:int" minOccurs="0" />
              <xsd:element name="ProductName"
                  type="xsd:string" minOccurs="0" />
              <xsd:element name="SupplierID"
                  type="xsd:int" minOccurs="0" />
              <xsd:element name="CategoryID"
                  type="xsd:int" minOccurs="0" />
              <xsd:element name="QuantityPerUnit"
                  type="xsd:string" minOccurs="0" />
              <xsd:element name="UnitPrice"
                  type="xsd:decimal" minOccurs="0" />
              <xsd:element name="UnitsInStock"
                  type="xsd:short" minOccurs="0" />
              <xsd:element name="UnitsOnOrder"
                  type="xsd:short" minOccurs="0" />
              <xsd:element name="ReorderLevel"
                  type="xsd:short" minOccurs="0" />
              <xsd:element name="Discontinued"
                  type="xsd:boolean" minOccurs="0" />
            </xsd:sequence>
          </xsd:complexType>
        </xsd:element>
```

Note how this schema defines an element named Products and a bunch of elements under it named ProductID, ProductName, SupplierID, and so on. This is equivalent to describing a SQL Server table named Products with fields named ProductID, ProductName, SupplierID, and so on.

Manual XML

If your goal is to manually produce an XML file on disk, then the XMLTextWriter class is what
you'll probably use. This class contains methods for creating node structures of any complexity level. The following method creates an XML document using the XMLTextWriter class,
and methods on that class like WriteComment, WriteStartElement, WriteElementString, and
so on. These methods make it easy to create well-formed XML documents.

```
Private Sub WriteTheFile()

    Dim oW As New XmlTextWriter(cXMLFilename, Nothing)

    Try
        oW.Formatting = System.Xml.Formatting.Indented
        oW.WriteStartDocument(False)
        oW.WriteComment("This file represents another " & _
        "fragment of a book store inventory database")

        oW.WriteStartElement("order")

        oW.WriteStartElement("customer", Nothing)
        oW.WriteAttributeString("custid", "123456-Q")
        oW.WriteElementString("firstname", Nothing, _
        "matthew")
        oW.WriteElementString("lastname", Nothing, _
        "tagliaferri")
        oW.WriteEndElement()

        oW.WriteStartElement("ItemList", Nothing)

        oW.WriteStartElement("Item", Nothing)
        oW.WriteAttributeString("ItemID", "XD-1267")
        oW.WriteElementString("Description", "PowerBar")
        oW.WriteElementString("Quantity", "2")
        oW.WriteElementString("Price", "2.99")
        oW.WriteEndElement()

        oW.WriteStartElement("Item", Nothing)
        oW.WriteAttributeString("ItemID", "DE-2322")
        oW.WriteElementString("Description", "Grape-Ade")
        oW.WriteElementString("Quantity", "1")
        oW.WriteElementString("Price", ".89")
        oW.WriteEndElement()

        oW.WriteEndElement()
        oW.WriteEndElement()
```

```
        'Write the XML to file and close the writer
        oW.Flush()
        oW.Close()

    Finally
        oW.Close()
    End Try

End Sub

<?xml version="1.0" standalone="no"?>
<!--This file represents another fragment of a
book store inventory database-->
<order>
  <customer custid="123456-Q">
    <firstname>matthew</firstname>
    <lastname>tagliaferri</lastname>
  </customer>
  <ItemList>
    <Item ItemID="XD-1267">
      <Description>PowerBar</Description>
      <Quantity>2</Quantity>
      <Price>2.99</Price>
    </Item>
    <Item ItemID="DE-2322">
      <Description>Grape-Ade</Description>
      <Quantity>1</Quantity>
      <Price>.89</Price>
    </Item>
  </ItemList>
</order>
```

As you can see, actually writing out the XML code is pretty easy. As with any set of structured data, the hard part is organizing the data in a coherent manner that is understandable by whomever or whatever needs to read it.

80 Using XML from SQL Server

 The code accompanying this section can be found in the folder prjSQLXML.

Everyone quickly started catching on that XML could be a powerful tool for communication between disparate computing environments. More and more information is being stored in XML format (check out .NET application config files, for example), which means that all of the .NET XML support will be useful in managing this information.

Microsoft is putting XML support just about everywhere, including in their database engine SQL Server. You can add the keywords FOR XML to the end of any SQL Select statement to return the data in a standard XML format. There are several modifiers for the FOR XML statement that allow different types of XML formats to be generated. The simplest modifier to use is the AUTO keyword. For example, the query

```
SELECT EmployeeID, LastName, Firstname, Title
FROM Employees WHERE LastName LIKE 'D%' FOR XML AUTO
```

yields the following XML data:

```
- <Northwind xmlns:sql="urn:schemas-microsoft-com:xml-sql">
  <employees EmployeeID="1" LastName="Davolio" Firstname="Nancy" Title=
    ➥"Sales Representative" />
  <employees EmployeeID="9" LastName="Dodsworth" Firstname="Anne" Title=
    ➥"Sales Representative" />
  </Northwind>
```

With all the .NET Framework tools at your disposal for manipulating XML data, you can use the XML generation capabilities of SQL Server to whip up some great reporting in just a few lines of VB code.

XSL to the Rescue

An XSL stylesheet is a description of how to write XML data into another format. To add a layer of complexity to confuse you further, XSL stylesheets are in an XML format themselves. Here is an example of an XSL stylesheet:

```
<?xml version="1.0"?>
<xsl:stylesheet xmlns:xsl="http://www.w3.org/1999/XSL/Transform" version="1.0">
<xsl:output method="html"/>
<xsl:template match="/">
<HTML>
<HEAD>
<TITLE>Sales Summary</TITLE>
</HEAD>
<BODY bgcolor="lightsteelblue">
<!--Part 2-->

<xsl:for-each select="//c">
<p>
<table border='1' style="font-family: Tahoma; font-size: 10pt">
<tr><td colspan='4'><strong>
<xsl:value-of select="@CompanyName" />
</strong></td></tr>
<tr>
<th>Order#</th>
```

```
<th>Date</th>
<th>Subtot</th>
<th>Freight</th>
</tr>

<xsl:for-each select="o">
<tr>
<td><xsl:value-of select="@OrderID" /></td>
<td><xsl:value-of select="@OrderDate" /></td>
<td>
<xsl:for-each select="tot">
<xsl:value-of select="@SubTotal" />
</xsl:for-each>
</td>
<td><xsl:value-of select="@Freight" /></td>
</tr>
</xsl:for-each>

</table>
</p>
</xsl:for-each>

</BODY>
</HTML>
</xsl:template>
</xsl:stylesheet>
```

This section will not attempt to explain all the complexities of writing XSL stylesheets. Suffice to say that XSL stylesheets are a somewhat simple form of programming that take an XML document as input and create another document as output. This particular stylesheet creates an HTML document that can be viewed in any browser.

It only takes a few lines of VB .NET code to pull data out of SQL Server and run it through this stylesheet:

```
Private Sub BuildSalesPage()
    Const CONNECTIONSTRING As String = "DATABASE=Northwind;SERVER=localhost;
        ➡UID=sa;PWD=;"

    Dim cPath As String

    cPath = mappathsecure("")
    If Not cPath.EndsWith("\") Then cPath &= "\"

    Dim SQL As String
    SQL = "select top 25 c.CompanyName, c.CustomerID, "
```

```
SQL &= "o.OrderID, o.OrderDate, o.Freight, tot.SubTotal "
SQL &= "from [Order Subtotals] tot "
SQL &= "inner join Orders o on o.OrderId = tot.OrderID "
SQL &= "inner join Customers c on o.CustomerID = c.CustomerID "
SQL &= "order by c.CustomerID, o.OrderDate FOR XML AUTO"

Dim oConn As New SqlConnection(CONNECTIONSTRING)
Dim oCmd As New SqlCommand(SQL, oConn)
oConn.Open()
Try
    Dim oReader As XmlReader = oCmd.ExecuteXmlReader
    Dim oXslXForm As XslTransform
    Dim oXPDoc As XPathDocument

    oXPDoc = New XPathDocument(oReader)
    oXslXForm = New XslTransform()
    oXslXForm.Load(cPath & "orderxform.xsl")

    Dim stWrite As System.IO.StringWriter = New System.IO.StringWriter()
    oXslXForm.Transform(oXPDoc, Nothing, stWrite)

    Dim sOut As New StreamWriter(cPath & GENERATEDFILE)
    Try
        sOut.Write(stWrite.ToString)
    Finally
        sOut.Close()
    End Try

Finally
    oConn.Close()
End Try
End Sub
```

The code that performs the XML-to-HTML translation happens right after the first Try statement. The results of the SQLCommand are passed to an XMLReader. (Note that the SQL query specifies the FOR XML AUTO statement at the end.) From there, the XMLReader is loaded into an XMLDocument instance. That document and a standard StringWriter are passed as the parameters to an XSLTransform object instance, which performs the translation. From there, the XSLTransform contents are exported to a file.

This might seem like a convoluted way to get XML data into HTML format, but note how generic this code is. It could easily be converted into a generic class that is given an SQL statement, an XSL stylesheet filename, and an output name, and the conversion specified by the stylesheet would be performed. This could make the basis for a fairly robust web-based reporting engine done entirely with XSL stylesheet programming.

81 Special Delivery: Sending E-mail

 The code accompanying this section can be found in the folder prjEmail.

I write quite a few programs that run unattended at night, and one way I use to report on their success (or failure) is to have the program send me an e-mail that I can read in the morning. The contents of the e-mail tells me if everything ran smoothly or—in the most dire cases—the failure to receive said e-mail tells me something ran less than smoothly.

Sending an e-mail in Visual Basic .NET takes only a few lines of code, but getting those few lines to work takes a bit of background work. E-mail is sent using the SMTP services in Windows NT or 2000, and therefore this service must be installed and running on your server to send the mail. To add this service, open the Control Panel, the Add/Remove Programs section, and then the Windows Components section. Under Internet Information Services (IIS), you should find an entry named SMTP Service. Get this utility installed and running, and you'll be able to send e-mail from your PC using the .NET Framework.

Sending mail is done using two classes, the SMTPMail class and the MailMessage class, both of which are found in the System.web.Mail namespace. Following is the sample code that sends a test message:

```
Private Sub cbSend_Click(ByVal sender As System.Object,_
  ByVal e As System.EventArgs) Handles cbSend.Click

        Dim m As New MailMessage()

        lbStatus.Text = "Sending Message"
        Application.DoEvents()

        m.From = "nobody@somewhere.net"
        m.To = tbTo.Text
        m.Subject = tbSubject.Text
        m.Body = tbMessage.Text
        m.BodyFormat = MailFormat.Text

        Try
            Call SmtpMail.Send(m)
            lbStatus.Text = "Message Sent"
        Catch oEx As Exception
            lbStatus.Text = oEx.Message
        End Try

    End Sub
```

This code takes the mail recipient, the subject, and the body from textboxes found on the form in the following illustration, and sends off the mail message. The sender is the made-up address nobody@somewhere.net. I implemented some simple exception handling because, as I mentioned, my first attempts at sending e-mail were not successful (because I didn't have the SMTP service installed), and I wanted as much information as possible about why the e-mail wasn't being sent properly.

82   Message for You, Sir

 The message queue code can be found in the folder prjMessageQueues.

A few years back, Microsoft introduced message-queuing technology as part of their Microsoft Message Queue 1 product (called MSMQ for short). This product worked pretty well, assuming you could get the thing installed on your NT 4 client machines in order to use it. (Oh, the horror stories I could tell…)

Message queuing is a technology that allows a client machine to send asynchronous messages back to a server without needing to worry about the current connectivity state. The client application doesn't have to contact the server to check if it's up, establish a connection, or anything of that nature. In fact, the destination server in question need not even be up and running at the time the message is sent. The best analogy for message queuing is to think of it as *e-mail for code*. The client application can create an object instance, package it up in a message, and send it off. If the client is connected to the server and all is well, the message flows to the server at that time. If the client machine and server are currently not in contact (perhaps the client simply isn't dialed in), the object is stored in the client queue and shipped off automatically when connectivity is established.

The release of Windows 2000 made message queuing part of the operating system as a Windows NT service, so the installation woes of MSMQ version 1 pretty much vanished. Microsoft also removed the requirement that the client machine be attached to the message queue server when configuring the client service, which made client machine rollout a much simpler proposition. And now, with the advent of the .NET Framework, Microsoft has introduced some ready-made classes for taking advantage of this technology in your applications.

> **NOTE** The Message Queuing Service can be found under IIS Services in the Windows Components portion of Add/Remove Programs in your Control Panel. Make sure this service is running on your local development box or on a connected Windows Server before you take advantage of Message Queuing Services.

The sample program acts as both the sender and receiver, so you might have to study it for a minute or two to assure yourself that it is really two distinct processes communicating with each other. Let's see how to send things from a client perspective first.

Sending a Message

The most obvious data that you might want to send along in a message queue is a string. The code behind the Send String button in the application performs that task with under a dozen lines of code:

```
Private Sub cbSendString_Click(ByVal sender As _
System.Object, ByVal e As System.EventArgs) _
Handles cbSendString.Click

    Try
        Dim mq As MessageQueue = New MessageQueue(QUEUEPATH)
        mq.Formatter = New BinaryMessageFormatter()
        Call mq.Send(tbOut.Text, "StringMessage")
    Catch oEX As Exception
        MsgBox(oEX.Message)
    End Try
End Sub
```

First, a `MessageQueue` object instance is created, with the name of the queue as the parameter into its constructor. (A message queue server can communicate via any number of queues. These queues can be split up by application, type of message, or function.) The message is set to be a binary format by attaching a `BinaryFormatter` instance to the message. Then, the message is sent. The first parameter in this example is the contents of a `Textbox` control on the main form of the application, but the data type of this parameter can be any object instance. (Remember, simple strings are also inherited from `Object`.) The second parameter is known as the *label* of the message. This is equivalent of the subject of the e-mail, to further that analogy.

Sending a more complex object isn't much more difficult than sending a simple string. First, you need to make sure that the object you want to send is marked as `Serializable`, which is done using an attribute. The following code shows the beginning of a simple class definition with the `Serializable` attribute attached:

```
<Serializable()> _
Public Class PolygonDescriptor

    Private FNumSides As Integer
    Private FName As String

    Sub New()
        MyBase.New()
        FName = "Undefined"
        FNumSides = 0
    End Sub
    ...
End Class
```

Now that the class definition is marked as such, you can send it off in an MSMQ message, the same way a string was sent:

```
Private Sub cbSendObject_Click(ByVal sender As _
System.Object, ByVal e As System.EventArgs) _
Handles cbSendObject.Click

    Dim p As New PolygonDescriptor("Square", 2)

    Select Case iCtr Mod 3
        Case 0
            p.Name = "Triangle"
            p.NumSides = 3
        Case 1
            p.Name = "Rectangle"
            p.NumSides = 4
        Case Else
            p.Name = "Pentagon"
            p.NumSides = 5
    End Select
    iCtr += 1

    Try
        Dim mq As MessageQueue = _
        New MessageQueue(QUEUEPATH)
        mq.Formatter = New BinaryMessageFormatter()
```

```
        Call mq.Send(tbOut.Text, "StringMessage")
    Catch oEX As Exception
        MsgBox(oEX.Message)
    End Try
End Sub
```

The bottom of this procedure is identical to the string-sending code, with the exception of the send method. The first parameter is the object instance you're sending, and the second parameter is again the label. This implementation uses the label to determine what type of object the message contains.

The top of the procedure just sets up a simple iterative loop so that the object's properties are different each time you send an object into the queue (with three different variations on the object).

Get the Message (?)

You've got code to send the message; now you need to receive them on the server side. This is also done using the MessageQueue object:

```
If (Not MessageQueue.Exists(QUEUEPATH)) Then
    MessageQueue.Create(QUEUEPATH)
End If

oMSMQ = New MessageQueue(QUEUEPATH)
oMSMQ.Formatter = New BinaryMessageFormatter()

AddHandler oMSMQ.ReceiveCompleted, New _
ReceiveCompletedEventHandler(AddressOf _
ReceiveCompleted)
oMSMQ.BeginReceive()
```

The first part of this code checks to see if a queue exists and creates it if it does not. Note that both the test and queue creation is done using the static functions MessageQueue.Exists and MessageQueue.Create, as opposed to creating an instance of the MessageQueue class and then calling methods off the instance.

Now that the queue is set up, you can open it up and start looking for messages. This program uses a form-level variable named oMSMQ. This object is instantiated, the formatter is attached (make sure to use the same formatter class that the client programs are using), and then code is attached to the ReceiveCompleted event of this object using the AddHandler statement. This event fires whenever a message comes into the queue. Once that event is set up, the MessageQueue variable is instructed to start listening for messages using the BeginReceive method. All you need to see now is the contents of that `ReceiveCompleted` event so you know what the program does with the message when it receives it:

```
Protected Sub ReceiveCompleted(ByVal sender _
As Object, ByVal args _
As ReceiveCompletedEventArgs)

    Dim mq As MessageQueue = CType(sender, MessageQueue)
    mq.Formatter = New BinaryMessageFormatter()
    Dim m As System.Messaging.Message = _
    mq.EndReceive(args.AsyncResult)
    Dim p As PolygonDescriptor
    Dim cLine As String = Format(Now, "hh:mm:ss") & " - "

    Try
        If m.Label = "StringMessage" Then
            cLine = cLine & CStr(m.Body)
        Else
            p = CType(m.Body, PolygonDescriptor)
            cLine = cLine & p.ToString
        End If
        lbOutput.Items.Add(cLine)

    Catch oEX As Exception
        Call MsgBox(oEX.Message)
    Finally
        mq.BeginReceive()
    End Try
End Sub
```

First, the message queue is responsible for firing this event resolved to a local `Message-Queue` object, since it comes through as a parameter having the data type `Object`. Then, the `EndReceive` method is issued on the queue, which retrieves the actual message sent.

Next, the label of the message object (named simply `m` in the code) is checked to see if a string or `PolygonDescriptor` object was sent. (These are the only two things this program sends; your client app would have to be smarter if different objects were being passed in the queue.) Depending on what's being sent, the message is extracted from the body of the message and reported on using the `Listbox` on the form.

The last step is very important: The `BeginReceive` method is reissued inside a `Finally` block. This method must be reissued to make sure that the queue resumes looking for messages, no matter what happened while processing this current message. Without this call, further messages would never be extracted from the queue. Issuing the command inside a `Finally` block guarantees that it is called.

The following illustration shows the program after sending a few of each message type:

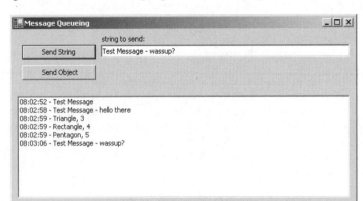

83   Application Transactions: A Big COM+

The COM+ code can be found in the folders prjComPlusServer and prjComPlusClient.

COM+ is a set of services that help you in writing multi-tier, distributed applications. These services provide much of the advanced functionality that people writing large-scale, distributed applications used to have to write on their own. Some of these services include object and thread pooling, advanced transaction support, and security.

As you would expect, the .NET Framework contains ample support for COM+ development. Much of this support is built directly into existing Framework classes, meaning that you get much of the functionality that COM+ provides simply by inheriting your business objects off of existing classes.

Transactions are a way to group a series of related programming tasks into a single unit. An often-used example is an ATM transaction. The act of withdrawing money from an account involves several sub-steps, such as checking the account for available balance, deducting the proper amount from the checking account balance, and dispensing the money. If any of these sub-steps fails (say, due to power failure), you do not want any of the other steps to succeed. You don't want the customer to receive money if you can't deduct the amount from his account. (The user probably wouldn't mind, though!) You wouldn't want to give the user funds if you can't check the available balance first.

Transactions are important enough that many of the computing tools you already use, such as Microsoft Message Queue and SQL Server, have them built in. However, you don't always have control over the data stores you need to interface with. You may need to read or write data from a legacy mainframe database system that may not have access to transaction support. You may also need to perform tasks *across* systems, so while both SQL Server and Message Queue have transactional support within them, there is no support in either one that allows it to control the other.

This is where COM+ transaction support comes in. You can easily write method calls that provide transaction support in several different ways. This functionality works hand in hand with the existing transaction support in products like SQL Server and Message Queue, and also provides the framework for writing transactional code for things like legacy databases. The code examples in the following sections demonstrate two types of COM+ transaction support available in the .NET Framework classes: automatic and manual transactions.

Automatic Transactions

A COM+ component is created simply by inheriting off of the ServicedComponent class. This class is found in the System.EnterpriseServices namespace, so you need to add a reference to this namespace before you can create a class of this type first, as follows:

```
Imports System.EnterpriseServices
Imports System.Data
Imports System.Data.SqlClient

<Transaction(TransactionOption.Required)> _
  Public Class CompPlusDemos
    Inherits ServicedComponent

    <AutoComplete()> Public Sub AutoTransaction()

    End Sub
```

This piece of code declares a class named CompPlusDemos and declares a method named AutoTransaction. Note the attributes in front of both the class and method declarations (the part within the angle brackets). The Transaction attribute in front of the class declaration tells COM+ what type of transaction support this class requires. (In this case, the class requires a transaction and will share an existing transaction if it is available.) The AutoComplete attribute in front of the AutoTransaction method sets up an implied transaction within that method. If the method executes with no exceptions, then the transaction is committed. If there is any exception in the method, then the code within the transaction (meaning all the code in the method) is rolled back.

To demonstrate the transaction code, I purposely wrote some code that would generate an exception within this method. It attempts to add the same primary key to the Region table in the Northwind database twice:

```
Const CONNECTIONSTRING As String = "DATABASE=Northwind;SERVER=localhost;UID=sa;
    ➥PWD=;"

        Dim aConn As New SqlConnection(CONNECTIONSTRING)
        Dim SQL As String

        Dim aSQL As New SqlCommand()
        With aSQL
            .Connection = aConn
            SQL = "insert into Region (RegionID, RegionDescription) "
            SQL &= " Values (5, 'Northwest')"
            .CommandText = SQL
            aConn.Open()
            Try
                .ExecuteNonQuery()
                .ExecuteNonQuery()
            Finally
                aConn.Close()
            End Try
        End With
```

Note the two ExecuteNonQuery lines in a row. This situation produces a database exception. Now, without transaction support on this method, the Regions table would have the first row inserted, and the second insert would fail because of the primary key error. Because of the COM+ transaction, however, the first insert is automatically rolled back because of the exception.

Remember, all this transaction handling is done by COM+, not by SQL Server. This becomes important when doing updates across multiple servers (where a transaction on one server cannot affect updates on another), or among disparate data sources that might not even have transaction support.

Manual Transactions

It's great to get all of this transaction handling for free, but it doesn't do much good when performing I/O against data sources that don't have transaction-handling capabilities. In this case, you have to roll your own transaction support. For example, you might have to perform an Insert in a legacy system database in the Try block of your method, and then run a Delete command in the exception handler should some other part of the method generate an exception.

When you desire more control over when you commit or roll back your COM+ transaction, you can use the ContextUtil object, as shown in the second example:

```
Public Sub ManualTransaction()

    Const CONNECTIONSTRING As String = "DATABASE=Northwind;SERVER=localhost;
        ➥UID=sa;PWD=;"

    Dim aConn As New SqlConnection(CONNECTIONSTRING)
    Dim SQL As String

    Dim aSQL As New SqlCommand()
    With aSQL
        .Connection = aConn
        SQL = "insert into Region (RegionID, RegionDescription) "
        SQL &= " Values (5, 'Northwest')"
        .CommandText = SQL
        aConn.Open()
        Try
            .ExecuteNonQuery()
            .ExecuteNonQuery()
            ContextUtil.SetComplete()
        Catch oEX As Exception
            ContextUtil.SetAbort()
        Finally
            aConn.Close()
        End Try
    End With

End Sub
```

This method performs the same exception-forcing double database update as the previous example. However, the AutoComplete attribute is not placed on the method call. Instead, the transaction is committed or aborted manually using the ContextUtil.SetComplete or SetAbort methods, within the exception block.

Writing the COM+ Client

Writing a client application that uses your COM+ class library is done exactly as you would use any other class library, with one exception that I found. I was getting some strange design-time errors the first time I attempted to write a .NET client that used my COM+ component. I ended up resolving the problem by including a reference to the System .EnterpriseServices namespace in my client project. This is the same namespace you need to reference in your COM+ component project. Once I figured this little problem out, I was able to access my COM+ component easily and get all the great transaction support.

The following example client program calls both the automatic and manual transaction methods, and displays the generated exception text in the box. Because the entire method is wrapped in a transaction, none of the database inserts should succeed, and your Northwind Regions table should remain unchanged.

84   Remoting Control

 The remoting code can be found in the folder `prjRemotingServer`.

The computing universe is ever expanding, and your programs are expected to communicate over ever-widening boundaries. Point-of-sale systems are expected to be able to send data to the home office retail system and retrieve information on an ad hoc basis from that same system. Never mind if the home office and the retail outlet are in different cities, states, or countries. A remote sales force requires instant access to up-to-the-second inventory information. If the company just filled a order this morning and emptied the warehouse out of a hot item, the remote salesman needs to know.

Remoting is a term used to describe .NET Framework objects talking to each other across application domains. The two domains might be on the same computer or on computers with an ocean or two between them.

Developing applications using remoting concepts in the .NET Framework can be very powerful. Your all-important business logic can be coded into objects that stay close to home and in a single place and that require remote users to access from their own location. Changes or new functionality to these classes don't require distribution of new code to the entire remote force (a pretty daunting task for a 250-store retail chain or a sales force of 100+).

A remoting framework requires three parts: a server-based class, a server-based "listener" program to wait for requests, and a client program to request instances of the server class. This section will demonstrate the two server-side components.

The Server Class

The server class that will be used to create remote instances from a client has but one requirement: It should be a descendant of the MarshalByRefObject class. This class uses the Northwind database to report on the total amount spent by a customer, given the customer ID:

```
Imports System
Imports System.IO
Imports System.Data
Imports System.Data.SqlClient

Public Class OrderServantClass
    Inherits MarshalByRefObject

    Const CONNECTIONSTRING As String = _
    DATABASE=Northwind;SERVER=localhost;UID=sa;PWD=;"

    Public Function Test() As Integer
        Return 41
    End Function

    Public Function GetCustSpentAmount _
    (ByVal cCustID As String) As Single

        Dim SQL as String
        SQL = " SELECT ISNULL(SUM(ExtendedPrice),0) "
        SQL = SQL & " as TotalSpent "
        SQL = SQL & "FROM [Order Details Extended] OD "
        SQL = SQL & "INNER JOIN Orders O ON "
        SQL = SQL & "O.OrderID = OD.OrderID "
        SQL = SQL & "WHERE O.CustomerID = '" & cCustID & "'"

        Dim oConn As New SqlConnection(CONNECTIONSTRING)
        Dim oCmd As New SqlCommand(SQL, oConn)
        oCmd.CommandType = CommandType.Text

        Dim iSpent As Single = 0
        Dim oRD As SqlDataReader
```

```
        oConn.Open()
        Try
            oRD = _
            oCmd.ExecuteReader(CommandBehavior.CloseConnection)
            If oRD.Read() Then
                iSpent = oRD.Item("TotalSpent")
            End If
        Finally
            oRD.Close()
        End Try

        Return iSpent

    End Function

End Class
```

This class should look no different than any other VB .NET class you've seen so far, except for it being a descendant of the `MarshalByRefObject` class. The `Test` method is used purely as a debugging placeholder—it provides something to call that returns a given value when making sure that the remoting itself is working, rather than trying to track down a bug in the larger functions. The real function, `GetCustSpentAmount`, takes the passed-in customer ID and runs it up against a view in the Northwind database to see how much that customer spent. Exception handling is used to make sure the remote object doesn't behave poorly for the client application in the case of an error.

This object is compiled into its own assembly named `OrderServant.DLL`. Now that you have an object ready to be called remotely, you need a simple "listener" program to load up that class and prepare it to receive requests.

Listen Up!

The purpose of the listener program is to register the server class on either an HTTP channel or a TCP channel. This listener program in the following class uses an HTTP channel for purposes you'll learn about later:

```
Imports System
Imports System.IO
Imports System.Runtime.Remoting
Imports System.Runtime.Remoting.Channels
Imports System.Runtime.Remoting.Channels.Http
Imports OrderServant

Class OrderServerClass

    Shared Sub Main()

        Const PORT As Integer = 5001
        Const URI As String = "Orders"
```

```
ChannelServices.RegisterChannel(New HttpChannel(PORT))

Dim oAsm As System.Reflection.Assembly
Dim oTyp As Type
Dim cMsg As String

oAsm = System.Reflection.Assembly.Load("OrderServant")
oTyp = oAsm.GetType("OrderServant.OrderServantClass")

RemotingConfiguration.RegisterWellKnownServiceType( _
  oTyp, URI, WellKnownObjectMode.SingleCall)

System.Console.WriteLine("")
System.Console.WriteLine("")
cMsg = "server '" & URI
cMsg = cMsg & "' active on port " & PORT
cMsg = cMsg & Environment.NewLine
cMsg = cMsg & "to test in browser: "
cMsg = cMsg & "http://localhost:" & PORT
cMsg = cMsg & "/" & URI & "?WSDL" & Environment.NewLine
cMsg = cMsg & "hit <enter> to stop"
System.Console.WriteLine(cMsg)
System.Console.ReadLine()

    End Sub

End Class
```

The channel you choose (5001 in this example) needs to be known by clients designed to use the remote object. This channel is registered in the first line of the listener program. Then the server class that is to serve as the remoting object is registered using the `Register-WellKnownServiceType` method. This method takes the type of the class as its first parameter. (The type of a class can be described using a class itself. This class is called `Type` and is part of the reflection abilities of the .NET Framework.) The second parameter is the name that the class will be known as by clients. In this case, the more common name `Orders` is used instead of the actual name of the class, `OrderServantClass`. The third parameter specifies that each object created from the clients will be a distinct object (`SingleCall`), rather than each client call sharing a single, global object instance (`Singleton`). The latter type of remoting might be useful when objects have to share amongst themselves and the remote object is brokering that object sharing.

Running the previous listener program gives the following results:

```
server 'Orders' active on port 5001
to test in browser: http://localhost:5001/Orders?WSDL
hit <enter> to stop
```

The URL displayed here can be entered into your favorite browser to test if the server is working. The results you see in the browser represent the WSDL (Web Services Description Language) of the remote class. The WSDL is an XML description that describes the class, as you can see here:

```
<?xml version="1.0" encoding="UTF-8" ?>
- <definitions name="OrderServantClass" targetNamespace=
  "http://schemas.microsoft.com/clr/nsassem/OrderServant/
  OrderServant" xmlns="http://schemas.xmlsoap.org/wsdl/"
   xmlns:tns="http://schemas.xmlsoap.org/wsdl/"
   xmlns:xsd="http://www.w3.org/2001/XMLSchema"
   xmlns:xsi="http://www.w3.org/2001/XMLSchema-instance"
   xmlns:suds="http://www.w3.org/2000/wsdl/suds"
   xmlns:wsdl="http://schemas.xmlsoap.org/wsdl/"
   xmlns:soapenc="http://schemas.xmlsoap.org/soap/encoding/"
   xmlns:ns2="http://schemas.microsoft.com/clr/nsassem/
   OrderServant.OrderServantClass/OrderServant"
   xmlns:ns0="http://schemas.microsoft.com/clr/nsassem/
   OrderServant/OrderServant"
   xmlns:ns1="http://schemas.microsoft.com/clr/ns/System"
   xmlns:soap="http://schemas.xmlsoap.org/wsdl/soap/">
 - <types>
   <schema targetNamespace="http://schemas.microsoft.com/
   clr/nsassem/OrderServant/OrderServant"
   xmlns="http://www.w3.org/2001/XMLSchema"
   elementFormDefault="unqualified" attributeFormDefault
   ="unqualified" />
   </types>
   <message name="OrderServantClass.TestInput" />
 - <message name="OrderServantClass.TestOutput">
   <part name="return" type="xsd:int" />
   </message>
 - <message name="OrderServantClass.GetCustSpentAmountInput">
   <part name="cCustID" type="xsd:string" />
   </message>
 - <message name="OrderServantClass.GetCustSpentAmountOutput">
   <part name="return" type="xsd:float" />
   </message>
 - <portType name="OrderServantClassPortType">
 - <operation name="Test">
   <input name="TestRequest"

     message="ns0:OrderServantClass.TestInput" />
   <output name="TestResponse"
   message="ns0:OrderServantClass.TestOutput" />
   </operation>
 - <operation name="GetCustSpentAmount">
```

```
<input name="GetCustSpentAmountRequest"
message="ns0:OrderServantClass.GetCustSpentAmountInput" />
<output name="GetCustSpentAmountResponse"
message="ns0:OrderServantClass.GetCustSpentAmountOutput" />
</operation>
</portType>
- <binding name="OrderServantClassBinding"
type="ns0:OrderServantClassPortType">
<soap:binding style="rpc"
transport="http://schemas.xmlsoap.org/soap/http" />
<suds:class type="ns0:OrderServantClass"
rootType="MarshalByRefObject" />
- <operation name="Test">
<soap:operation soapAction=
"http://schemas.microsoft.com/clr/nsassem/
OrderServant.OrderServantClass/OrderServant#Test" />
- <input name="TestRequest">
<soap:body use="encoded"
encodingStyle="http://schemas.xmlsoap.org/soap/encoding/"
namespace="http://schemas.microsoft.com/clr/nsassem/
OrderServant.OrderServantClass/OrderServant" />
</input>
- <output name="TestResponse">
<soap:body use="encoded"
encodingStyle="http://schemas.xmlsoap.org/soap/encoding/"
namespace="http://schemas.microsoft.com/clr/nsassem/
OrderServant.OrderServantClass/OrderServant" />
</output>
</operation>
- <operation name="GetCustSpentAmount">
<soap:operation soapAction=
"http://schemas.microsoft.com/clr/nsassem/
OrderServant.OrderServantClass/
OrderServant#GetCustSpentAmount" />
- <input name="GetCustSpentAmountRequest">
<soap:body use="encoded"
encodingStyle="http://schemas.xmlsoap.org/soap/encoding/"
namespace="http://schemas.microsoft.com/clr/nsassem/
OrderServant.OrderServantClass/OrderServant" />
</input>
- <output name="GetCustSpentAmountResponse">
<soap:body use="encoded"
encodingStyle="http://schemas.xmlsoap.org/soap/encoding/"
namespace="http://schemas.microsoft.com/clr/nsassem/
OrderServant.OrderServantClass/OrderServant" />
</output>
</operation>
```

```
        </binding>
-   <service name="OrderServantClassService">
-   <port name="OrderServantClassPort"
      binding="ns0:OrderServantClassBinding">

      <soap:address location=
      "http://24.51.177.153:5001/Orders" />
      </port>
      </service>
      </definitions>
```

When beginning with remoting, I recommend using the HTTP protocol to test out your objects because you can test the communication in a browser as just shown. You can't perform a test like this when using the TCP protocol. However, once you're confident in the new technology, you might consider switching to the binary (and therefore faster) TCP protocol.

Now that you've got a remote class and a listener, you're ready to write a client that calls it.

85 Remoting Control Calling

 The remoting client code accompanying this section can be found in the folder prjRemotingClient.

To write a client application that calls your remote object, you can test the client application on the same PC or on a different PC that has connectivity to the server PC. Setting up the remoting call and using the remote object instance is done as follows:

```
Imports System
Imports System.Runtime.Remoting
Imports System.Runtime.Remoting.Channels
Imports System.Runtime.Remoting.Channels.http
Imports OrderServant

Public Class OrderClient

    Shared Sub Main()

        ChannelServices.RegisterChannel(New HttpChannel())

        Dim oObj As OrderServantClass

        Dim oAsm As System.Reflection.Assembly
        Dim oTyp As Type
        Dim cMsg As String
```

```
oAsm = System.Reflection.Assembly.Load("OrderServant")
oTyp = oAsm.GetType("OrderServant.OrderServantClass")

oObj = CType(Activator.GetObject(oTyp, _
"http://localhost:5001/Orders"), _
OrderServantClass)

If oObj Is Nothing Then
    System.Console.WriteLine("Could not locate server")
Else
    Dim cCust As String
    Dim iSpent As Single

    Console.WriteLine("")
    Console.Write("Enter a valid Customer ID: ")
    cCust = Console.ReadLine()

Try
        iSpent = oObj.GetCustSpentAmount(cCust)
        If iSpent = 0 Then
            Console.WriteLine("customer " & _
            "ID invalid or spent $0.00")
        Else
            Console.WriteLine("customer spent $" & _
            iSpent)
        End If
    Catch oEX As Exception
        Console.WriteLine(oEX.Message)
    End Try
    Console.WriteLine("")
    Console.WriteLine("")
End If
Console.WriteLine("hit enter key to end")
Console.ReadLine()

End Sub

End Class
```

The critical call in the client program is the `Activator.GetObject` call. This object creates an instance of the remote object using the port and URL defined by the listener application and then typecasts that object to the appropriate type for use in this application.

Remoting is a large topic that can warrant an entire book in its own right. There are many design issues to consider, such as what type of connection the end user might have to the remote server or how much data will be sent back and forth. A remoting solution won't work in cases where a network or Internet connection is not 100 percent available. (How can the client create the remote object instance without a connection to the server?) Do you want your application to "hang" while it instantiates the remote object, or is there something it can do in the meantime? All of these design issues will influence the design of your application and whether remoting is the correct solution in your environment.

86 Web Service Creation

 The web service code can be found in the folder prjWebService.

Remoting represents one way for client applications to access components on remote servers. This method of object invocation is powerful and easy to use, but it is not open-ended. Only .NET clients can invoke .NET remote objects. Microsoft was looking to provide a means of remote object invocation using standard Internet protocols like HTTP and XML, as well as a means of creating objects from any source. This was the idea that gave rise to web services.

Web services are defined strictly in terms of the functions that communicate with the outside world. In that respect, they are not "complete" objects like regular .NET objects; you don't create web services with properties or events. Instead, the set of methods exposed by the object defines the web service.

To demonstrate that most .NET Framework classes can be exposed as a web service, I decided to take the same server class used in the remoting examples and modify the classes for use as a web service. Here is part of the code to describe the new server class:

```
Imports System
Imports System.IO
Imports System.Data
Imports System.Data.SqlClient
Imports System.Web.Services

Public Class OrderServantClass
    Inherits MarshalByRefObject

    <WebMethod()> _
    Public Function Test() As Integer
        Return 41
    End Function

    <WebMethod()> _
        Public Function GetCustSpentAmount(ByVal cCustID _
        As String) As Single

<stuff deleted>

        Return iSpent
```

```
    End Function

  End Class
```

I removed much of the guts of the `GetCustSpentAmount` method so you can focus on the details of setting up the web service itself. After some study, you'll discover that the only difference between this object and the remoting server is the addition of the `WebMethod` attribute at the start of each of the methods. This attribute tells the .NET Framework to expose this method as part of the web service.

Could that be it? In short, yes. You use the VB .NET you already know to create the class and then signify which methods make up the web service with the `WebMethod` attribute. Time for testing.

Testing, Testing...

To test your web service, create a new application in IIS. Take your compiled DLL and place it into a BIN folder underneath the IIS application virtual directory. Then, create a file named `orders.asmx` that contains the following line of text:

```
<%@ WebService Class="OrderServant.OrderServantClass" %>
```

The name in the quotes should match the `assemblyname.classname` of the .NET class created in the previous step. (The assembly is the DLL name, and the class name is just that: the name of the class created.) The actual name of the .asmx file can be anything; you just need to know it when you want to test or use the web service.

Now the service is all configured, so you can go to your browser and type the following URL to test it all out:

```
http://localhost/prjwebservice/orders.asmx
```

The `prjwebservice` component of the URL is the virtual directory that was created in IIS, and the `orders.asmx` component is the name of the file that was just created. If all is working correctly, you should see something resembling the following description:

Note how the two web methods defined in the `OrderServantClass` class have been exposed in this sample web page. Clicking each method in the browser allows you to enter any necessary parameters and test the functionality of the web service, all without the need to set up a client application before testing. This allows a great division of labor. The web service component developers don't have to mess around with writing client code to test their services, and the client developers can see an exact description of the available services by typing the URL.

Note that all of this fancy DLL-to-browser communication is happening via XML over standard HTTP on plain old HTTP port 80. The object is described using an XML specification named SOAP, which you can see if you add `?WSDL` to the end of the URL in the browser. Because the communication is happening over standard HTTP port 80, communications problems due to pesky firewalls are eliminated. As long as your client can see your server over a standard Internet connection, web services are a viable way to have the two communicate.

87   Web Service Usage

 The web service client code can be found in the folder `prjWebServiceClient`.

Microsoft's vision of the future is that every online business and programmer will want to expose business functionality via the Internet and web services. If this is true, your client applications will link to and use all of these web services all over the world. The remote salesman with a laptop may dial up, check inventory levels using a web service you wrote, enter the order using another web service, look up an address using a U.S. Postal Service web service, and then check shipping schedules and rates using yet another web service provided by UPS.

If all this comes true, we client-side developers will have to become experts in linking to and consuming web services, both our own and those from third parties. Fortunately for us, doing so couldn't have been made any easier.

To add a web service to your current project, go to the Solution Explorer and right-click the Web References item in the `Treeview`. Select Add Web Reference. A dialog box appears that allows you to enter a URL. Simply add the exact URL that you entered to test the web service in the previous step. The lower half of the dialog box displays the same browser output you saw when testing your service. If all looks well, click Add Reference, and the web service is ready for use.

Here is the code for a simple client to consume the customer order totals web service:

```
Imports System
Imports prjWebServiceClient.localhost

Public Class WebServiceClient
```

```
Public Shared Sub Main()

    Dim cCust As String
    Dim iSpent As Single
    Dim oObj As OrderServantClass

    Console.WriteLine("")
    Console.Write("Enter a valid Customer ID: ")
    cCust = Console.ReadLine()

    oObj = New OrderServantClass()
    iSpent = oObj.GetCustSpentAmount(cCust)
    If iSpent = 0 Then
        Console.WriteLine("customer ID " & _
        "invalid or spent $0.00")
    Else
        Console.WriteLine("customer spent $" & iSpent)
    End If
    Console.WriteLine("")
    Console.WriteLine("")
    Console.WriteLine("hit enter key to end")
    Console.ReadLine()
End Sub


    End Class
```

Note that this code can declare a variable of the `OrderServantClass` class directly, because the SOAP description of the service tells your application that this class (and all of its methods) are part of that service. In order to most easily use this class, the `Imports` section at the top of the project includes a reference to the `projectname.referencename` displayed in the Solution Explorer.

Once all the linkage is done, the `OrderServantClass` can be used as easily as a class built right into our application.

88   Talking to Microsoft TerraServer

 The TerraService code can be found in the folder `prjTerraService`.

One of the largest parts of the Microsoft vision of the future, and therefore a big part of the .NET initiative, is the concept of the *web service*. The web service is a piece of code that does its job over the Internet. This job can be anything from calculating a monetary exchange rate or returning a credit history or package status to locating and/or retrieving files.

In this new vision, Internet access is built into almost every program, not just programs that use the browser as the interface. Regular desktop programs will call upon code across the world via the Internet to provide their functionality as well.

An early example of a program that follows this new programming model is Gnutella. This program attaches via the Internet to other Gnutella users and provides a list of shared files on all of those users' hard drives. These files can be MP3s (which makes Metallica, et al. nervous), pictures, or any file deemed sharable by a group of people. These types of programs provide all the power of the vast world-encompassing network that the Internet has become, but not at the expense of the slimmed-down, wizard-like simplicity of a browser-based application.

As a programmer in this new world, Microsoft hopes that you'll all play nice with their new toys and share. If you write a useful piece of code from which other programmers would benefit, you can use the .NET technology to expose that code as a web service. Once installed as such, other programmers can call your code over the Internet, have it do its job, and return information back to the caller.

Accessing a Web Service

Web services use the common framework of XML to send the required information back and forth across the .NET. However, you don't need to be an XML expert to call an existing web service. In fact, you may write an entire application that talks to a web service and not know that XML was involved at all.

One of the first interesting, nontrivial web services to spring up is the .NET version of Microsoft TerraServer, which is a huge database of aerial and satellite images of the earth, stored in a SQL Server database and available online.

The first glimpses into the vast quantity of TerraServer information came via the browser-based interfaces at www.terraserver.com. You could use the supplied programs to look at a map by latitude/longitude, famous place name, city name, or several other interfaces.

Close to the time that Visual Studio .NET beta 1 was released, a .NET-programmed web service version of TerraServer was announced, called the TerraService. This exposes the enormous collection of TerraServer data to the programmer. After licking my chops for a few seconds, I decided to dive in and try to grab some data for my own little program: a TerraServer ballpark viewer.

To use a web service in your program, you need to know its URL. The file extension at the end of the URL is always .asmx. To add the web service to your project, go into the Solution Explorer and right-click the Web References line in the Treeview. The first menu option is Add Web Reference. Selecting this option brings up the following dialog box.

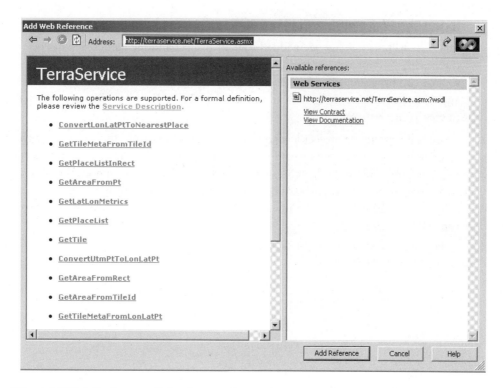

The Add Web Reference dialog box works just like a mini-web browser application. In the Address field at the top of the dialog box, enter the web service URL (the one that ends in .asmx). This begins the communication process between Visual Studio .NET and the web service. If the communication works properly, the large box on the left side of the dialog box will be populated with the interfaces available to you as the user of this web service. Once everything appears to be working, simply click the Add Reference button on the dialog box and the connection has been made.

At this point, you might want to rename the web reference in the Solution Explorer to match your own naming scheme. I decided to leave my name as it was defined: net.terraservice. The name you select for the service is important in the next step.

To expose all of the classes described by the web reference, you should also include the full namespace of the web reference in the Imports section of your main form. The full namespace is the project name of the current project, a period, and then the web reference name you used in the previous step. The Imports section of my project is as follows:

```
Imports System.IO
Imports System.Drawing.Imaging
Imports prjNewTerraservice.net.TerraService
```

Using the Web Service Classes

Once the web service has been added to your project and the namespace has been added to the `Imports` section of your main form, Visual Studio .NET has all the information it needs to help you program using the new web service classes. The information for these classes will appear in Intellisense along with all of the other .NET Framework classes you have exposed to your project.

My ballpark viewer project leverages the fact that Microsoft TerraServer has thousands of "famous places" stored in it by name and the ability to display the geographic region surrounding that famous place. I selected a dozen baseball ballparks throughout the Major Leagues and included their names in a `Listbox` on the left side of the form. Once the user selects one of the ballparks and hits the View button, the display routine kicks in. That routine is reproduced here:

```
Protected Sub CreatBitmapBasedOnPlaceName(ByVal _
cPlaceName As String)

    Const IWIDTH As Integer = 600
    Const IHEIGHT As Integer = 400

    Dim theme As Theme = New Theme()
    Dim scale As Scale = New Scale()
    Dim ts As TerraService
    Dim abb As AreaBoundingBox
    Dim iImage As Image
    Dim pfs() As PlaceFacts

    Me.Cursor = Cursors.WaitCursor
    lbWait.text = "retrieving image data"
    application.DoEvents()

    Try
        ts = New TerraService()
        pfs = ts.GetPlaceList(cPlaceName, 1, False)
        If pfs.Length = 0 Then Exit Sub

        If rbAerial.Checked Then
            theme = Theme.Photo
        Else
            theme = Theme.Topo
        End If

        scale = Scale.Scale2m
```

```
        abb = ts.GetAreaFromPt(pfs(0).center, _
        theme, scale, IWIDTH, IHEIGHT)

        Dim pf As PixelFormat = PixelFormat.Format32bppRGB
        Dim compositeImage As Image = _
        New Bitmap(IWIDTH, IHEIGHT, pf)

        Dim compositeGraphics As Graphics = _
        Graphics.FromImage(compositeImage)

        Dim xStart As Integer = abb.NorthWest.TileMeta.Id.X
        Dim yStart As Integer = abb.NorthWest.TileMeta.Id.Y
        Dim x, y As Integer

        For x = xstart To abb.NorthEast.TileMeta.Id.X
            For y = ystart _
            To abb.SouthWest.TileMeta.Id.Y Step -1

            Dim tid As TileId
            Dim tileimage As Image

            tid = abb.NorthWest.TileMeta.Id
            tid.X = x
            tid.Y = y
                tileImage = Image.FromStream(New _
                MemoryStream(ts.GetTile(tid)))
                    compositeGraphics.DrawImage(tileImage, _
                (x - xStart) * tileImage.Width - _
                abb.NorthWest.Offset.xOffset, _
                (yStart - y) * tileImage.Height - _
                abb.NorthWest.Offset.yOffset, _
                tileImage.Width, tileImage.Height)
        Next
        Next

        Compositeimage.Save(DUMMYNAME, imageformat.BMP)
    Finally
        Me.Cursor = Cursors.Arrow
        lbWait.text = ""
    End Try
End Sub
```

The name of the famous place to display is passed in as the sole parameter. The first statement after the `Try` statement initializes the `TerraService` class. This is the "main" class in the web service, and you must create an instance of it to use any TerraServer functionality in your project. The second line after the `Try` statement retrieves what's known as a `PlaceFacts` object, based on the passed-in place (ballpark) name. The `PlaceFacts` class is a `Collection` class that contains within it some number of `PlaceFact` classes. The `GetPlaceList` method allows you to specify the maximum number of `PlaceFact` objects to return in the collection.

NOTE   Places like Cleveland or Los Angeles can have thousands of `PlaceFact` objects associated with them in TerraServer. My program chooses to return only one `PlaceFact` object, since I know that each ballpark is at the most granular level of place data in TerraServer.

Working with the Graphics

The hardest part about working with TerraServer image data is that it is returned in 200×200 pixel tiles. Usually, a single tile does not display enough visual information by itself to be useful to an end user, so the programmer will almost always have to "stitch together" several adjacent tiles to display a map with meaningful value.

The stitching process in the previous procedure takes up most of the routine. My final output picture is 600×400, or three tiles across by two down. I have set up constants at the top of the routine to specify this image size—the final routine can be changed to output different size pictures by changing these constants.

The next important TerraServer-related line in the routine is the following:

```
abb = ts.GetAreaFromPt(pfs(0).center, _
theme, scale, IWIDTH, IHEIGHT)
```

This line passes in the `PlaceFact` object received about the ballpark, along with the intended width and height of the final image, and returns another structure known as an `AreaBoundingBox` structure. This structure contains the four geographic corner coordinates, as well as the center, of the `PlaceFact` that is passed to it. You now have enough info to begin stitching the final image together. The next three lines set up the destination bitmap in memory:

```
Dim pf As PixelFormat = PixelFormat.Format32bppRGB
Dim compositeImage As Image = _
New Bitmap(IWIDTH, IHEIGHT, pf)

Dim compositeGraphics As Graphics = _
Graphics.FromImage(compositeImage)
```

The object that you are going to draw into is an instance of the `Graphics` class. This class is the encapsulation of a GDI+ drawing surface. You set up a `Graphics` instance from a `Bitmap` instance. The `Bitmap` instance is created by specifying the intended height and width, as well as a `PixelFormat` (number of colors in the bitmap).

Finally, the stitching loop begins (shown in the next code example). Actually, there are two loops, one inside the other. Both loops begin in the northwest corner of our map. The x loop travels east, and the y loop travels south. For each tile, the GetTile method is called off the TerraService object instance. The tile image data is loaded into a MemoryStream instance and in turn into an Image instance. Finally, this single image is drawn into the compositeGraphics instance. Some reasonably tricky math has to be done to turn the coordinates of the tile into the bitmap coordinates that you draw into:

```
For x = xstart To abb.NorthEast.TileMeta.Id.X
    For y = ystart To abb.SouthWest.TileMeta.Id.Y Step -1

        Dim tid As TileId
        Dim tileimage As Image

        tid = abb.NorthWest.TileMeta.Id
        tid.X = x
        tid.Y = y
        tileImage = Image.FromStream(New _
        MemoryStream(ts.GetTile(tid)))

        compositeGraphics.DrawImage(tileImage, _
        (x - xStart) * tileImage.Width - _
        abb.NorthWest.Offset.xOffset, _
        (yStart - y) * tileImage.Height - _
        abb.NorthWest.Offset.yOffset, _
        tileImage.Width, tileImage.Height)
    Next
Next
```

Once the loop is complete, the compositeGraphics instance contains the completed image.

The next step is to save this image to disk as a BMP file so you can load it into the form:

```
Compositeimage.Save(DUMMYNAME, imageformat.BMP)
```

The constant DUMMYNAME is a temporary filename that I used just for the life of this application. The routine to load the BMP file into the PictureBox.pbImage is fairly simple:

```
Public Sub LoadAndDeleteTheDiskFile()

    Dim f As file
    Dim s As New FileStream(DUMMYNAME, FileMode.Open)

    pbImage.Image = system.Drawing.image.FromStream(s)
    s.Close()

    Try
        f = New File(DUMMYNAME)
```

```
        f.delete()
    Catch ert As Exception
        msgbox(ert.Message)
    End Try

  End Sub
```

This code loads the BMP file into a `FileStream` object, and the `pbImage` object uses a method known as `FromStream` to copy that stream data into itself for display, which can be seen in the following illustration. The dummy file is then deleted. I wrapped the file delete routine around a simple `Try…Except` block because my first pass at this program was written in VB .NET beta 1, and I had uncovered a small bug in the language that prevented the file from being deleted in all cases. I decided to leave the handler in for the final version, because it helps warn the user if the program is going to leave the dummy bitmap file on disk.

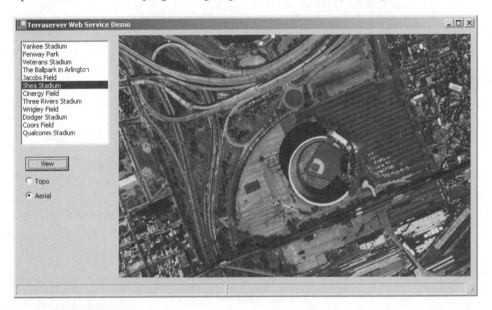

89 More Web Services

 The additional web services examples can be found in the folder `prjMoreWebServices`.

Microsoft envisions that XML web services will be as important to the future of programming as ActiveX controls (and their precursors, like VBX controls) were to the earlier versions of Visual Basic. In those days, third-party developers would create new functionality and sell it as a library that other developers could purchase and use. XML web services provide the same type of functionality, but in a more modern, distributed development environment that uses the Internet as a means of communication.

Part of the fun in these early days of the web service will be learning about all the new web services that are available to us. As the .NET tools become more and more mature, web services are becoming more and more prevalent. This section describes a few of the useful web services I found, and two ways for you to locate web services.

I did? No, UDDI!

The Universal Description, Discovery, and Integration Service, affectionately known as UDDI, is a web service that serves as a directory of other web services. There is an implementation of UDDI on the Add Web Reference dialog box in Visual Studio .NET, as you can see in the following illustration:

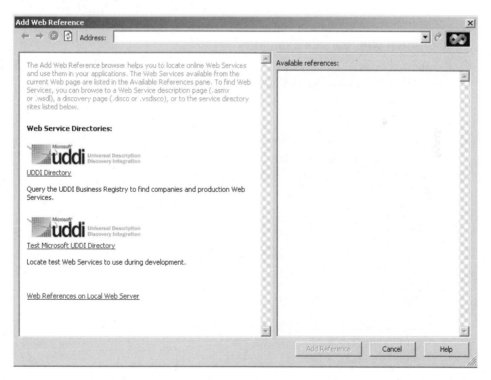

From this dialog box, you need to know the company name that supplies the web services you want to find (or at least the starting characters of the company name). For example, if you type **Microsoft** into the search box, you'll find web services that Microsoft provides (like the UDDI service itself).

The UDDI service is in its infancy, but it's a good start for locating web services.

SalCentral.com

One web site is billing itself as "The Napster of Web Services," a description that might not be too far off. The site is http://www.salcentral.com, which attempts to serve as "The world's largest brokerage for schemas, reviews and quality assurance information on web services." SalCentral provides both a "latest" list of new web services and a "most popular" list right on their home page. SalCentral also contains a keyword text search through their entire catalog. Thus, if you are looking for a web service that provides credit card authorization, you can easily find it by typing **credit** into the search engine. A representative of SalCentral also let me know that they will interface to the UDDI service in the near future.

Additional Web Service Examples

Using somebody else's web service is so fun at first, I decided to interface to a few of the web services I found on the SalCentral website, just as a reminder of how powerful the web services concept will be in the future.

The first web service to which I linked returns sales rank and price information from Amazon and/or Barnes and Noble's websites. You can see the simple user interface I whipped up to present rank and price information from Amazon. I filled a list box with the ISBN and title of three books I knew of (wink, wink), and then called the service from a button-click with the following code:

```
Private Sub cbGet_Click(ByVal sender As System.Object, _
ByVal e As System.EventArgs) Handles cbGet.Click

    Dim b As New SalesRankNPrice()
    Dim r As SalesRankNPrice1

    Me.Cursor = Cursors.WaitCursor

    r = b.GetAmazonSalesRankNPrice(lbBooks.SelectedValue)
    lbPrice.Text = "Price: " & r.Price
    lbRank.Text = "Rank: " & r.SalesRank

    Me.Cursor = Cursors.Default
End Sub
```

The interface to the service is a single method call. It returns a structure known as a `SalesRankNPrice1`. This structure contains the current Amazon sales rank and price for the passed-in ISBN. Here's the output of the program:

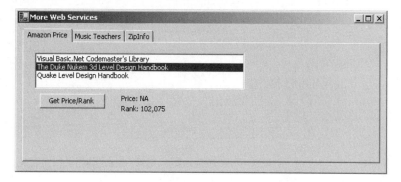

The second web service returns information about local music teachers in an area. You pass in a zip code and some optional information such as the desired skill level of the teacher and the instrument taught, and the web service returns a `DataSet` of available music teachers around that zip code. Here's the code that sets up the call to that web service:

```
Private Sub cbGetTeacher_Click(ByVal sender As System.Object, _
    ByVal e As System.EventArgs) Handles cbGetTeacher.Click

    Dim oDS As New DataSet()
    Dim cXML As String
    Dim oRead As StringReader
    Dim o As New wsMusicTeachers.SearchMusicTeachers()

    Me.Cursor = Cursors.WaitCursor
    cXML = o.FindMusicTeachers2(tbMusicZip.Text, "0", "0", "0", "0", "-1")

    oRead = New StringReader(cXML)
    oDS.ReadXml(oRead)
    dgMusic.DataSource = oDS
    dgMusic.NavigateTo(0, "Details")

    Me.Cursor = Cursors.Default
End Sub
```

NOTE   At press time, the music teacher web service was written in a beta version of .NET, and in working with the author, I discovered an incompatibility with the `DataSet` that was returned. The author of the service, Darshan Singh, whipped up a new method that returned the same data as straight XML, and left it up to the caller to import that data into a `DataSet`. The preceding code performs this conversion.

You can see some test results of the music teachers service in the following illustration:

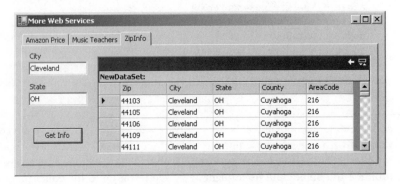

Finally, I discovered a nifty little zip code web service that returns a list of zip codes found within the passed-in city and state. The code is as follows:

```
Private Sub cbGetZip_Click(ByVal sender As System.Object, _
        ByVal e As System.EventArgs) Handles cbGetZip.Click

        Dim oDS As DataSet
        Dim o As New wsZipInfo.ZipCodes()

        Me.Cursor = Cursors.WaitCursor
        oDS = o.rtnZipDS(tbCity.Text, tbState.Text)
        dgZip.DataSource = oDS
        dgZip.NavigateTo(0, "ZIPDATA")

        Me.Cursor = Cursors.Default
    End Sub
End Class
```

You can see the output from this web service in the following illustration:

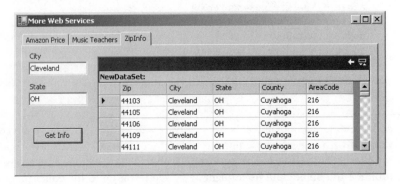

The code that calls all of the services described in this section borders on trivial, and of course that's the fun and power of the whole XML web services concept. What you're doing is finding a fellow programmer who has done some of the work of your own project for you, and VB .NET provides the glue to trivially link his code into your project.

90   Getting Mobile

 The mobile code can be found in the folder `prjMobile`.

Good developers are often victims of their own success. Say you write the killer app that your company has been pining over for years. You save hours of productivity, make the company smarter and richer, and land that promotion you've been seeking. Your application is used by everyone from the CEO down to administrative assistants and the mailroom guy. The data and reporting within your app becomes indispensable.

Sounds like a great story with a happy ending, right? Usually in the software world, this story is just the beginning. "We need our remote sales force to have access to the numbers in the kill app," cries the sales department. "We need our managers at the corporate regional conference call in Boston, Atlanta, and Paris to see the data. Oh yeah, and one of the managers will be stuck in Boise, Idaho for the conference call, and he needs to see the data, too."

As the world gets more connected (via the Internet as well as via private networks that piggyback off the Internet), more and more types of hardware platforms are taking advantage of the ability to log in and browse. "Smart devices," such as portable phones and wireless PDAs, are starting to become affordable and powerful. Microsoft recognizes the importance of these devices in the near future and has done some incredible things with adding mobile device support into the .NET Framework.

Actually, there is a subset of the .NET Framework available known as the *.NET Compact Framework*. This library allows you to develop applications for PDAs and mobile phones in exactly the same way you would develop a normal .NET application. It also contains emulators so that you can begin to test these applications without even needing a device. This makes it easy to prototype the mobile version of your killer app in order to justify the purchase of the dozens of PDAs that will be handed out to the sales force so they can use your mobile app.

I'd love to spend pages upon pages writing a detailed example of all the tips and tricks required to write a mobile app, but the truth is that you already know just about everything you need to if you've written a few regular Windows Forms apps. Once the .NET Compact Framework is installed, you'll see some new project types when you begin a new project, as seen here:

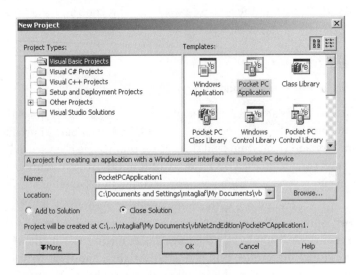

My test mobile application uses a wireless connection to get back to my corporate Northwind database and display a list of products after some first letters of the product name are typed. The results shown include the product name, the price, and the units in stock. (Showing units in stock is especially difficult unless you're wirelessly connecting to your corporate database.) The code that displays this information is standard, good-old ADO.NET code:

```
Private Sub cbGo_Click(ByVal sender As System.Object, _
    ByVal e As System.EventArgs) Handles cbGo.Click

    Const CONNECTIONSTRING As String = "DATABASE=Northwind;SERVER=TAGLIUS;
        ➡UID=sa;PWD=;"

    Dim SQL As String

    SQL = "Select ProductName, UnitPrice, "
    SQL &= "UnitsInStock, UnitsOnOrder"
    SQL &= " from Products "
    SQL &= " where ProductName like '"
    If Not rbSearch.Checked Then
        SQL &= "%"
    End If
    SQL &= tbProd.Text.Trim & "%'"

    Dim oConn As New SqlConnection(CONNECTIONSTRING)
```

```
Dim oCmd As New SqlCommand(SQL, oConn)
Dim oRD As SqlDataReader
Dim lvItem As ListViewItem
Dim cVal As String

Call lvProd.Items.Clear()
Try
    oConn.Open()
    oRD = oCmd.ExecuteReader(CommandBehavior.CloseConnection)
    Do While (oRD.Read())
        lvItem = New ListViewItem(oRD.Item("ProductName").ToString)
        lvItem.SubItems.Add(oRD.Item("UnitPrice").ToString)

        cVal = oRD.Item("UnitsInStock").ToString
        If CInt(cVal) = 0 Then cVal = "-"
        lvItem.SubItems.Add(cVal)

        Call lvProd.Items.Add(lvItem)
    Loop

Finally
    oRD.Close()
End Try

End Sub
```

I decided to ditch the standard 3D appearance of the forms and went back to a flat, white display for the wireless application. (Looks like Windows 3.1, doesn't it? How things travel in cycles…) You can see the application running in the emulator here:

NOTE When this section was written, I was using Release Candidate 1 of Visual Studio .NET, which was released with a very early version of Smart Device Extensions and the Compact Framework (version 7.00.0648). This early version did not come with a visual Forms designer for mobile applications. However, it was not too difficult to work around this problem. All I had to do was start up two versions of Visual Studio .NET, and begin a PocketPC application in one instance and a standard Windows Forms application in the second instance. I did all the form designing in the Windows Forms app. When I had the form the way I wanted it, I copied the code from this application into the PocketPC app. There were a few properties that weren't supported in the Compact Framework version of the form (like Dock, Font, and AutoScaleBaseSize), but the Visual Studio Task List quickly pointed these out. Once these initial errors were removed, I could easily continue development on my mobile app.

PART IX

.NET Delegates: A C# (and Now VB .NET) Bedtime Story

- Intra-class communication

- Communicating via events

- Events as delegates

- Asynchronous notification

The web is a fabulous place for the software developer to learn his craft, research new tools, styles, and programming methods, and meet peers in the industry. I came across this wonderful explanation of .NET Delegates in a .NET developers listserv. In this explanation, a program goes through several iterations to meet the changing requirements of a background story. It represents an excellent method of not only teaching how something is done in the .NET world, but why it is done that way. With permission from the author, Chris Sells, I have reprinted the story here. Because Chris uses C# as his language of choice, I have altered the story only by adding the VB .NET equivalent to each of the code examples in his story (where possible; see each example for details). I want to thank Chris for the great job on this little story, and I feel fortunate that he allowed its inclusion in this book. You can see more of Chris's work at `http://www.sellsbrothers.com`.

91 Type Coupling

 The type-coupling code in C# can be found in the folder `csBedtime01`, and the VB .NET code can be found in the folder `prjBedtime01`.

Once upon a time, in a strange land south of here, there was a worker named Peter. He was a diligent worker who would readily accept requests from his boss. However, his boss was a mean, untrusting man who insisted on steady progress reports. Since Peter did not want his boss standing in his office looking over his shoulder, Peter promised to notify his boss whenever his work progressed. Peter implemented this promise by periodically calling his boss back via a typed reference like so:

C# code (on CD in the folder *csBedtime01*)

```
class Worker {
    public void Advise(Boss boss) { _boss = boss; }
    public void DoWork() {
        Console.WriteLine("Worker: work started");
        if( _boss != null ) _boss.WorkStarted();

        Console.WriteLine("Worker: work progressing");
        if( _boss != null ) _boss.WorkProgressing();

        Console.WriteLine("Worker: work completed");
        if( _boss != null ) {
            int grade = _boss.WorkCompleted();
            Console.WriteLine("Worker grade= " + grade);
        }
    }
    private Boss _boss;
}
```

```csharp
class Boss {
    public void WorkStarted() { /* boss doesn't care. */ }
    public void WorkProgressing() { /* boss doesn't care. */ }
    public int WorkCompleted() {
        Console.WriteLine("It's about time!");
        return 2; /* out of 10 */
    }
}

class Universe {
    static void Main() {
        Worker  peter = new Worker();
        Boss        boss = new Boss();
        peter.Advise(boss);
        peter.DoWork();

        Console.WriteLine("Main: worker completed work");
        Console.ReadLine();
    }
}
```

VB code (on CD in the folder *prjBedtime01*)

```vb
Module BedtimeStory

    Public Class Boss
        Public Sub WorkStarted()
            'boss doesn't care
        End Sub

        Public Sub WorkProgressing()
            'boss doesn't care
        End Sub

        Public Function WorkCompleted() As Integer
            Console.WriteLine("It's about time!")
            Return 2
        End Function

    End Class

    Public Class Worker
        Private FBoss As Boss
        Public Sub Advise(ByVal b As Boss)
            FBoss = b
        End Sub
```

```
    Public Sub DoWork()
        Console.WriteLine("Worker: work started")
        If Not (FBoss Is Nothing) Then FBoss.WorkStarted()

        Console.WriteLine("Worker: work progressing")
        If Not (FBoss Is Nothing) Then FBoss.WorkProgressing()

        Console.WriteLine("Worker: work completed")
        If Not (FBoss Is Nothing) Then
            Dim Grade As Integer = FBoss.WorkCompleted
            Console.WriteLine("Worker grade= " & Grade)
        End If

    End Sub

End Class

Class Universe
    Shared Sub Main()

        Dim Peter As New Worker()
        Dim Boss As New Boss()

        Peter.Advise(Boss)
        Peter.DoWork()

        Console.WriteLine("Main: worker completed work")
        Console.ReadLine()

    End Sub
End Class
End Module
```

92   Interfaces

 The interface code in C# can be found in the folder csBedtime02, and the VB .NET code can be found in the folder prjBedtime02.

Now Peter was a special person. Not only was he able to put up with his mean-spirited boss, but he also had a deep connection with the Universe around him, so much so that he felt that the Universe was interested in his progress. Unfortunately, there was no way for Peter to advise the Universe of his progress unless he added a special Advise method and special callbacks just for the Universe, in addition to keeping his boss informed. What Peter really wanted to do was to separate the list of potential notifications from the implementation of those notification methods. And so he decided to split the methods into an interface:

C# code (on CD in the folder *csBedtime02*)

```csharp
interface IWorkerEvents {
    void WorkStarted();
    void WorkProgressing();
    int WorkCompleted();
}

class Worker {
    public void Advise(IWorkerEvents events) { _events = events; }
    public void DoWork() {
        Console.WriteLine("Worker: work started");
        if( _events != null ) _events.WorkStarted();

        Console.WriteLine("Worker: work progressing");
        if(_events != null ) _events.WorkProgressing();

        Console.WriteLine("Worker: work completed");
        if(_events != null ) {
            int grade = _events.WorkCompleted();
            Console.WriteLine("Worker grade= " + grade);
        }
    }
    private IWorkerEvents _events;
}

class Boss : IWorkerEvents {
    public void WorkStarted() { /* boss doesn't care. */ }
    public void WorkProgressing() { /* boss doesn't care. */ }
    public int WorkCompleted() {
        Console.WriteLine("It's about time!");
        return 3; /* out of 10 */
    }
}
```

VB code (on CD in the folder *prjBedtime02*)

```vb
Interface IWorkerEvents
    Sub WorkStarted()
    Sub WorkProgressing()
    Function WorkCompleted() As Integer
End Interface

Public Class Boss
    Implements IWorkerEvents

    Public Sub WorkStarted() _
        Implements IWorkerEvents.WorkStarted
```

```vb.net
            'boss doesn't care
        End Sub

        Public Sub WorkProgressing() _
            Implements IWorkerEvents.WorkProgressing

            'boss doesn't care
        End Sub

        Public Function WorkCompleted() As Integer _
            Implements IWorkerEvents.WorkCompleted

            Console.WriteLine("It's about time!")
            Return 3          'out of 10
        End Function

    End Class

    Public Class Worker
        Private FWorkerEvents As IWorkerEvents

        Public Sub Advise(ByVal we As IWorkerEvents)
            FWorkerEvents = we
        End Sub

        Public Sub DoWork()
            Console.WriteLine("Worker: work started")
            If Not (FWorkerEvents Is Nothing) Then FWorkerEvents.WorkStarted()

            Console.WriteLine("Worker: work progressing")
            If Not (FWorkerEvents Is Nothing) Then FWorkerEvents.WorkProgressing()

            Console.WriteLine("Worker: work completed")
            If Not (FWorkerEvents Is Nothing) Then
                Dim Grade As Integer = FWorkerEvents.WorkCompleted
                Console.WriteLine("Worker grade= " & Grade)
            End If

        End Sub

    End Class
```

93   Delegates

The delegates code in C# can be found in the folder csBedtime03, and the VB .NET code can be found in the folder prjBedtime03.

Unfortunately, Peter was so busy talking his boss into implementing this interface that he didn't get around to notifying the Universe, but he knew he would soon. At least he'd abstracted the reference of his boss far away from him so that others who implemented the IWorkerEvents interface could be notified of his work progress.

Still, his boss complained bitterly. "Peter!" his boss fumed. "Why are you bothering to notify me when you start your work or when your work is progressing?!? I don't care about those events. Not only do you force me to implement those methods, but you're wasting valuable work time waiting for me to return from the event, which is further expanded when I am far away! Can't you figure out a way to stop bothering me?"

And so, Peter decided that while interfaces were useful for many things, when it came to events, their granularity was not fine enough. He wished to be able to notify interested parties only of the events that matched their hearts' desires. So, he decided to break the methods out of the interface into separate delegate functions, each of which acted like a little tiny interface of one method each:

C# code (on CD in the folder *csBedtime03*)

```csharp
delegate void WorkStarted();
delegate void WorkProgressing();
delegate int WorkCompleted();

class Worker {
    public void DoWork() {
        Console.WriteLine("Worker: work started");
        if( started != null ) started();

        Console.WriteLine("Worker: work progressing");
        if( progressing != null ) progressing();

        Console.WriteLine("Worker: work completed");
        if( completed != null ) {
            int grade = completed();
            Console.WriteLine("Worker grade= " + grade);
        }
    }
    public WorkStarted started;
    public WorkProgressing progressing;
    public WorkCompleted completed;
}

class Boss {
    public int WorkCompleted() {
        Console.WriteLine("Better...");
        return 4; /* out of 10 */
    }
}
```

```
class Universe {
    static void Main() {
        Worker   peter = new Worker();
        Boss         boss = new Boss();
        peter.completed = new WorkCompleted(boss.WorkCompleted);
        peter.DoWork();

        Console.WriteLine("Main: worker completed work");
        Console.ReadLine();
    }
}
```

VB code (on CD in the folder *prjBedtime03*)

```
Module BedtimeStory

    Delegate Sub WorkStarted()
    Delegate Sub WorkProgressing()
    Delegate Function WorkCompleted() As Integer

    Public Class Boss

        Public Function WorkCompleted() As Integer
            Console.WriteLine("Better...")
            Return 4          'out of 10
        End Function

    End Class

    Public Class Worker

        Public started As WorkStarted
        Public progressing As WorkProgressing
        Public completed As WorkCompleted

        Public Sub DoWork()
            Console.WriteLine("Worker: work started")
            If Not (started Is Nothing) Then started()

            Console.WriteLine("Worker: work progressing")
            If Not (progressing Is Nothing) Then progressing()

            Console.WriteLine("Worker: work completed")
            If Not (completed Is Nothing) Then
                Dim Grade As Integer = completed()
                Console.WriteLine("Worker grade= " & Grade)
            End If
```

```
        End Sub

    End Class

    Class Universe
        Shared Sub Main()

            Dim Peter As New Worker()
            Dim Boss As New Boss()

            Peter.completed = New WorkCompleted(AddressOf Boss.WorkCompleted)
            Peter.DoWork()

            Console.WriteLine("Main: worker completed work")
            Console.ReadLine()

        End Sub
    End Class
End Module
```

94   Static Listeners

 The static listeners code in C# can be found in the folder csBedtime04, and the VB .NET code can be found in the folder prjBedtime04.

   This accomplished the goal of not bothering his boss with events that he didn't want, but still Peter had not managed to get the Universe on his list of listeners. Since the Universe is an all-compassing entity, it didn't seem right to hook delegates to instance members. (Imagine how many resources multiple instances of the Universe would need...) Instead, Peter needed to hook delegates to static members, which delegates support fully:

C# code (on CD in the folder *csBedtime04*)

```
class Universe {
    static void WorkerStartedWork() {
        Console.WriteLine("Universe notices worker starting work");
    }

    static int WorkerCompletedWork() {
        Console.WriteLine("Universe pleased with worker's work");
        return 7;
    }
}
```

```csharp
static void Main() {
    Worker  peter = new Worker();
    Boss boss = new Boss();
    peter.completed = new WorkCompleted(boss.WorkCompleted);
    peter.started = new WorkStarted(Universe.WorkerStartedWork);
    peter.completed = new WorkCompleted(Universe.WorkerCompletedWork);
    peter.DoWork();

    Console.WriteLine("Main: worker completed work");
    Console.ReadLine();
}
}
```

VB code (on CD in the folder *prjBedtime04*)

```vb
Class Universe

    Shared Sub WorkerStartedWork()
        Console.WriteLine("Universe notices worker starting work")
    End Sub

    Shared Function WorkerCompletedWork() As Integer
        Console.WriteLine("Universe pleased with worker's work")
        Return 7
    End Function


    Shared Sub Main()

        Dim Peter As New Worker()
        Dim Boss As New Boss()

        Peter.completed = New WorkCompleted(AddressOf Boss.WorkCompleted)
        Peter.started = New WorkStarted(AddressOf Universe.WorkerStartedWork)
        Peter.completed = New WorkCompleted(AddressOf Universe.
            ➥WorkerCompletedWork)

        Peter.DoWork()


        Console.WriteLine("Main: worker completed work")
        Console.ReadLine()

    End Sub
End Class
```

95 Events

The events code in C# can be found in the folder csBedtime05, and the VB .NET code can be found in the folder prjBedtime05.

Unfortunately, the Universe, being very busy and unaccustomed to paying attention to individuals, has managed to replace Peter's boss's delegate with its own. This is an unintended side effect of making the delegate fields public in Peter's Worker class. Likewise, if Peter's boss gets impatient, he can decide to fire Peter's delegates himself (which is just the kind of rude thing that Peter's boss was apt to do):

```
// Peter's boss taking matters into his own hands
if( peter.completed != null ) peter.completed();
```

Peter wants to make sure that neither of these can happen. He realizes he needs to add registration and unregistration functions for each delegate so that listeners can add or remove themselves, but they can't clear the entire list or fire Peter's events. Instead of implementing these functions himself, Peter uses the event keyword to make the C# compiler build these methods for him:

C# code (on CD in the folder *csBedtime05*)

```
class Worker {
...
    public event WorkStarted started;
    public event WorkProgressing progressing;
    public event WorkCompleted completed;
}
```

VB code (on CD in the folder *prjBedtime05*)

```
Public Class Worker
...
        Public Event started As WorkStarted
        Public Event progressing As WorkProgressing
        Public Event completed As WorkCompleted
End Class
```

NOTE This is the point where the differences between C# and VB start to affect the example. In Visual Basic, events cannot be created against delegates with a return type. The Work-Completed delegate is a function with an integer return type, so setting up the event as shown in the preceding code isn't valid. The delegate can be modified to become a sub that passes in the grade as a parameter, as in this line of code: Delegate Sub Work-Completed(ByRef Grade As Integer).

Peter knows that the event keyword erects a property around a delegate, only allowing C# clients to add or remove themselves with the += and -= operators, forcing his boss and the Universe to play nicely:

C# code (on CD in the folder *csBedtime05*)

```
static void Main() {
    Worker  peter = new Worker();
    Boss boss = new Boss();
    peter.completed += new WorkCompleted(boss.WorkCompleted);
    peter.started += new WorkStarted(Universe.WorkerStartedWork);
    peter.completed += new WorkCompleted(Universe.WorkerCompletedWork);
    peter.DoWork();

    Console.WriteLine("Main: worker completed work");
    Console.ReadLine();
}
```

VB code (on CD in the folder *prjBedtime05*)

```
Shared Sub Main()

    Dim Peter As New Worker()
    Dim Boss As New Boss()

    AddHandler Peter.completed, New WorkCompleted(AddressOf Boss.WorkCompleted)
    AddHandler Peter.started, New WorkStarted(AddressOf
    ➥ Universe.WorkerStartedWork)
    AddHandler Peter.completed, New WorkCompleted(AddressOf
    ➥ Universe.WorkerCompletedWork)

    Peter.DoWork()


    Console.WriteLine("Main: worker completed work")
    Console.ReadLine()

End Sub
```

96   Harvesting All Results

The harvesting-all-results code in C# can be found in the folder csBedtime06.

At this point, Peter breathes a sign of relief. He has managed to satisfy the requirements of all his listeners without having to be closely coupled with the specific implementations.

However, he notices that while both his boss and the Universe provide grades of his work, he's only receiving one of the grades. In the face of multiple listeners, he'd really like to harvest all of their results. So, he reaches into his delegate and pulls out the list of listeners so that he can call each of them manually:

```
C# code (on CD in the folder csBedtime06)
public void DoWork() {
    ...
    Console.WriteLine("Worker: work completed");
    if( completed != null ) {
        foreach( WorkCompleted wc in completed.GetInvocationList() ) {
            int grade = wc();
            Console.WriteLine("Worker grade= " + grade);
        }
    }
}
```

NOTE   VB .NET doesn't allow events to be looped through in this way. You could change the event back to a static listener, but then you wouldn't be able to hook up multiple listeners via the registration/unregistration functions. Consider the elements in this section and the ones that follow to be "advanced" delegate manipulation that would require you to switch over to C# to accomplish properly. Future versions of VB .NET may address these differences.

97   Async Notification: Fire & Forget

 The async-notification code in C# can be found in the folder csBedtime07.

In the meantime, his boss and the Universe have been distracted with other things, which means that the time it takes them to grade Peter's work is greatly expanded:

C# code (on CD in the folder *csBedtime07*)

```
class Boss {
    public int WorkCompleted() {
        System.Threading.Thread.Sleep(3000);
        Console.WriteLine("Better..."); return 6; /* out of 10 */
    }
}

class Universe {
    static int WorkerCompletedWork() {
        System.Threading.Thread.Sleep(4000);
        Console.WriteLine("Universe is pleased with worker's work");
```

```
        return 7;
    }
    ...
}
```

Unfortunately, since Peter is notifying each listener one at a time, waiting for each to grade him, these notifications now take up quite a bit of his time when he should be working. So, he decides to forget the grade and just fire the event asynchronously:

```
public void DoWork() {
    ...
    Console.WriteLine("Worker: work completed");
    if( completed != null ) {
        foreach( WorkCompleted wc in completed.GetInvocationList() )
        {
            wc.BeginInvoke(null, null);
        }
    }
}
```

98   Async Notification: Polling

 The async-polling code in C# can be found in the folder csBedtime08.

This allows Peter to notify the listeners while letting Peter get back to work immediately, letting the process thread pool invoke the delegate. Over time, however, Peter finds that he misses the feedback on his work. He knows that he does a good job and appreciates the praise of the Universe as a whole (if not his boss specifically). So, he fires the event asynchronously, but polls periodically, looking for the grade to be available:

C# code (on CD in the folder *csBedtime08*)

```
public void DoWork() {
    ...
    Console.WriteLine("Worker: work completed");
    if( completed != null ) {
        foreach( WorkCompleted wc in completed.GetInvocationList() ) {
            IAsyncResult res = wc.BeginInvoke(null, null);
            while( !res.IsCompleted ) System.Threading.Thread.Sleep(1);
            int grade = wc.EndInvoke(res);
            Console.WriteLine("Worker grade= " + grade);
        }
    }
}
```

99   Async Notification: Delegates

The async-delegates code in C# can be found in the folder `csBedtime09`.

Unfortunately, Peter is back to what he wanted his boss to avoid with him in the beginning, i.e., looking over the shoulder of the entity doing the work. So, he decides to employ his own delegate as a means of notification when the async delegate has completed, allowing him to get back to work immediately, but still be notified when his work has been graded:

C# code (on CD in the folder *csBedtime09*)

```csharp
public void DoWork() {
    ...
    Console.WriteLine("Worker: work completed");
    if( completed != null ) {
        foreach( WorkCompleted wc in completed.GetInvocationList() ) {
            wc.BeginInvoke(new AsyncCallback(WorkGraded), wc);
        }
    }
}

private void WorkGraded(IAsyncResult res) {
    WorkCompleted wc = (WorkCompleted)res.AsyncState;
    int grade = wc.EndInvoke(res);
    Console.WriteLine("Worker grade= " + grade);
}
```

Happiness in the Universe

Peter, his boss, and the Universe are finally satisfied. Peter's boss and the Universe are allowed to be notified of the events that interest them, reducing the burden of implementation and the cost of unnecessary round-trips. Peter can notify them each, ignoring how long it takes them to return from their target methods, while still getting his results asynchronously. Peter knows that it's not *quite* that easy, because as soon as he fires events asynchronously, the target methods are likely to be executed on another thread, as is Peter's notification of when the target method has completed. However, Peter is good friends with Mike, who is very familiar with threading issues and can provide guidance in that area.

And they all lived happily ever after. The end.

Index

Note to the reader: Throughout this index **boldfaced** page numbers indicate primary discussions of a topic. *Italicized* page numbers indicate illustrations.

TELL US WHAT YOU THINK!

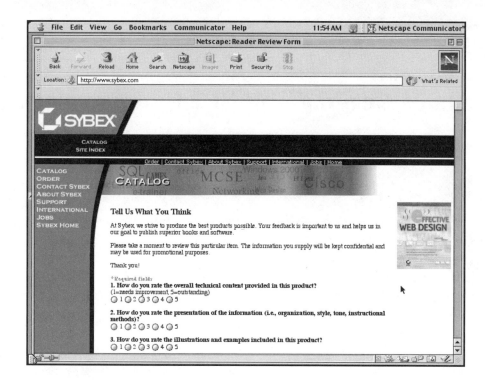

Your feedback is critical to our efforts to provide you with the best books and software on the market. Tell us what you think about the products you've purchased. It's simple:

1. Visit the Sybex website
2. Go to the product page
3. Click on **Submit a Review**
4. Fill out the questionnaire and comments
5. Click **Submit**

With your feedback, we can continue to publish the highest quality computer books and software products that today's busy IT professionals deserve.

www.sybex.com

SYBEX Inc. • 1151 Marina Village Parkway, Alameda, CA 94501 • 510-523-8233

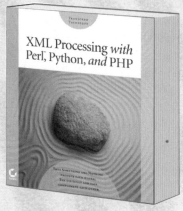

The quotation on the bottom of the front cover is taken from the sixty-third chapter of Lao Tzu's Tao Te Ching, the classic work of Taoist philosophy. This particular verse is from the translation by D. C. Lau (copyright 1963) and is part of a larger exploration of the qualities of the sage, who "meets with no difficulty...because he is alive to it."

It is traditionally held that Lao Tzu lived in the fifth century B.C. in China, during the Chou dynasty, but it is unclear whether he was actually a historical figure. It is said that he was a teacher of Confucius. The concepts embodied in the Tao Te Ching influenced religious thinking in the Far East, including Zen Buddhism in Japan. Many in the West, however, have wrongly understood the Tao Te Ching to be primarily a mystical work; in fact, much of the advice in the book is grounded in a practical moral philosophy governing personal conduct.